Crime Files

Series Editor
Clive Bloom
Middlesex University
London, UK

Since its invention in the nineteenth century, detective fiction has never been more popular. In novels, short stories and films, on the radio, on television and now in computer games, private detectives and psychopaths, poisoners and overworked cops, tommy gun gangsters and cocaine criminals are the very stuff of modern imagination, and their creators a mainstay of popular consciousness. Crime Files is a ground-breaking series offering scholars, students and discerning readers a comprehensive set of guides to the world of crime and detective fiction. Every aspect of crime writing, from detective fiction to the gangster movie, true-crime exposé, police procedural and post-colonial investigation, is explored through clear and informative texts offering comprehensive coverage and theoretical sophistication.

Sarah J. Link

A Narratological Approach to Lists in Detective Fiction

palgrave
macmillan

Sarah J. Link
University of Wuppertal
Wuppertal, Germany

ISSN 2947-8340   ISSN 2947-8359   (electronic)
Crime Files
ISBN 978-3-031-33226-5   ISBN 978-3-031-33227-2   (eBook)
https://doi.org/10.1007/978-3-031-33227-2

Cover illustration: William Whitehurst/Getty Images

This Palgrave Macmillan imprint is published by the registered company Springer Nature Switzerland AG.
The registered company address is: Gewerbestrasse 11, 6330 Cham, Switzerland

ACKNOWLEDGMENTS

This book has its origin in a dissertation in English philology written at the University of Freiburg and submitted in 2021. First of all, my heartfelt thanks go to my supervisor Eva von Contzen, without whose constructive feedback, keen insight, and encouragement this book would not have been possible. I am profoundly grateful for many inspiring conversations, crucial advice, and unwavering enthusiasm for my project. I am grateful as well to Katharina Boehm, for her support and expertise, and for fostering my early interest in detective fiction. I would also like to thank Roman Barton, Anne Rüggemeier, Stefanie Lethbridge, and Miriam Nandi for their continuous support and advice. Thank you as well to Nicole Bancher and Gert Fehlner, for their help with administrative matters.

At various stages of this book's development, I was able to present my ideas at workshops and conferences, and I am grateful to the organizers for the opportunity to do so. Special thanks are due to the organizers of the annual conferences of the International Society for the Study of Narrative 2019 in Pamplona and 2020 in New Orleans, and to the organizers of the conference "Beyond Narrative" in Leipzig in 2019, for providing supportive environments for helpful exchange. I am grateful for stimulating conversations with Jared Gardner, Sebastian M. Herrmann, Katja Kanzler, Maurice S. Lee, Regina Schober, and Stefan Schubert.

I am likewise grateful to my colleagues at the University of Wuppertal—first and foremost to Sandra Heinen and Katharina Rennhak, for their support, advice, and insightful feedback, and for granting me the time to complete this book. I am further grateful to Carolin Gebauer and Lance Pettitt for countless thought-provoking conversations.

I wish to thank the editing and production team at Palgrave Macmillan for being immensely helpful and supportive: Allie Troyanos, Eliana Rangel, Paul Smith, and V. VinodhKumar. I am furthermore indebted to my insightful peer reviewer for their detailed, thoughtful, and valuable comments.

A huge thank-you is due to my friends and colleagues Julia Böckling, Stephan Bosch, Thomas Brachtendorf, Anne Engel, Felix Ettensperger, Fabian Fischer, Ester Gnandt, Nikolina Hatton, Stefan and Stephanie Heyl, Marlene Jäger, Andreas Kattler, Franca Leitner, Laura Maretzky, Undine Remmes, Golnaz Shams, Hanna Specker, Leonie Wanitzek, and Eli Watts for their aid, for their wit, and for being such wonderful people.

Finally, and most importantly, I wish to thank my loving family, for their continuous support and unwavering encouragement.

My project would not have been possible without the funding provided by the European Research Council for the project "Lists in Literature and Culture: Towards a Listology" (Grant No. 715021).

CONTENTS

ABBREVIATIONS

Ackroyd	*The Murder of Roger Ackroyd.* Agatha Christie. 2013 [1926]. London: Harper Collins.
"Bachelor"	"The Adventure of the Noble Bachelor." In *The Adventures of Sherlock Holmes.* Arthur Conan Doyle. 2013 [1892]. London: Harper Collins.
"Bohemia"	"A Scandal in Bohemia." In *The Adventures of Sherlock Holmes.* Arthur Conan Doyle. 2013 [1892]. London: Harper Collins.
"Brodski"	"The Case of Oscar Brodski." In *Dr. Thorndyke Collection: Vol. 2.* R.A. Freeman. 2017 [1912]. n.p.: Neo Books.
Cases	*John Thorndyke's Cases.* In *Dr. Thorndyke Collection: Vol. 2.* R.A. Freeman. 2017 [1909]. n.p.: Neo Books.
Clouds	*Death in the Clouds.* Agatha Christie. 2015 [1935]. London: Harper Collins.
"Creeping Man"	"The Adventure of the Creeping Man." In *The Case-Book of Sherlock Holmes.* Arthur Conan Doyle. 2011 [1927]. London: Penguin.
"Gables"	"The Adventure of the Three Gables." In *The Case-Book of Sherlock Holmes.* Arthur Conan Doyle. 2011 [1927]. London: Penguin.
Hickory	*Hickory Dickory Dock.* Agatha Christie. 2015 [1955]. London: Harper Collins.
"Identity"	"A Case of Identity." In *The Adventures of Sherlock Holmes.* Arthur Conan Doyle. 2013 [1892]. London: Harper Collins.
"League"	"The Red-Headed League." In *The Adventures of Sherlock Holmes.* Arthur Conan Doyle. 2013 [1892]. London: Harper Collins.

New Inn	*The Mystery at Number 31, New Inn.* R. A. Freeman. 2004 [1912]. Greenville, SC: JourneyForth.
Orient Express	*Murder on the Orient Express.* Agatha Christie. 2015 [1934]. London: Harper Collins.
Osiris	*The Eye of Osiris.* R.A. Freeman. 1989 [1911]. Oxford: Oxford University Press.
"Romance"	"A Wastrel's Romance." In *Dr. Thorndyke Collection: Vol. 2.* R.A. Freeman. 2017 [1912]. n.p.: Neo Books.
Scarlet	*A Study in Scarlet.* Arthur Conan Doyle. 2014 [1887]. London: Penguin.
Sign	*The Sign of Four.* Arthur Conan Doyle. 2010 [1890]. London: Penguin.
"Soldier"	"The Adventure of the Blanched Soldier." In *The Case-Book of Sherlock Holmes.* Arthur Conan Doyle. 2011 [1927]. London: Penguin.
"Pips"	"The Five Orange Pips." In *The Adventures of Sherlock Holmes.* Arthur Conan Doyle. 2013 [1892]. London: Harper Collins.
Thumb	*The Red Thumb Mark.* R.A. Freeman. 2010 [1907]. Rockville, MD: Serenity Publishers.
"Vampire"	"The Adventure of the Sussex Vampire." In *The Case-Book of Sherlock Holmes.* Arthur Conan Doyle. 2011 [1927]. London: Penguin.
Witness	*A Silent Witness.* R.A. Freeman. 2001 [1914]. Cornwall: House of Stratus.

LIST OF FIGURES

CHAPTER 1

Introduction: Reading Lists, Listing Clues

[T]attoos, knots, ears, ciphers, bicycle tires, tobacco ash, newspaper types, perfumes, the development of English script, and names of American gunsmiths.

The items on this list seem fairly unrelated. Some are visible material objects (bicycle tires), some are abstract (names), some seem to be consumer goods, some are part of the human body, and one item even designates a timespan rather than a concrete entity. Lists invite us to group items together and to find a connecting principle that allows us to make sense of them as a unit. The above list makes this difficult because its items come from such a broad range of categories. However, once we can find a common heading to sort things by, their relation becomes immediately apparent, no matter how obscure it might have seemed a moment ago. The above list is taken from Ian Ousby's *Bloodhounds of Heaven*, and it designates the various areas of knowledge in which Arthur Conan Doyle's detective Sherlock Holmes claims expertise (1976, 162). Seen from this perspective, the very variety of categories that initially made it confusing becomes the point of the list: it demonstrates the great range of areas in which Sherlock Holmes is considered an expert, and the uncommon, almost absurd, scope and unrelated nature of the list items create the impression that Holmes's knowledge is so all-encompassing that potentially anything could fall within its range.

© The Author(s) 2023
S. J. Link, *A Narratological Approach to Lists in Detective Fiction*,
Crime Files, https://doi.org/10.1007/978-3-031-33227-2_1

When looking at a list, readers have to perform cognitive work and actively fill in missing links to make sense of the listed items. The readers' activity, in a way, resembles detective work in that they have a number of clues that need to be put together in order to reveal the bigger picture those clues represent. "To list," writes Stephen Barney, "is to attempt to comprehend" (1982, 223); he thus points out the central role that cognitive processes occupy in the making and decoding of lists. It is, perhaps, not surprising that the popular literary genre of detective fiction teems with lists; they are used as meaning-making and ordering tools by fictional detectives and, at the same time, as devices to involve readers in the act of detection. Detective fiction often invites readers to put together clues in a way similar to how they would make sense of a list; frequently, the genre even chooses the form of the list to present readers with clues to make sense of.

The strategies that readers use to piece together information presented in lists are inextricably linked with epistemological concerns about how knowledge is generated, delimited, or manipulated within any particular story world. The various conceptions of knowledge that can be found in detective fiction are closely connected to the forms through which they are conveyed to readers and thus also to the readers' positioning with regard to the story world. This tightly knit relation between the form of the list, the genre of detective fiction, and different conceptions of knowledge has hitherto remained unexplored but deserves critical attention. The study at hand is an attempt to close that gap.

Detective fiction is a well-researched genre with regard to its history,[1] and much attention has been paid to the work of individual authors.[2] Considerably less attention has been paid to the genre with regard to its formal properties.[3] Recent years have seen a revived interest in literary form across a wide variety of contexts. Caroline Levine's study *Forms* (2015) makes a case for the importance of literary form for social, cultural, and political contexts, Verena Theile and Linda Tredennick's edited volume *New Formalisms and Literary Theory* (2013) brings together scholars who explore the merits of new formalist approaches to literary criticism, and Elizabeth Kovach, Imke Polland, and Ansgar Nünning's edited volume *Forms at Work* (2021) builds on Levine's work to discuss the relevance of new formalism in the study of literature, culture, and different media.

Lists can be considered as forms in the sense proposed by Caroline Levine: they are structures crafted for a specific purpose (see 2015, XI), they are carefully arranged to assert a certain kind of order (ibid.), they stay recognizable throughout a variety of different settings and can thus be considered portable (see ibid., 7), and they are inextricable from practices that shape them into material form (ibid., 10). Levine's new formalist approach to form carries explicitly political connotations, but it overlaps to a significant degree with approaches that focus on *narrative* form, for example, in its focus on the patterns and structures that underlie (narrative) texts. My analysis is centered on narrative representation and thus draws on the methodology and theoretical framework of postclassical narratology; at the same time, I am interested in the impact form unfolds beyond its strictly narrative contexts. As both a narrative and a Levinean form, the list is particularly well suited to an approach that views formal and narratological aspects of texts in conjunction with their wider sociocultural implications.

The list's ubiquity and adaptability to a sheer infinite number of different contexts may be the reason why the form, in both its literary and everyday variations, has drawn an increasing amount of critical attention across disciplines in the humanities over the past decade. As early as the late 1970s, Jack Goody has examined lists in the context of anthropology and administrative practices,[4] and decades later, scholars such as Liam Cole Young still draw on his work. Young refers to Goody's study to examine lists from the perspective of media studies in a variety of cultural and historical contexts. Lucie Doležalová's edited volume *The Charm of a List* (2009) takes a transdisciplinary approach to the study of lists that emphasizes the form's ubiquitous presence across a wide variety of scientific disciplines. Both Doležalová and Young focus on demonstrating the omnipresence of lists across cultural and historical contexts. Rebecca Laemmle et al. place their focus on classical scholarship and explore the poetics of enumerative modes in an edited volume on *Lists and Catalogues in Ancient Literature and Beyond* (2021). Most recently, the edited volume *Forms of List-Making: Epistemic, Literary and Visual Enumeration* (2022b) presents a selection of case studies that throws light on list-making as a cultural, visual, and literary practice. From a sociological point of view, Urs Stäheli focuses on the politics of the lists and on the power relations that lists can generate, conceal, or reveal (see 2011, 2016, 2017).[5]

A more specific focus on literary lists can be found in Robert Belknap's seminal study *The List: the Uses and Pleasures of Cataloguing* (2004), which provides a much quoted definition of the form of the list and highlights the form's importance in the works of four canonical American authors. Sabine Mainberger's *Die Kunst des Aufzählens* (2003) discusses lists and enumerations with a particular regard for the rhetorical and poetological aspects of the form in literary writing. Umberto Eco's *The Infinity of Lists* (2009) presents a kind of list of lists in the history of art and literature that aims for demonstrating the form's prominence across times and contexts.[6] More recently, a special issue of the journal *Style* edited by Eva von Contzen provides a diachronic perspective and engages with *Lists in Literature from the Middle Ages to Postmodernism* (2016). Furthermore, in *Literary Lists: A Short History of Form and Function* (2023), Barton et al. trace the history of the literary list from the early modern period to postmodernism. A genre-specific approach is taken by a recent issue of the journal *a/b Autobiography Studies* (2020), which contains a forum that turns its attention to lists within the particular genre of life writing.[7]

My own study of lists in detective fiction and their relation to readers and reading practices draws on the work of Eva von Contzen, who explores the cognitive dimensions that are inseparable from the simple form of the list.[8] Von Contzen's approach to lists and list-making allows for seeing lists on a sliding scale of narrativity rather than positing the form as automatically opposed to narrative. According to Eva von Contzen, lists need not be considered as inherently narrative, but narratives can use lists as a mode to achieve certain effects. "[A]pprehended as narrative elements of change and transformation," von Contzen argues, lists can "considerably shape the perception of a work" (2021, 45). This holds true for the lists that appear in detective fiction as well: although they tend to interrupt the continuous progression of plot in a text, lists hold great potential to engage readers and often function as triggers for the reader to fill in textual gaps and reshuffle information previously presented in the text.

A Narratological Approach to Lists in Detective Fiction does not pursue a cognitive approach in the narrow sense—it neither investigates narratives as a "resource for sense making" (see Herman 2013b, x) nor elaborates on the role of embodied cognition for the reading process in any detail. However, my exploration of how features of narrative discourse enable particular kinds of processing strategies strongly overlaps with cognitive approaches to literary studies, such as Torsa Ghosal's cognitive approach to multimodality in contemporary fiction (see 2021). In investigating how readers engage with elements of a text that (seemingly) interrupt the continuous flow of narration, this book furthermore shares an interest with Karin Kukkonen's recent study on *Probability Designs* (2020).

A Narratological Approach to Lists in Detective Fiction proposes to investigate how lists can facilitate access to story worlds through their capacity to both transport and shape knowledge about the fictional world. Starting from a conceptualization of the list that assumes this form requires readers to actively make sense of it, this book explores the functional potential of lists in detective fiction with regard to how they frame knowledge in the fictional world and thus guide the cognitive work readers perform when engaging with texts. My reader-based approach to the topic focuses on the idea of describing narrative potential, and thus aims to avoid discussing the responses of individual readers. In order to better be able to describe such narrative potential, this study will work with the concept of affordances. The concept of affordances originates in design theory and describes how a great number of potential uses can be inherent in one form or material, and that objects or situations can have different affordances relative to the person (or entity) interacting with them (see Gibson 1979, 127). Psychologist James Gibson argues that looking at objects in terms of what they afford may be a useful way of avoiding limiting and necessarily incomplete definitions (see ibid., 134). New formalist scholar Caroline Levine applies his concept to literary studies.[9] According to Levine, affordances "describe the potential uses or actions latent in materials and designs" (2015, 6). In her monograph, Levine outlines the affordances, or potential uses of four exemplary forms, and lists, among others, the affordances of connectedness and a potentially infinite extensiveness as characteristic for the form she designates as "network" (see ibid., 113–117). The idea of form itself could be said to carry a number of affordances.

Eva von Contzen has explored the notion of affordances with regard to the form of the list. Drawing on Levine, she argues that affordance is an apt concept to describe "those aspects of an object or form that it is capable of" (2018, 317); it constitutes a way of illustrating both the specific properties and the general scope of an object of scrutiny (see ibid., 325). Von Contzen has used affordances to describe the reactions lists are capable of eliciting in readers. The concept is so useful because it can outline capacities without the need for making normative statements. Just because a list has the potential to evoke a certain response, that potential need not be actualized for every single reader confronted with the list (see ibid., 326). The same holds true for the study of lists in detective fiction. The capacity that the use of lists in this genre holds for involving readers merits closer attention even if individual readers may have different reactions.[10]

But what exactly counts as a list? Even though the form looks deceptively simple and appears to be intuitively recognizable, as soon as one attempts to find a definition for the list, it is difficult to come up with one that is specific enough to be useful, yet inclusive enough to account for less prototypical specimen. There are a number of different approaches to defining lists, with the focus reaching from formal features to functions to aspects of reception. One list definition that has been quoted often, perhaps for its general scope, and that focuses on formal features is that of Robert Belknap:

> At their most simple, lists are frameworks that hold separate and disparate items together. Lists are plastic, flexible structures in which an array of constituent units coheres through specific relations generated by specific forces of attraction. (2004, 2)

One of the merits of Belknap's definition is that he draws attention to the twofold nature of lists and invites us to take into consideration both "the immediately recognizable form of the list as a whole, and the individual items that make up the list" (von Contzen 2022, 132). What makes a list cohere can either be found in what Belknap calls "specific relations" between the individual items on the list, or in the way it is framed as a whole, for instance, by a heading such as "stolen items" or "to do" (see ibid.). Von Contzen herself has proposed the minimalist definition of a list as "a set of items assembled under some principle in a formally distinctive unit" (2021, 36). Formally, lists are "characterised by several (usually three or more) distinct elements employed in direct succession and in loose, if at all, syntactic and conceptual coherence to both the other elements and the surrounding narrative material" (ibid.). Belknap's definition is general enough to be fairly comprehensive, but it is also so broad that its usefulness in identifying concrete lists is doubtful. Yet, a more narrow determination of a list's properties may exclude arrangements that readers would intuitively consider lists.

To circumvent the problem of being too general, von Contzen, and Sabine Mainberger, who defines lists and enumerations on a formal level as dependent on their characteristic visual appearance (see 2003, 5), add a cognitive dimension to their formal list definitions. Von Contzen states that "a list, even though it is defined by its form, is always also more than this form because of the cognitive processes required to decode its meaning(s)" (2021, 38). In a similar vein, Mainberger emphasizes that lists are tools for certain intellectual operations such as memorization or categorization (see 2003, 6). Others highlight aspects of reception in addition to form as playing a crucial role when thinking about lists (see Doležalová 2009, 5).[11]

Yet another approach to defining lists that is, for example, taken by Jack Goody (1978) and Stephen Barney (1982) is to incorporate functional features of the list into its definition and to thus focus on what lists *do*. Goody combines formal and functional features when he writes that:

> [t]he list relies on discontinuity rather than continuity; it depends on physical placement, on location; it can be read in different directions, both sideways and downwards, up and down, as well as left and right; it has a clear-cut beginning and a precise end, that is, a boundary, an edge, like a piece of cloth.[12] Most importantly it encourages the ordering of the items, by number, by initial sound, by category, etc. And the existence of boundaries, external and internal, brings greater visibility to categories, at the same time as making them more abstract. (1978, 81)

A functional approach to the form can be especially useful to describe lists as they appear within a certain professional or thematic field, and using a cluster of affordances as the basis for a definition raises the level of specificity and usefulness of the definition for a particular purpose. However, once again, it is impractical, if not impossible to phrase a definition of lists that includes all their potential affordances, and the more contradictory affordances a definition contains, the less useful it becomes. This is why, for the purposes of this book, I have chosen to merely outline a number of formal features that may help to identify lists and place them on a sliding scale of more or less prototypical with regard to their appearance. To do justice to the great variety of affordances that the form of the list can have, I will then discuss specific affordances with regard to my material in the individual chapters.

I propose to view the list through a model that is based on prototypical features rather than a strict definition, which always runs the risk of being too general or too restrictive. Prototype models are, for example, used in linguistics in the field of cognitive semantics to describe basic-level categories in a language (see Rosch et al. 1976), and they derive their appeal from their non-binary structure. Prototype theory is an area of cognitive science that features prominently in the work of cognitive literary scholars such as Monika Fludernik (1996) or David Herman (see f.e. 2008), perhaps because it allows to move away from the idea that we can draw clear-cut boundaries around (narratological) categories (see Alber and Fludernik 2010, 22).

A prototype-based approach to lists is thus in line with this book's idea of form as a flexible and dynamic concept. The idea of prototypes draws together a number of phenomena (such as footnotes, maps, inventories, suspect profiles, and lists of questions) that may initially appear to be unrelated, but work according to the same list-based principles. There simply is "no one theory that allows for encompassing the many formal and functional facets of lists and the processes of sense-making their reception involves" (von Contzen 2021, 40–41). Von Contzen also speaks of "prototypical list[s]" (ibid., 36), and Mainberger comments on the restrictive nature of definitions and proposes to look at lists and enumerations in terms of family resemblances (see 2003, 6).

I consider the following formal properties as typical features of lists:

- Lack of or minimal syntax
- Visually distinct from the text surrounding it
- Short enough to be taken in at one glance
- Consists of three or more consecutive items
- Individual items are marked with numbers, letters, or bullet points
- Items are words of the same order, often nouns (see also Belknap 2004, 19)
- The transition from one item to the next contains a visible gap that also exists on the level of content

A list need not contain all these characteristics to function as one, but the more boxes it ticks, the more obviously it can be identified as a list. I use the word *list* as an umbrella term for a number of enumerative forms that share a prototypical list's formal properties or affordances but may have more specific applications. Items in catalogs, for example, tend to be more expansive than a single noun and frequently consist of full sentences (see von Contzen 2021, 37), and a table could be considered a list that extends to two or more dimensions.[13] While my definition focuses on formal criteria to define lists, these formal aspects need not necessarily be restricted to the written word and could, with only minor modifications, be used to describe enumerative structures in images as well. Barton et al. (2022a, esp. 12–15) also conceptualize the list as a phenomenon that is not limited to textual representations and, for example, discuss the idea of visual lists as defined by "the manifestation of a pattern of repetition and variation" and "the highlighting of the relationship between a whole and its parts" (ibid., 13).[14]

The visual-formal level of the list, which my own definition is based on, also makes visible functional criteria that are inseparable from the dimension of form. Lists, for example, decontextualize items on the levels of both form and content—the (prototypical) list's lack of syntax and its distinctness from the surrounding text, therefore, mirror, on a formal level, the decontextualization that also takes place on the level of content. Furthermore, the use of visual markers such as bullet points or numbering also takes on a dual role on the levels of both (textual) form and content if thought of as a framing device. Such parallels make it possible to project the formal criteria that are crucial to my definition of the list onto a conceptual-metaphorical level. A prototype-based and, therefore, flexible approach to defining the form of the list can therefore also accommodate forms such as diagrams or maps that can be considered list-like through conceptual-metaphorical extension (i.e., forms that share some prototypical features of textual lists through a conceptual-metaphorical link).[15]

Lists can work as a tool to visualize thought processes. The following chapters will demonstrate their capacity to do so on both the level of (detective) characters and that of the reader. This book approaches narrative meaning-making from the perspective of postclassical narratology and also draws on the methodology of cognitive narratology[16] in order to examine ways in which lists can make visible shifting horizons of expectations (of both readers and characters). Lists, therefore, can be used as a means to examine how readers construct story worlds. Since readers play a crucial role when it comes to making sense of lists, I will combine my narratological analysis with considerations that have their origin in reception theory, more specifically in the work of Wolfgang Iser (1926–2007). My interest in the reading process lies in a text's affordances and the sense-making strategies that can be employed to decode it rather than in an empirical study of the responses of individual readers. Therefore, when I speak of how a text affects the reader, I refer to a hypothetical reader, who interacts with a text through its formally given properties.

In *The Act of Reading*, Iser refers to such a reader as the *implied reader*. The implied reader has all the attributes (such as cultural background knowledge or context- and period-specific attitudes) that allow them to decode the entire spectrum of potential meaning encoded in a text. According to Iser, the concept of the implied reader "provides a link between all the historical and individual actualizations of the text and makes them accessible to analysis" (1978, 38).[17] Any (fictional) text offers its readers a variety of perspectives (such as the narrator, the characters, or the plot). Each perspective invites the audience to take a certain stance with regard to the text and "provide[s] access to what the reader is meant to visualize" (ibid., 35). The implied, or ideal, reader is able to connect such perspectives with one another to draw meaning from the text (see ibid.). Furthermore, the implied reader is distinct from the narratee (a fact that takes on particular importance in the context of detective fiction), who may, for example, not be intended to be able to actualize the full meaning of a text.

Iser's aesthetics of reception highlights how text and reader interact to produce meaning. According to Iser, texts contain "gaps" and "blanks" that interrupt the continuous flow of narration and thus stimulate the "constitutive activity of the reader, who cannot help but try and supply the missing links" (ibid., 186).[18] Iser's text/reader model is of particular appeal for the analysis of lists and list-like structures, in which the reader's involvement in creating meaning becomes especially obvious. Eva von Contzen similarly points out that "enumerative structures require the reader's input in order to be rendered meaningful: the 'gaps' or 'blanks' that necessarily exist between the items of a list need to be filled" (2021, 49).[19] Iser's notion of gaps and blanks provides a model to explain how readers supplement missing bits of information and integrate this information into the text (or under which circumstances they fail to do so). Although gaps and blanks exist in all kinds of texts, lists put them on display through their loose grammatical relations and, often, through the visual space left between items listed on a page. For this reason, enumerative structures are an ideal starting point to examine reader involvement and its close connection to knowledge in detective fiction.

Detective fiction, especially the clue puzzle subgenre, invites readers to guess at the solution of the mystery they present. George Dove even goes as far as claiming that "the reader cannot be excluded from the definition of the tale of detection" (1997, 1). It is perhaps no coincidence that lists abound in detective fiction; after all, their fragmented nature requires reading strategies that may also come in useful when trying to piece together the clues scattered through the text. The simple form and loose structuring of the list afford flexibility and allow for a number of different reading strategies. In the context of detective fiction, lists invite readers to create ever-new potential patterns of meaning.

Detective fiction plays with different ways of constructing knowledge that involve a reader's familiarity with genre conventions as well as intra-textual clues and extratextual reference points. The following chapters will take a closer look at different ways of positioning readers in relation to story worlds and detective characters through distinct ways of transmitting (or sometimes producing) knowledge that is necessary to solve the cases.

This book draws attention to three specific conceptions of knowledge in detective fiction: knowledge based on textual clues, knowledge based on referents outside the text, and knowledge as a signifier without a concrete signified. Intratextual knowledge, that is, knowledge situated inside the story world depends on clues explicitly presented in the texts. Bodies of knowledge will be labeled as extratextual if they comprise professional expertise that exists in real-world scientific fields and that characters lay claim to even though it is not explicitly presented on the discourse level. What I call imaginary knowledge, finally, is knowledge that detective characters draw on without referencing either real-world scientific contexts or clues that have been presented in the texts. A text's choice of how knowledge is to be presented to readers crucially influences the role texts assign to readers and thus their (potential) degree of involvement in the investigation. To convey knowledge of any kind to readers, detective fiction resorts to the form of the list with particular frequency. In addition to being tools for narrators and detective characters to focus or divert the reader's attention, lists can thus also serve as pointers to distinct knowledge conceptions evoked by a text.

The central aim of this book will be to show how detective fiction makes use of lists in order to frame various conceptions of knowledge that are crucial to decoding the texts and to demonstrate how readers can be engaged in the act of detection or manipulated into accepting certain propositions through their interaction with those lists. The second chapter of this book provides a brief overview over the history of the detective fiction genre and its close affinity for list-like structures in order to situate the analysis of select texts in their wider socio-cultural framework. My material, which ranges from one of the first detective novels published in 1865 to an early twenty-first-century TV show, is based around two moments of genre consolidation—the late nineteenth century and the Golden Age of detective fiction. During these periods, detective fiction was not only an especially salient genre, but many of the narrative strategies and ways of transmitting knowledge that still form part of the genre's conventions were negotiated during that time. This selection is complemented by a reference to a contemporary TV show to demonstrate the list's relevance across time periods and media. My material is grouped thematically rather than historically—according to different reader positions and conceptions of knowledge—because this structure better enables me to indicate parallels in the ways in which readers interact with lists.

The third chapter examines lists in the context of dossier novels and uses Charles Warren Adams's *The Notting Hill Mystery* (1865) and the *Murder Dossier* novels (1936–1939) by J.G. Links and Dennis Wheatley as case studies. The chapter shows how the dossier format relies on list-based structures, such as footnotes, tables of contents, suspect profiles, and inventories to involve readers in tracking and (re-)organizing information and to invite them to act *as* detectives. The files collected in these dossiers contain the central clues necessary to solve the mystery. The lists the dossiers contain function as organizational tools that mobilize readers to reorganize fragmented pieces of information into a pattern that proves the guilt of a particular suspect. Dossier novels frame knowledge as the result of a process and as something attainable through diligence and exactitude. The communicative situation in all dossiers discussed in this chapter has the reader take on the role of the addressee of the text and imparts on them not only the power but also the (at least implied) responsibility to solve the crime.

Chapter 4 analyzes lists in novels written by Agatha Christie with regard to how they invite readers to adopt certain patterns of thinking. The chapter draws on sociologist Urs Stäheli's work on the political dimension of lists to demonstrate how lists create naturalized patterns of classification and reduce complexity in order to conceal connections. The visible gaps that lists contain can be used to gloss over gaps in a text's content or chain of logic. Christie systematically uses lists and their affordances to mislead readers through playing with their genre expectations, or what George Dove calls the "detection formula[, which] 'programs' the gaps and blanks of the text" (1990, 27), and thus predetermines the most likely patterns in which gaps will be filled. Christie uses the list itself as a device that becomes tied to her readers' expectations about order structures. Like the dossier novels, Christie's texts promise the reader that the knowledge necessary to solve the case can be found in the text in the shape of clues. Yet, what these texts readily present as knowledge concerning the investigation is deceptive and thus requires a reading strategy different from the diligent cross-referencing in the dossier novels. To successfully compete with the fictional detective in finding the solution, readers need to think outside the knowledge structures that lists present as seemingly evident. Christie seems well aware of the importance of all aspects of order in her genre and uses the list's close entanglement with classification structures as the basis for manipulating her readers' attention.

Chapter 5 consists of a short excursus that focuses on Austin Freeman's detective Dr. Thorndyke. Contrary to Christie's novels, Freeman's Dr. Thorndyke stories do not invite readers to take on the role of detective themselves and solve the mystery based on clues provided in the text. To corroborate Thorndyke's conclusions, the stories instead rely on expert knowledge that can only be verified by readers with real-world expertise in a range of scientific disciplines. Knowledge in these novels is situated outside the story world, and the reader is supposed to share the role of Thorndyke's assistant. Rather than becoming active as a co-detective, the reader's role is to constantly be amazed by Thorndyke's exceptional deductive powers and, through him, by the explanatory power of science itself.[20] Thorndyke's lists of hypotheses and the list-like explanations—that at times verge on the didactic—become a narrative strategy to endow Thorndyke's statements and interpretations with an air of being scientific and objective. The list's close entanglement with a number of scientific practices allows the form to transport the authority and semblance of objectivity from the scientific contexts in which it originates to the contexts in which Thorndyke uses it (e.g., when he analyzes evidence). Such list-based references to real-world scientific practices endow Thorndyke's statements and interpretations with authority and a veneer of scientificity. The scientific nature of Thorndyke's statements is thus based on a narrative strategy that relies on listing techniques for its effect.

Chapter 6 expands on the previous chapter's exploration of how lists discursively construct knowledge. The chapter takes a closer look at the famous detective Sherlock Holmes in both Arthur Conan Doyle's original *Sherlock Holmes* stories and the BBC show *Sherlock* (2010–2017), which features a modernized version of the character. Both versions of Sherlock Holmes capitalize on the affordances of visibility and comprehensiveness inherent in the form of the list in order to make the mere reference to the bodies of knowledge they draw on stand in for the knowledge itself. The actual referent remains unmentioned and thus interchangeable at will. Doyle's detective uses the list-like paper technologies of sorting, selecting, and summarizing,[21] and the frequent mentioning of reference works to create the illusion that his deductions are based on a reliable and sound method, and Sherlock Holmes in the BBC's *Sherlock* makes use of the

Internet in a similar manner. Through enumerative practices, references to knowledge are made visible in these texts and ultimately make Holmes himself appear like a personified encyclopedia that promises a comprehensive explanation for every conceivable problem. Since visualization is a central element of this strategy, the chapter uses Bruno Latour's essay "Drawing Things Together" (1990) as a basis to point out the shared affordances of lists and related forms such as maps that are not usually the center of narrative analysis. The BBC's *Sherlock* serves as a case study to discuss how both maps and lists can function to visualize cognitive processes and thus unfold their persuasive force by ordering, illustrating, and conveying knowledge.

The concluding chapter highlights how the various conceptions of knowledge discussed in the previous chapters are inseparable from the roles the novels assign to their readers and from the lists and list-like devices that are crucial to defining those roles. It draws together the previous chapters' findings about the affordances and functions that lists take within the genre of detective fiction, and it points out how epistemological concerns are closely linked to the forms that transport them and to the ubiquitous form of the list in particular.

Detective fiction's concern with order[22] makes it particularly receptive to the workings of form. A study of the form of the list as a dynamic and flexible category makes it possible to put forms that have hitherto been considered as unrelated—such as lists and maps—in dialogue with one another. The shared affordances and strategies of meaning-making between these forms are not restricted to the genre of detective fiction and can easily be transferred to other contexts.

NOTES

1. See, for example, the seminal studies by Stephen Knight (1980) and Julian Symons (1985).
2. The keyword "Arthur Conan Doyle," for example, yields more than 2000 search results in the MLA international bibliography.
3. Notable exceptions are Tzvetan Todorov's "The Typology of Detective Fiction" (1966), George Dove's *The Reader and the Detective Story* (1997), and the essay collection *The Cunning Craft* (1990) edited by June Frazer and Ronald Walker, which takes a look at the detective fiction genre through the lens of various literary theories.
4. For further studies on lists in the context of administrative practices, see also Hess and Mendelsohn (2010) and Gitelman (2014).

5. On the politics of the list, see also the special issue of *Environment and Planning D: Society and Space* edited by Marieke de Goede et al. (2016).

6. Francis Spufford's *The Chatto Book of Cabbages and Kings* (1989) takes a similar approach that focuses on demonstrating the form's ubiquity rather than situating it within theoretical or diachronic frameworks.

7. See Rüggemeier (2020). For a study of the writer Dashiell Hammet's use of lists in the context of both factual and fictional detective work, see Link (2020).

8. See, for example, von Contzen (2017, 2018, 2021).

9. In *The Epic Catalogue: List Form, Cognition, and Reception from Paradise Lost to Beowulf* (forthcoming), Eva von Contzen points out that the first person to adapt the concept of affordances to literary studies was James Gibson's wife Eleanor Gibson (see E. Gibson and Levin 1975; see also von Contzen n.d. forthcoming).

10. From this perspective, arguments such as the one made by Robert Rushing that "real readers" may not or "do not attempt to solve the puzzle" presented in a work of detective fiction (2005, 90) miss the mark. The interest of the study at hand lies with potentials and affordances rather than empirical studies.

11. Some scholars, such as Müller-Wille/Charmantier at least implicitly include the reader in their definition when they write that "the simplest form of a list—that is, the arrangement of entries in a linear series that is *read* from top to bottom, while each individual entry is to be *read* from left to right" (2012, 748, my emphasis).

12. Etymologically, the term "list" goes back to the Old English *líste*, which was used to designate a strip of cloth or a hem. The OED lists "A border, hem, bordering strip" as by now obsolete meaning of the word "list" (see *OED Online*, s.v. list, n.3, accessed 15.12.2022).

13. The OED lists "an orderly arrangement of particulars, a list" as an obsolete meaning of the word *table* (see *OED Online*, table, n.14. Accessed 15 December 2022).

14. Barton et al. also point toward a conceptual distinction between the terms "list" and "series" (see 2022b, 13–14). While the term series suggests a strong semantic relation between items, the unifying effect of a visual list can follow more variable principles of coherence (such as the relationship between a whole and its parts (see ibid.)).

15. The idea that a strong link exists between visual signs and cognitive processes has been emphasized by scholars such as Bruno Latour (see 1990) and will be the basis for my discussion of the relation of lists and maps in Chap. 5.

16. Cognitive narratology is considered a branch of postclassical narratology (see Herman 2013a, §5).

17. The term *implied reader* was coined by Wayne C. Booth (see 1983). Iser's concept of the implied reader remains highly contested in narratological debates and has, for example, been criticized for its lack of precision (see Schmid 2014). I see merit in Iser's concept for the study of lists in detective fiction and do not wish to get entangled in the ongoing debates around the term. For a detailed discussion of the term, see Schmid (2014).

18. Iser's aesthetics of reception draws on Roman Ingarden's conception of literary schemata proposed in *Das literarische Kunstwerk*, which lie at the heart of the indeterminacy inherent in literary works (see Ingarden 1931).

19. See also Mainberger, who writes that enumerations depend on practices that give them meaning (2003, 12).

20. S.E. Sweeney considers this reader role the norm for all detective fiction and argues that the detective's sidekick "personifies the ideal reader of the text" (1990, 8).

21. In *Too Much to Know*, Ann Blair discusses these paper technologies in the context of knowledge production in more detail (see 2010, 3).

22. While detective fiction foregrounds the ordering and structuring functions of lists, other genres employ the form to evoke a fundamentally chaotic impression of linguistic proliferation. For an exploration of the functions of lists in postmodern literature, see Jan Alber's article on Absurd Catalogues: The Functions of Lists in Postmodernist Fiction (2016). For further examples of lists that evoke chaos, see f.e. Eco (2009).

CHAPTER 2

Defining Detective Fiction

The popularity of mystery/detective fiction is only matched by the popularity of received ideas about what it is and what it does.
—*Kayman (1992, 104)*

Detective characters in fiction appear long before there is a coherent genre of detective fiction, and crime has been a popular topic in writing for centuries. Recognizable and clean-cut as the term detective fiction might initially seem, it is surprisingly hard to find a definition that fits all representatives of the genre. A rather frequent approach is to work inductively and determine common features from a very narrow corpus, such as that of Edgar Allan Poe's detective Dupin stories. T.J. Binyon argues that "the [detective] genre grew out of the character, rather than vice versa" (Binyon 1989, 1) and builds his definitions around Arthur Conan Doyle's *Sherlock Holmes* stories.

Frequently, such attempts to define the genre seem too narrow and too broad at the same time. Julian Symons's often quoted suggestion that "[t]he two qualification everybody has thought necessary are that [detective fiction] should present a problem, and that the problem should be solved by an amateur or professional detective through processes of deduction" (1985, 13) excludes much of the hardboiled detective genre, where deduction tends to play only a minor role. W.H. Auden's plot-based definition that "[t]he basic formula is this: a murder occurs: many are

© The Author(s) 2023
S. J. Link, *A Narratological Approach to Lists in Detective Fiction,*
Crime Files, https://doi.org/10.1007/978-3-031-33227-2_2

suspected; all but one suspect, who is the murderer, are eliminated; the murderer is arrested or dies" (1948, n.p.) only applies to a very narrow set of text from the clue puzzle subgenre.[1] Out of the first twelve Sherlock Holmes short stories (usually printed and sold as *The Adventures of Sherlock Holmes*), for example, only three revolve around (attempted) murder. Furthermore, "[m]ost major Victorian novels contain at the very least a mystery, and many feature both a crime and a character who performs the work of detection" (Reitz 2006, n.p.), yet the majority of them would not be considered detective novels.

An attempt to give a comprehensive definition of detective fiction that tries to be precise enough to be useful, and still holds for all representatives of the genre, is destined to fail, it seems. Therefore, in accordance with my discussion of the form of the list, I will describe the genre in terms of family resemblances and provide a number of common and recurring features that I consider central to detective fiction, even if some of them rarely occur together within the same text.[2] Such an approach allows to combine aspects of several definitions, all of which have their merit, and situate texts along an axis of more or less prototypical—rather than sort them into a binary and often arbitrary in-or-out model. The following list provides an overview of frequent features and addresses thematic, formal, and ideological aspects:

- Detectives and detection: an obvious starting point included in almost all definitions is the presence of a detective character, professional or amateur. This figure is centrally involved in a plot, which "describe[s] the effects of detection" (Knight 2004, 28).
- Crime and investigation: thematically, detective fiction plots are characterized by an "interest in the nature of, motives for, and results of, [sic] a crime" (Symons 1985, 16), which are then explored in an investigation.
- Documents and documentation: in terms of content, another reoccurring topic in detective fiction is a concern with written documents and their role in conveying and preserving knowledge. Especially early detective stories show a heightened interest in practices of recording and the documentation of knowledge.
- The power of reason: the detective most frequently relies on reason and rationality when solving problems. Such reliance often expresses itself in an affinity for or references to scientific procedures, which are conceptually tied to ideas of objectivity.

- Containing disorder: regardless of specific themes or plot points, detective stories tend to engage in empowering fantasies of controlling and containing disorder and disruption. Such control is frequently achieved through the power of reason, but can also arise from the detective's physical prowess. This tendency for containing disorder is also reflected in the ways in which the genre makes use of lists.
- Clue puzzles: a feature that is strongly indicative of detective fiction and typically found in the subgenre of Golden Age clue puzzles is the presence of textual clues that hint toward the central mystery throughout the novel. These clues can be spotted and pieced together by the reader to solve the puzzle on their own.
- Reader participation: a rarely discussed, but frequent feature of detective fiction is that it encourages "reader participation" (see Bleiler 1980, 1540).[3] John Gruesser refers to a similar phenomenon when he points out the competitive nature of detective fiction that often involves the level of the reader, for example, by encouraging readers to piece together the clues before the fictional detective does (see 2020, n.p.).

None of these features can be considered as genre-defining on its own, but together, they form a pattern that can be recognized because it has been internalized by readers.[4] Recent studies have employed such pattern recognition on an empirical level and used computer-based, statistical models to establish patterns of coherence within a group of texts considered to belong to the same genre. Ted Underwood, for example, identifies a pattern in detective fiction that is "textually coherent across a period of 160 years (1829–1989)" (2016, 15). Underwood's pattern is consistent across subgenres from the clue puzzle to hardboiled fiction that at first glance to differ widely in theme and plot mechanics, while at the same time it proves clearly delimitable from Newgate and sensation fiction, which are generally considered to be closely related to detective fiction (ibid.).[5]

The idea of pattern recognition also forges a strong conceptual link between the form of the list and the genre of detective fiction. Lists become a tool for both detectives and readers that enables them to recognize patterns and to (re-)order information. This book's underlying assumption that detective fiction uses lists as formal devices to represent ideas about order is rooted in the genre's history. On the following pages, a closer look at this history will demonstrate how the clearly marked reader positions that develop across various subgenres of detective fiction are linked to different conceptions of knowledge, which, in turn, crucially influence how information is conveyed. Examining different reader positions and ideas about knowledge in the context of their development can thus shed light on the different ways in which lists—as textual tools of both creating order and representing knowledge structures—are used in detective fiction.

This chapter will thus provide an overview over the genre history of detective fiction in order to highlight different reader positions and their connections to distinct conceptions of knowledge, and to embed the subsequent analysis in a cultural and historical context. The following summary by no means aims to be a comprehensive overview of the genre but is rather meant to establish some common terms and reference points for the further discussion of selected texts from the genre.[6] The chapter concludes with a brief excursion on the numerous rule catalogs produced in the Golden Age period, which will highlight the conceptual link between lists and detective fiction from an additional perspective.

PRECURSORS, INFLUENCES, DEVELOPMENTS: FROM THE *NEWGATE CALENDAR* TO THE GOLDEN AGE

Beginnings: The Newgate Calendar

The *Newgate Calendar*, a collection of crime stories which first appeared as a printed anthology in the eighteenth century, is often quoted as an important predecessor to detective fiction. The *Newgate Calendar* was initially issued as a monthly record of executions by the chaplain of Newgate prison, where criminals were held to await their sentence or execution, but the pamphlets were adapted by publishers into collections of morally edifying crime stories in multiple volumes which collectively came to be known as *The Newgate Calendar* (see Knight 2004, 5–6).

The (allegedly true) stories in the *Newgate Calendar* are a testimony to shifting views on crime and mark the transition from a theological to a more secular frame of reference for criminality (see ibid., 9). They feature no special agent of detection because they are situated in a social context in which the belief is still prevalent that crime and deviance cannot go unnoticed in a tightly knit community (see Knight 1980, 18). Ideologically, the *Newgate Calendar* is thus based around what Stephen Knight calls an "organic model of society" that is founded on the idea that society can negotiate aberrant behavior without the interference of a mediating instance (ibid., 13). At the same time, the stories make evident the fissures between such a belief and a social and economic reality which has long moved on from the religious views and the political system of feudalism that gave birth to those beliefs (see Knight 2004, 8).

Since personal guilt and social observation are central factors in exposing crimes in the stories related in the *Newgate Calendar*, the plots of these stories are often resolved by what appears to be coincidence from a modern point of view. But within a framework in which individual humans exert only little control over events, such solutions become acceptable (see Knight 1980, 18).

Newgate stories remained in fashion into the early 1830s, when a number of novelists resorted to the *Newgate Calendar* for inspiration for their works. Newgate novels, which enjoyed enormous popularity during that decade, were centered around criminals and the spectacle of punishment rather than disciplinary power that would become inseparable from the figure of the detective (see Pykett 2006, 34).

Influences: Edgar Allan Poe, Eugène Vidoq, and Émile Gaboriau

The first English language texts in which both a detective figure and the act of detection play a major role are Edgar Allan Poe's C. Auguste Dupin short stories. Poe's stories are frequently considered to be the origin of detective fiction, and both French and British crime writers were greatly influenced by the pattern Poe established.[7] *The Cambridge Companion to Crime Fiction* references the notion that Poe's first Dupin story "Murder in the Rue Morgue" (1841) is to be considered the first detective story as "standard view" (Priestman 2006b, 3), and even computer-based, statistical models identify Poe's Dupin stories as prototypical representatives of the genre (see Underwood 2016, 13).

Poe's short stories are centered around the steps his detective takes in order to resolve a number of incidents that leave the police in the stories at a loss. Detective Dupin, Stephen Knight argues, was to become the model for the "intelligent, infallible, isolated hero so important to the crime fiction of the last 100 years" (1980, 39). Poe's stories suggest that "isolated intellectual and imaginative life is a sufficient and successful response to the world and its problems" (ibid., 39) and thus address nineteenth-century values about individualism, reason, order, and, implicitly, even reflect contemporary concerns about state power growing out of perspective. Dupin presents Poe's readers with a set of values that they can both share and admire, and his emphasis on the analysis of physical data (see Knight 1980, 42) is a testament to an ever-growing interest and belief in the power of science and human reason to explain the world.[8]

Both Dupin's character traits, which mark him as a somewhat aloof genius, and his methods, which (he claims) are firmly grounded in observation and scientific reason, and that hence seem demystified and reproducible, exerted a strong influence on numerous detective figures that were to follow him. Most notably among them is Arthur Conan Doyle's Sherlock Holmes, who shares Dupin's intellectual prowess and his predilection for empiricism.

The French tradition of detective fiction also exercised considerable influence over the genre's development in Britain. Two French detective figures that should be mentioned here are the criminal-turned-detective Eugène Vidoq, whose (partly ghost-written) autobiography *Mémoires de Vidocq, chef de la police de Sûreté, jusqu'en 1827* (1828–1829) is often quoted as a possible first detective novel, and Émile Gaboriau's detective Monsieur Lecoq. Lecoq served as a role model for Doyle's Sherlock Holmes (see Knight 2004, 52), and according to E.F. Bleiler, Gaboriau's novels already assemble all the features that would later become central to the detective novel (see 1980, 1540).[9]

Precursors: Sensation Fiction

Poe is often considered as a notable influence on the sensation fiction writer Wilkie Collins, whose 1868 novel *The Moonstone* is commonly regarded as the first novel-length piece of detective fiction in Britain.[10] The establishment of a detective department at the London Metropolitan Police in 1842 sparked a new wave of interest in the topic of crime and detection. This renewed interest found its expression, among other things, in the abundance of sensational crime stories featured in newspapers, which recent innovations in printing culture made cheaply available and which, due to ever-growing literacy rates, were widely distributed and read.

Sensation fiction takes its name from its appeal to and stirring effect on the senses, that is, from supposedly causing excitements and other sensations in its readers. This preoccupation with readers and their involvement in fictional texts already foreshadows the keen interest that detective fiction was soon to take in its readers. Sensation novels draw on topics which hitherto had been the hallmark of Gothic fiction but relocate issues such as "social transgressions and illicit passions" and "nervous, psychological, sexual and social shocks" (Pykett 2006, 34) from remote Gothic castles in faraway times and countries to modern British middle- and upper-class homes in order to directly affect their readers and "preach [...] to the nerves" (ibid., 33).

Not unlike the genre of Newgate fiction that arose out of the eighteenth century *Newgate Calendar* in the early 1830s, the immense popularity of sensation fiction sparked concerns about the genre's possibly corrupting influence on its middle class, largely female readership, and on culture in general (see Reitz 2006, n.p.). The genre raised particular concern with contemporary reviewers and critics because it not only treated unseemly and indecorous topics, but moreover had them play out in "the drawing room rather than the drinking den" (Pykett 2006, 34).[11]

Two examples of immensely popular sensation novels that had a great influence on the reading public are Wilkie Collins's *The Woman in White* (1859) and Mary Elizabeth Braddon's *Lady Audley's Secret* (1861–1862). *Lady Audley's Secret* includes all the hallmark features of sensation fiction: a concern with the (in)stability of class boundaries, transgressions of gender roles, a "mix of thrillingly gendered crime and sexually exciting beauty" (Knight 2004, 42), and a secret that revolves around the rift between seeming and being with regard to (social) appearances and respectability.

Due to its fascination with secrets and concealment, sensation fiction frequently features elements of detection, just as many aspects of detection—such as the detective's supposed ability to see through the surface of things—are portrayed as sensational. One criterion that distinguishes sensation fiction from detective fiction such as Wilkie Collins's *The Moonstone*, however, is that detective fiction "shifts the focus from the crime itself [...] to its investigation" (Priestman 2006b, 4). While many sensation novels exhibit an interest in letters, descriptions, documents, and the display of realistic detail—features they share with detective fiction—they "tend to have deeply improbable lurches in the plot that suggest there are strange forces in the world beyond mere realism" (Knight 2004, 43).[12]

According to T.S. Eliot, Collins's *The Moonstone*, which revolves around the theft of an Indian diamond, is to be considered "the first and greatest of English detective novels" (1934, 426), and Dorothy Sayers has called it "the finest detective story ever written" (1928, 25). The novel was inspired by a true crime case[13] and features not one but several detectives (both amateur and professional).[14] *The Moonstone* contains many features that have become central constituents of detective fiction, such as a plot focused on an investigation, the examination of evidence, so-called *red herring* clues supposed to lead the reader astray, a grand revelation, and the reestablishment of order at the end of the story—the latter also being a typical trait of sensation fiction.[15]

Detectives and the Police

With all the popular attention paid to stories revolving around crime and detection in fiction and newspapers, and with a newly established detective department in London, one might wonder why the great majority of (successful) fictional detectives in the nineteenth century were individual amateurs or, like Sherlock Holmes, private investigators. This has a lot to do with the English public's attitude and relation toward the police. Before the establishment of the Metropolitan Police in 1829, crime was dealt with locally or regionally by the constables that individual country parishes employed, a system established in Tudor times.[16] With the advent of the London Metropolitan Police, for the first time, police organizations were centralized and became immediately subordinate to the home office. This centralized police force was generally regarded with suspicion and hostility by the British public, to a degree where police officers initially had to wear their uniforms even when they were off duty in order to alleviate fears of state espionage (see Shpayer-Makov 2010, 674–675).[17]

Such distrust toward the police is deeply intertwined with Victorian anxieties about privacy and class stability and turns police officers (and later, detectives) into projection surfaces for misgivings ranging from surveillance to class affiliation. The fact that the first detectives employed in the newly established detective departments were recruited from the ranks of the working classes further fueled such fears among the bourgeoisie, "whose normality has been hitherto defined as a matter of not needing the police" (Miller 1988, 3). Even in fictional contexts, the detectives' ability to move between social strata and blend in anywhere stimulated the fear that class boundaries were not fixed and threatened to expose the instability of class-based identities as such (see Milton 2011, 519).

The invisibility and undetectability awarded to detectives by their exemption from having to wear a uniform fostered the fear of state espionage and increased the perceived threat emanating from the existence of such a position (see Shpayer-Makov 2010, 673). The threatening nature of the detective's newly established role as unseen observer largely resulted from a perceived imbalance of power: while detectives themselves were all but invisible because they did not have to wear a uniform, they still supposedly were able to see through what others wished to conceal. The powers of observation ascribed to detectives, and their alleged ability to endow seemingly irrelevant details with incriminating meaning, according to D.A. Miller, appeared almost superhuman to those not capable of drawing the same conclusions (see 1988, 28). For a society obsessed with visibility, the anonymity of detectives and the opacity of their power were particularly disconcerting. A detective's outstanding "super-vision" is closely connected to the "police supervision that it embodies," as Miller points out (ibid., 35),[18] and indeed the words *detective* and *spy* were used synonymously long into the nineteenth century (see Knight 2004, 10). In this context, it is hardly surprising that lists, as tools that visualize a certain way of ordering the world, feature so prominently in many texts in which detection plays a central role.

While detectives as agents of the state were regarded with considerable suspicion, the idea of an art of detection as a way of thinking and looking at the world sparked widespread fascination among the public. Caroline Reitz argues that "[d]etective fiction gave a particular expression to what was arguably a much larger cultural methodology, detection itself" and that the detective profession can be considered as only one among many professions emerging in the nineteenth century "who use observation and deduction to grapple with the challenges of modernity" (2006, n.p.). One factor for the enormous success of the character Sherlock Holmes toward the end of the nineteenth century may have been that Doyle's detective caters to the fascination with the detective's alleged power of vision and absolute command over human reason. At the same time, Doyle sidesteps anxieties about class and surveillance by making Holmes a private investigator, who is asked for help by his clients rather than intruding on their privacy unwanted.

Doyle and Positivism

The nineteenth century's fascination with detective fiction, Caroline Reitz observes, is "part of an emerging faith in observation and empirical data shared broadly by the Victorians" (2006, n.p.). However, despite the detective's ability to reimpose order on social problems that appeared increasingly unmanageable toward the beginning of the nineteenth century (ibid.), the image of the detective as a protector of society only took hold gradually and only slowly superseded that of the criminal as a romantic outlaw hero (see Symons 1985, 45). It was only with the creation of Arthur Conan Doyle's Sherlock Holmes that this development achieved its full momentum.

Stephen Knight sees two main reasons for the appeal that the character of Sherlock Holmes held for a Victorian audience: "Doyle has two premises: the rational scientific idea that events are really linked in an unaccidental chain, and the individualistic notion that a single inquirer can—and should—establish the links" (1980, 68). Such an approach both separates the enormous power Holmes commands from an obscure and untrustworthy state institution and, by implicitly linking rationalism and individualism, creates the illusion that Holmes's powers of observation and his command over logic and reason are qualities potentially attainable by anyone. Through listing and referencing techniques, Doyle's short stories and novels suggest to readers that replicating Holmes's methods of investigation should be as easy as looking up a reference in an encyclopedia. Yet, at the same time, his abilities make Holmes an idealized hero figure than can be admired. Such alluring power fantasies of "individualized rationality" (ibid., 68) of course appealed to an audience grappling with rapid technological developments, the crumbling certainties of class stability, and changes in societal structure.

The early *Holmes* stories do not share sensation fiction's fascination with murder but instead foreground Holmes's amazing observational and problem-solving abilities that make him an embodiment of the "romance of science" (Knight 2004, 56) that constitutes a big selling point of these stories. Unlike sensation fiction, Doyle's *Sherlock Holmes* stories are no longer interested in the sensational aspects of crime. In fact, some of the stories from *The Adventures of Sherlock Holmes* do not feature a proper crime at all.[19] The focus of these stories is not the crime itself but rather the mystery it presents and the intellectual achievement displayed in resolving such mysteries. Holmes uses his capability for rational thought as a tool for maintaining order to champion his rather bourgeois values (see Knight 1980, 103)[20] and thus appears as a hero that seems tailor-made for the Victorians. Holmes's success in his investigations relies not only on his brilliant mind but at least as much on his exceptional command over recording and documentation techniques,[21] which themselves bear associations with the bourgeois virtues of exactitude and diligence.

The aloof attitude, trust in science, and emphasis on accuracy and rational thought that Holmes shares with earlier detectives such as Poe's Dupin[22] are all features that were to shape many of the detective figures that succeeded Sherlock Holmes. One such successor that deserves a brief mention here and that takes the detective fiction genre's fascination with science and positivism to a hitherto unreached level is Richard Austin Freeman's Dr. Thorndyke. Dr. Thorndyke is positivism personified. He emphasizes the prime importance of analyzing observable details (which he calls "data") when solving cases, and he uses his capacity for rational thought to create a number of hypotheses (based on what he at least claims to be observation and probability, and enumerated to the reader) for each puzzle he encounters. The pattern is that Thorndyke then eliminates all but one of those hypotheses with the help of classical observation-based investigation and logical thought.[23] Contrary to the allusions to science displayed in the *Holmes* stories that function more to convey a ritual of scientificity that is effect- and not content-based, the scientific facts in Freeman's *Thorndyke* stories are—so Freeman and his fans claim—all accurate to the last detail. Freeman provides detailed descriptions and explanations of the scientific procedures Thorndyke follows to solve his cases and thus, supposedly, lets his readers partake in these processes (see Symons 1985, 80). The didactic quality of Thorndyke's deliberations often puts readers in the position of a student to be educated about scientific principles and procedures.

Thorndyke represents the epitome of a strand of detective fiction that portrays the detective as a "rational superman" (Knight 2004, 68), that is, as an even more scientific, more intense version of the Sherlock Holmes model that proved so successful with its Victorian audience.[24] The American mystery writer Jacques Futrelle's detective Professor Augustus S.F.X. Van Dusen, PhD, LLD, FRS, MD, MDS, is another noteworthy figure within this tradition, and Futrelle's highly artificial puzzle plots have been considered as forerunners to the British clue puzzles of the 1920s (see Knight 2004, 69).

The Golden Age: Fair Play and the Clue Puzzle

The so-called Golden Age of detective fiction is usually dated between WWI and WWII.[25] In this period, the novel superseded the short story as prevalent medium and publishing channel for detective fiction. Changing reading habits after WWI may also have been responsible for the increasing popularity of novels. Such shifts in popular taste, Julian Symons argues, also influenced the audience the detective fiction genre drew. Besides an increasingly female readership, the genre also saw a rise in female writers during the Golden Age, so that, in this period, detective novels were written increasingly by and for women (see 1985, 86).

With such shifts in publication form and audience, the themes dealt with in these kinds of stories changed as well: in Agatha Christie's crime stories, for example, "[h]ard work, activity, professionalism and the positivistic mysteries of contemporary forensic science [...] are all thrown out together" and replaced by "peaceful reflection" (Knight 1980, 110). This not only makes detection more accessible to the general public but also caters to the "illusion of effective self-help and self-sufficiency" propagated in the post-WWI period (ibid.).[26]

In terms of the crimes covered in these texts, there is a clear shift from the non-violent offenses (such as theft) and concealed identities that characterize the early *Holmes* stories to murder. Yet, Golden Age murderers are rarely to never professional criminals and usually come from the same social (middle to upper class) circle as the victim, and they have personal rather than professional motives for crimes (see Knight 2004, 87–88; see also Symons 1985, 94). The crime typically takes place in an enclosed setting that allows for a limited number of suspects (Knight 2004, 87), and as a general rule, the setting disregards the real-world historical context of depression, trade unions, and other political developments (see Symons 1985, 96).

The most salient modification that came with the Golden Age, however, is a structural one. Golden Age fiction prides itself with making all the clues that the detective uncovers and needs to successfully complete the investigation available to the reader. Because of its emphasis on textual clues, the detective fiction of the Golden Age is frequently referred to as the *clue puzzle* (sub)genre.[27] In fact, the central idea associated with detective fiction literature of the Golden Age today is that the reader is supposed to be able to solve the puzzle the text presents along with or even before the fictional detective. For this purpose, clue puzzles frequently feature lists that summarize or order information as tools for readers. With the rise of the clue puzzle, maps of the crime scene, which served as an additional tool of detection for readers and made it easier to follow the detective's movements, became a standard feature included in detective novels of the period (see Knight 1980, 109–110).

Both writers and readers of such clue puzzles took the notion of *fair play*, which states that important clues must be made accessible to the reader and thus provide them with a fair chance of detecting the guilty party, very seriously. This becomes evident, for example, from the principle's inclusion in the "Detection Club Oath," which was drafted by a group of British writers including Agatha Christie and had to be sworn upon admission to the Detection Club. The "Detection Club Oath" includes a set of rules based around Ronald Knox's "Detective Story Decalogue" (1929), which members of the Detection Club were supposed to adhere to when writing their fiction. The Golden Age produced a plethora of such rule catalogs and investigations of the underlying principles and building blocks of the genre. Since those genre rules frequently appeared in or heavily relied on the form of the list as their mode of presentation, the remainder of this chapter will take a closer look at three such rule catalogs and elaborate on this curious connection to list-like structures that seems to be written into the detective fiction genre.

EXCURSUS: LISTS IN THE HISTORY OF DETECTIVE FICTION—THE RULE CATALOGS OF THE GOLDEN AGE

Susan Lanser argues that "form functions as social and cultural content" (2019, 10). This is certainly true when considering the significance that the form of the list takes on in the rule catalogs produced by detective fiction writers of the Golden Age. Those catalogs employ lists to support the genre's ideology of portraying a neatly ordered world that is logically structured and comprehensible through a commitment to human reason. At the same time, the normative authority that the list carries is used to support the authors' portrayal of the genre as serious and worth of critical attention. This excursus will consider three different rule catalogs from the Golden Age that take great pains to delineate the rules according to which the detective fiction genre works. In these catalogs, the form of the list is used to validate the rules and categorization strategies that the list-makers come up with in order to award their personal tastes normative force. Furthermore, I want to examine how two of these catalogs reference implied or actual readers to justify their claims—Austin Freeman does so by emphasizing the social status of his alleged readership, and Ronald Knox implicitly invokes the fair play principle as a justification for his rules.

The special status of the reader in detective fiction is thus already written into the rules that are meant to establish the foundations of the genre. W.H. Auden's (1907–1973) "The Guilty Vicarage" (1948) is an attempt to make the author's very personal taste in and ideas about what makes a good detective story appear as objectively valid criteria—something he shares with Freeman, who will be discussed below. Already in his introduction to his essay, Auden uses enumeration markers such as "[f]irstly," "[s]econdly," and "thirdly" (Auden 1948, n.p.) to evoke the impression of organized, logic thought, that mimics the (supposedly) orderly world and structure of the kind of fiction he describes. Even Auden's definition of detective fiction itself has an enumerative structure: "[t]he basic formula is this: a murder occurs; many are suspected; all but one suspect, who is the murderer, are eliminated; the murderer is arrested or dies" (ibid.).[28] The lack of causal connectors evokes the impression that his definition is descriptive rather than interpretative and hence objectively representative of the genre. Auden then further strengthens the supposed objectivity of his definition by following it with an elaboration on two special cases to be explicitly excluded from his considerations, and the length of these exceptions distinctly exceeds the length of the definition. These two exceptions are listed after a colon and each starts with a number. Auden thus makes use of the orderly impression that list-like structures create on the level of form to award the content he represents the same kind of orderly appearance.

This becomes evident at the latest when he proceeds to turn his "formula" (ibid.) into a table:

Peaceful state before murder	False innocence
|	|
Murder	Revelation of presence of guilt
|	|
False clues, secondary murder, etc.	False location of guilt
|	|
Solution	Location of real guilt
|	|
Arrest of murderer	Catharsis
|	|
Peaceful state after arrest	True innocence

The form of the diagram, similar to the list, carries vibes of scientificity, and the horizontally and vertically ordered structure evokes an empirical background that Auden's contentual speculations clearly do not live up to. It is through his clever choice of form that Auden lends credibility to his content.

In terms of content, Auden makes use of the biblical binary ideology of guilt and innocence and applies it as a classifying tool. The rigorous formal structure of binary classification forges a connection between his elaborations and the formal text structure of classification, compressed information, and objective fact.[29] Lisa Gitelman has argued that (written) documents are concrete in terms of their content, but always also represent an abstract heuristics. This heuristics stands behind the documents' immediately apparent meaning and is a result of "practices of expression and reception" (2014, 3) that can become manifest through form. Such formal practices are reflections of cultural beliefs, and Auden expertly avails himself of the connotations of objectivity and scientificity that are culturally associated with the form of the list as an ordering tool and categorizing device to strengthen his argument. By choosing the form of the diagram, Auden, for example, evokes the impression that there is an ordered plot structure identifiable in detective fiction that can be described to begin with. He thus creates the impression that the content, here, mirrors the form.

Following the presentation of this diagram, and very much in the classificatory spirit of his essay, Auden continues to sort elements he considers part of detective fiction into self-created categories and sub-categories. He, for example, states that "[t]here are three classes of crime: (A) offenses against God and one's neighbor or neighbors; (B) offenses against God and society; (C) offenses against God" (1948, n.p.). Such a classificatory system reminds of the lists of hypotheses that scientifically minded detectives such as Freeman's Dr. Thorndyke use to analyze their cases, and the classificatory lettering shows the heavy emphasis placed on categorization. The practice of classification here appears as *the* ordering tool par excellence, through which human reason dictates how to accurately and efficiently sort through the seemingly random material our surroundings present us with. Auden's act of classification mimics how the fictional detectives he writes about seem to be able to sort through and classify criminal motives and actions in the same way they can classify material clues.

Auden's choice of structure and his mode of expression in this essay thus mirror his beliefs about detective fiction as a genre. By using the classificatory structures which he tries to impose on the genre of detective fiction as structuring devices for his essay, Auden validates his own analysis and makes it appear comprehensive, logical, and empirically sound.

Despite all the emphasis Auden seems to place on structure, his conceptualization of good detective stories is content—rather than structure-based. Auden states that "[t]he detective story has five elements—the milieu, the victim, the murderer, the suspects, the detectives" (ibid.) and then proceeds to use these content-related elements as captions to structure the remainder of his essay. Hereby, Auden evokes the impression of definitional clarity and comprehensiveness. In his first category, which is concerned with the human milieu of detective fiction, he even goes so far as to establish two levels of subcategories, marked separately by letters and numbers (in the manner of "1 a, b, c; 2 a, b, c"). The letters and numbers draw attention to the list-like structure and intricate substructure of his classifications and evoke the impression of being comprehensive. At the same time, they conceal the fact that what is written down here shows Auden's specific preferences and ideas and is, in fact, far from comprehensive. Auden's text contains no tangible hints to humor; on the contrary, he seems to take his classifications very seriously and even references back to them later in his text. When listing possible causes of guilt in suspects, he, for example, writes "(1) the wish or even the intention to murder; (2) crimes of Class A or vices of Class C" (ibid.). By referring to his formerly established classes of crimes and vices not by their descriptive titles but by the classificatory letter assigned to them, Auden evokes the impression that his classification system can be taken for granted and should be so well known that it can be referred to by its abbreviated alphanumerical tag rather than its content. The actual content becomes secondary.

Austin Freeman (1862–1943), in his "The Art of the Detective Story" (1924), employs a similar strategy in awarding his personal opinions and preferences universal validity. Freeman's essay aims to defend detective fiction as a serious genre and purports that the rules he proposes will serve to guarantee that texts which follow them maintain a certain standard. To be able to produce good detective fiction, Freeman argues, a writer must possess an innate talent for both ratiocination and imagination, which he considers contradictory qualities that rarely coincide in the same person. Furthermore, detective fiction writers are in need of an "extensive outfit of special knowledge" (1976, 9), which, in contrast to the former two qualities, can be acquired by anyone.

Freeman's essay takes great pains to demonstrate how his own writing exhibits the analytical talent and extensive special knowledge he postulates in detective fiction writers. This becomes evident from the abundance of medico-mathematical vocabulary in his text and from his use of the list form to validate his arguments. Like his detective Dr. Thorndyke, Freeman employs mathematical vocabulary to convey the impression that the rather personal preferences he describes in his essay constitute objective assessments that are both measurable and quantifiable. When he writes that the pleasure an argument affords the reader is "*proportionate* to the intricacy of the proof" (ibid., 12, my emphasis), he suggests that both pleasure and intricacy are quantities that can be easily measured and that there exists a simple linear relation between them that offers itself to comparative analysis. Moreover, he repeatedly uses the word "data" to designate matters he discusses and thus evokes the contexts of science and objectivity.

Freeman also makes his own medical background obtrusively obvious when he uses medical vocabulary to discredit sensation fiction writers, who, he states, need to "penetrate [their] reader's mental epidermis" with their "literary projectiles," and who will hence inevitably "create a tolerance which has to be met by an increase of the dose" if they are to continue to engage their readers (ibid., 10). This mixed metaphor calls on the word fields of "medicine" and "war" to paint sensation fiction as an unwanted, unpleasant, and even violent intrusion upon the reader's well-being. The mention of tolerances and increased doses brings up medical contexts of addiction and floats the suggestion that there may be an overdose that could prove fatal to the reader's health. His choice of medical vocabulary aims at awarding Freeman's remarks the authority of a medical expert.

Freeman's medical background and his rather distinct ideas about what constitutes high and low culture also make their way into how he conceptualizes his readers and the kind of reading experience detective fiction is to afford them. He argues that detective fiction is to offer its readers "primarily an intellectual satisfaction" (ibid., 11), and consequently, he imagines his readers as "real connoisseurs" originating from a "definitely intellectual class" (ibid.) of male professionals. Freeman then enumerates professions (theologians, scholars, lawyers, doctors) that are likely to produce such intellectuals and thus uses the social status of his imagined class of readers to award a prestigious status to what happens to be his preferred class of fiction. An interesting parallel to his less scientifically minded fellow Golden Age writers arises when Freeman emphasizes that readers are to be "invited to take part" in the intellectual puzzle a detective novel poses and demands that "the excellence of the entertainment must be judged by the completeness with which it satisfies the expectations" of its addressee (ibid.).

In order to create such satisfaction with readers, Freeman argues, a good detective story needs to follow a certain structure. The structure Freeman proposes is presented in the form of a list and demands a proper detective story have:

> four stages: (1) statement of the problem; (2) production of the data for its solution ('clues'); (3) the discovery, i.e., completion of the inquiry by the investigator and declaration by him of the solution; (4) proof of the solution by an exposition of the evidence. (ibid., 14)

This list is followed by explanatory paragraphs for each step that refer back to the numbering of those steps. By stating his ideas about structure as a consecutively numbered list, Freeman creates the semblance of an incontestable causal relation between the items: just as the number two always inevitably follows the number one, his structure suggests, so must the second stage he proposes always follow the first. Freeman makes use of the unassailable sequential logic of numbers to present his steps of composition as a kind of natural order dictated by logic and to award them the argumentative force of mathematical logic.

Last but not least, Ronald Knox's "A Detective Story Decalogue" (1929) deserves mention among the Golden Age rule lists presented here.[30] The word "Decalogue" in the title is clearly aimed at awarding the ten rules that follow authority and speaks to Knox's aspiration to standardize genre conventions.[31] The reference to the ten commandments suggests that the rules Knox establishes are to be followed religiously and even implies that violating them may have severe consequences. The title functions to award Knox, as the creator of those rules, authority over seeing to their observance and poses his voice as one that is endowed with genre-defining authority. Knox's bold title may well have contributed to his rules being cited as a "moment [...] of genre consolidation" for detective fiction (Underwood 2016, 3).

Knox's ten commandments, unsurprisingly, are presented in the form of a list. The text consists of twenty paragraphs that state ten numbered rules in italics, each followed by an explanatory section that discusses specifications or exceptions of the previously stated rules. Even though the numbered rules and brief italicized statements formally create the impression of clarity and cast each rule as a clearly distinguishable entity, the sheer length of the explanatory paragraphs and the fact that four out of the ten rules come with exceptions already provides a hint that Knox's commandments cannot create the kind of orderly structured system their formal appearance simulates.

This becomes especially (and somewhat absurdly) evident from the phrasing of one of the rules, which seems explicitly designed to accommodate a text written by Knox himself. Rule III states that "[n]ot more than one secret room or passage is allowable" (1976, 195) in a detective novel and thus already inscribes the exception into the rule text itself. The explanatory paragraph that follows makes clear that Knox generally disapproves of secret passages because they can be used as the kind of unforeseeable surprise twist the fair play principle tries to do away with. At the same time, however, the explanation serves to justify an instance in which Knox himself resorted to this very device. The explanatory text comes up with the rather far-fetched addendum that secret passages should not be used "unless the action takes place in the kind of house where such devices might be expected" (ibid.), which, Knox emphasizes, is the case in his novel.

The cast-iron validity that the title and the orderly numbering suggest Knox's rules should have (and that would demand a phrasing such as "No secret room or passage is allowable" for rule III) is undermined by the—partly personalized—exceptions Knox has to allow to make at least his own published texts comply with his rules. Ultimately, the classificatory clarity that Knox aims for and that the list form coaxes readers into taking for granted is clearly a fantasy. All three texts discussed in this section use the list form to present subjective rules and impressions as founded in objective empirical evidence or a similarly irrefutable authority, and hence, as universally valid.

The historical overview I have provided in this chapter will serve as a framework that allows me to place the analysis of my material made in subsequent chapters in relation to the genre's history and to the cultural backdrop of the subgenres I discuss. Rather than trying to create a streamlined template that disregards specificity in favor of scope, the prototype-based approach I take to defining detective fiction enables readers to assess particular aspects of individual stories in relation to the historical background that produced (or obscured) them.

The rule catalogs discussed above make evident the difficulties of overgeneralizations. Nevertheless, these catalogs lay bare some of the formal features and persuasive strategies that underlie the genre, and they testify to the importance of form *as* cultural content.

NOTES

1. Auden's definition does not even account for all the works within that particular subgenre and, for example, excludes canonical work such as Agatha Christie's *Murder on the Orient Express* (1934), where none of the suspects can be eliminated because the crime was committed collaboratively.
2. For a similar approach, see Underwood, who also defines genre in terms of "overlapping features" (2016, 5).
3. Bleiler argues that the French crime writer Émile Gaboriau (1833–1873) was the first writer to establish a number of features that were to become common in novel-length detective stories.
4. Lisa Gitelman, too, speaks of genres in terms of pattern recognition (see 2014, 2) when she discusses documents as a genre and describes genres as "socially realized sites of coherence" (2014, 3).
5. Next to a thematic concern that revolves around the police, murder, and investigation, Underwood's statistical model also identifies the word field of "architecture and domestic furnishing" as indicative of the detective fiction genre (2016, 15). A possible explanation could be that the investigation of clues found in detective fiction usually necessitates descriptions of space.
6. For a more comprehensive over view of the detective fiction genre, see, for example, Knight (2004) and Symons (1985).
7. Martin Priestman cites Poe's influence on Emile Gaboriau and Wilkie Collins (see Priestman 2006b, 2), and Martin Kayman points out that Doyle's first Sherlock Holmes novel, *A Study in Scarlet*, has Sherlock Holmes compare himself to Poe's Dupin as if he were a real-world historical person (2006, 42).
8. This development marks a clear secular departure from community- and religion-based beliefs in the workings of order that are still prevalent around the time the *Newgate Calendar* appeared.
9. For more information on the French tradition of detective fiction, see, for example, Knight (2004, chapter 2); Schütt (2006); Fondanèché (2000).
10. See, for example, Priestman (2006b), who names *The Moonstone* as the first detective novel. Charles Dickens's *Bleak House* (1853) was published earlier and is often mentioned in the same breath. However, it only has a subplot that revolves around detection.
11. Lynn Pykett considers the difference between Newgate and sensation fiction as "the result of a change in the cultural meaning of crime and the criminal, and a movement from a society controlled by the spectacle of punishment to one morally managed by discipline" (2006, 34).
12. One example for such an improbable lurch would be when Walter Hartright, by a very lucky chance, visits the grave of Laura's mother at the exact same time Laura and Marian happen to be there, too, in *The Woman in White* (see also Knight 2004, 43).

13. For an examination of the Road Hill House murder case in relation to *The Moonstone*, see the study by Kate Summerscale (2008).

14. Incidentally, it also features a laundry list that serves as a central clue.

15. Knight furthermore draws attention to the "inherent stasis underlying the sensational form—and indeed the patterns of crime fiction as a whole" that is closely tied to this inevitable reestablishment of order at the end of detective and sensation novels (2004, 47).

16. Efforts to maintain a more transregional exchange of intelligence were already made in the second half of the eighteenth century, with the establishment of the Bow Street Runners, a paid task force for the pursuit of criminals (but not for the detection of crimes) (see Kayman 1992, 66–67).

17. Ernest Mandel proposes a somewhat simplistic correlation between the public's regard for the police and the type of crime the police most frequently investigated, and claims that once the prisons filled with more robbers and murderers than debtors, the status of the police in the eyes of the public improved (see 1987, 24).

18. Unless indicated otherwise, all emphases have been removed from quotations for better readability.

19. Instead, the cases featured in these stories revolve around impersonation or the concealing of one's identity for disreputable motives. The harmless nature of these crimes may also serve a distancing function from an everyday reality that seemed increasingly threatening and dangerous (see Knight 2004, 27). The infamous criminal mastermind Professor Moriarty as Holmes's nemesis only appears much later.

20. Interestingly, these values only very rarely seem to come into conflict with the character's bohemian tastes and often decadent and eccentric behavior.

21. The recording and documentation techniques that feature in the *Sherlock Holmes* stories will be discussed in more detail in Chap. 5.

22. T.J. Binyon argues that the traits of pride, alienation, and isolation make both Dupin and Holmes "a product of the Romantic Tradition" (1989, 10).

23. Or so he claims. The excursus that follows Chap. 4 will examine the stance that the *Thorndyke* novels take with regard to empirical observations and logical thought in more detail.

24. Some recent publications have questioned the idea of the (Victorian) detective as the epitome of reason and rationality. However, I argue that detective fiction's concern with lists makes evident a preoccupation with classification systems and ordering knowledge, and thus also with reason and rationality. For an approach that offers an explanation for the popularity of the character Sherlock Holmes that is rooted in media and material history, see, for example, Clarke (2019).

25. For a detailed discussion of the term *Golden Age* and some alternative suggestions for period dates, see Knight (2004, 85). While all period labels are naturally simplistic and somewhat restrictive, they can still be useful as umbrella terms to describe certain phenomena. It is in this way that period labels are used in this book.

26. For a discussion of the clue puzzle's relation to modernism, see Knight (2006). Knight argues with regard to the fiction of Agatha Christie that the clue puzzle's flat style, its interest in form, and particularly the way these texts repeatedly expose the constructed nature of identity are all features of modernism (see 2006, 90).
27. While the term *clue puzzle* is mostly associated with and originates in the literature produced during the Golden Age in Britain, not all clue puzzles are necessarily from this period or geographical origin. A notable exception are the novels of American crime writers Frederick Dannay and Manfred Bennington Lee, who published their novels under the pen name Ellery Queen. Ellery Queen's early novels went so far as to include a page with an explicit challenge informing the reader that all the clues necessary to solve the crime were now available to the reader (see Knight 2004, 91).
28. Interestingly, Auden's definition, unlike so many others, does not include a detective figure or an investigation among its criteria.
29. Auden's schema reminds of Propp's structuralist classification of fairy tales. Incidentally, Propp also uses a numbered list structure to present the elements he identifies and to underlie his claims (see 2004, 72–75).
30. Ronald Knox (1888–1957) was an English priest and detective fiction author.
31. In an American context, a similarly prescriptive rule catalog was created by American crime writer S.S. Van Dine [Willard Huntington Wright] in his "Twenty Rules for Writing Detective Stories" (1928). Although they were published in such close temporal proximity and overlap in some of their content, the two catalogs do not directly reference one another.

CHAPTER 3

Dossier Novels: The Reader as Detective

Detective fiction, it has been argued, engages readers in a special way and assigns them a more active role than other genre fiction does. The genre, Carl Lovitt remarks, "involve[s] two levels of detection: that of the detective, who investigates the murder, and that of the reader, who attempts to identify the criminal before the detective's revelation" (1990, 70). Read as a noun, the "detective" in the genre designation refers to the character who investigates the crime, but read as an adjective, it emphasizes the process of detection, the steps of logical reasoning to be taken to solve a puzzle or crime. This latter interpretation of the genre label does not specify who is to draw these conclusions and take the steps of reasoning, and thus potentially includes the reader in this process.[1] In different ways, the texts I will discuss in this chapter directly address the reader as detective and thus aim to merge the roles of attentive follower of the plot and proactive investigator. Both Charles Warren Adam's *The Notting Hill Mystery* (1865) and Dennis Wheatley and Joe Links's[2] *Murder Dossiers* (1936–1939) are presented to the reader in the form of a dossier, which provides the reader with the opportunity to track the course of the investigation and compile a variety of pieces of evidence from different sources. This formal setup contributes immensely to portraying the act of detection as a process and casting the reader as detective. The often fragmented and partial documents and files invite the reader to perform acts of comparing and cross-referencing in order to reconstruct the plot and extract meaning from them.

© The Author(s) 2023
S. J. Link, *A Narratological Approach to Lists in Detective Fiction*,
Crime Files, https://doi.org/10.1007/978-3-031-33227-2_3

The form and functions of the list play a central role in negotiating how readers engage with these texts. Scholars such as George Dove have already argued that it is in "the reading process itself, the interaction between text and reader, that the special quality of the tale of detection becomes evident" (1990, 37). I would like to take this statement as a starting point to explore how the use of lists and list-like forms such as footnotes or tables influences the reading experience. List formats encourage reading strategies that deviate from conventional reading practices, such as reading a text in the order of presentation from beginning to end. They both tease the reader to guess along and become involved in the act of detection and set up a structure that aids readers to do so if they choose to.

I will first discuss how Adams's *The Notting Hill Mystery* uses lists and list-like forms to emphasize the processual nature of detective work and portrays detection as an exact science. The high value this text places on reproducing "real" documents contributes to its semblance of objectivity and feeds into a positivist ideal of the objectivity of science that was common in the Victorian era.

Wheatley's *Murder Dossiers*, initially, place an equally high value on authenticity. By imitating the appearance of actual police files, they try to set themselves apart from other fiction of their age, which they consider artificial and purposefully misleading. Across volumes, however, they progressively expand on their playful and interactive elements to increase reader involvement. In both the representation of objectivity in *The Notting Hill Mystery* and in the *Murder Dossiers'* playful reader engagement, lists play a crucial role in negotiating between text and reader.

Detection as a Scientific Process: Charles Warren Adams's *The Notting Hill Mystery*

The Notting Hill Mystery is one of the first full-length detective novels written in Great Britain. It was serialized between 1862 and 1863 in the magazine *Once a Week* under the pseudonym Charles Felix and first appeared as a bound novel in 1865. The novel is presented as a collection of documents compiled by Ralph Henderson, an insurance investigator who works for a life insurance association and also serves as the first-person narrator for the frame narrative. The individual documents and witness statements contained in the dossier, however, are each narrated by the original witness. Wherever Henderson comments on or adds explanations to these statements, his additions are clearly marked as such, often in the form of footnotes.

Henderson is tasked with investigating a suspicious life insurance claim. From the beginning, his suspect is a certain Baron R., a famous mesmerist, who supposedly poisoned his wife; Madame R. Henderson's investigation uncovers that Madame R.'s twin sister and her husband, Mr. and Mrs. Anderton, also died under mysterious circumstances and that their deaths considerably increase the sum the Baron stands to gain from his wife's death. The temporal succession of events suggests the Baron may have been involved in those deaths as well. Henderson's collected evidence against the Baron hinges on the question whether mesmerism is scientifi-cally possible.

His findings are presented in a variety of reports, witness statements, and 'authentic' documents that offer readers the opportunity to examine all the clues and ensure themselves of the meticulousness and exactitude Henderson prides himself with. In terms of content, the novel presents a convoluted and sensational Victorian story that revolves around topics such as inexplicable mental bonds between twins or the power of rational-ity and science pitted against the preternatural forces of mesmerism. In terms of form, however, the novel is highly unusual and rather innovative. The multitude of documents and witness statements in the novel allows for a great number of different perspectives, and Henderson's role as nar-rator remains perfunctory. Furthermore, the emphasis on authentic docu-ments and the multitude of referencing tools at the reader's disposal—such as the footnotes or a table of contents that is part of the story world rather than the paratext—draw attention to form as a category relevant for analysis.

Henderson's profession of insurance investigator is a further curiosity. He stands in contrast to many private amateur investigators with a per-sonal interest in their cases (such as Wilkie Collins's Walter Hartright) that populate the plots of sensation fiction, and he also lacks the connections to the police that other private investigators of the era, such as Sherlock Holmes, claim for themselves. This purely professional interest and lack of connections has a profound influence on his methods of investigation: Henderson cannot rely on his knowledge of human nature or a particular person's character to judge statements by witnesses he never met in per-son. Moreover, he cannot draw on any kind of expert knowledge of scien-tific disciplines as detectives such as R. Austin Freeman's Dr. Thorndyke often do to solve their cases. Instead, in order to succeed in his investigation, Henderson has to first collect and compile and then methodically analyze, assess, and compare witness statements and expert opinions. In this compilation of documents, Henderson's notes and personal conclusions are placed among the witness statements he collected and constitute a frame narrative from his first-person perspective.

The Notting Hill Mystery's "documentary foundation" is a "constitutive component of the text" (Codebò 2007, n.p.) and shares a number of further features with texts that Marco Codebò considers as constitutive for so-called dossier novels. By presenting the case through a multiplicity of witness reports, *The Notting Hill Mystery* loosens plot connections, and through large parts of the novel silences Henderson's voice as a narrator. Furthermore, the records aim to create the illusion of being a collection of independent sources rather than a work of single-authored fiction.

The multiplicity of short forms of recorded documentation used to convey information in Henderson's dossier not only helps to assemble information efficiently but also, to a degree, depersonalizes the information.[3] It may seem a curious strategy that a genre such as detective fiction, which, on top of being fundamentally narrative, frequently relies on gathering personal information on suspects, makes such ample use of writing techniques that rely on forms that depersonalize, condense, and listify information. This circumstance, however, becomes less surprising when considering detective fiction's long-standing and tight entanglement with positivist beliefs about verifiable data, which, processed through logic and reason, are expected to yield unambiguous results. The numerous overlapping, yet not entirely congruous files seemingly authored by a variety of independent sources create the impression that the dossier presents documents that are both authentic and, at least when taken together, capable of conveying objective facts.

The Notting Hill Mystery uses the dossier format and its relation to short and concise forms such as lists and tables to engage the reader in the act of detection. Formal devices such as footnotes and summaries encourage readers to engage in non-linear reading strategies: the dossier format invites to skip back and forth between sections, to extract data, and to cross-reference dates and events from the separate witness statements with one another. Furthermore, the emphasis on authenticity and a (supposedly) neutral way of presentation encourage the reader to pursue positivist methods of investigation, and in the end challenge them to evaluate their conclusions. The reader not only acts as a second-order detective but also shares the position of the addressee of the dossier—the insurance company's board of directors—who are to judge the conclusions Henderson presents. The way the list form is used in this dossier is crucial to both how the process of the investigation is conducted and how the outcome is assessed.

The Role of the Reader

In his opening note, in which he presents his case file to his superiors, Henderson guarantees for the "accuracy and completeness" (2) of his source material and speaks of his investigation as "minute and laborious" (1). Already from the beginning, he hints at the kind of investigative role he is going to take and at the methods that will feature prominently in his investigation. Like many detectives to come after him, Henderson relies on his observation skills to draw connections between seemingly unrelated incidents; however, contrary to many later detectives, Henderson expounds right in his opening statement that his method of investigation is based on hard work, diligence, and accuracy rather than intuitive leaps, his ability to outwit or manipulate others, or physical prowess.

His choice of words from the word field of "exactitude" has a double function: it delineates the role the detective will take in this story, and it gives the reader hints as to which strategy of reading will most likely lead them to a successful reconstruction of the events depicted in his case file. As happens frequently in detective fiction, the detective's observational skills are not only closely related to their power of *seeing* but also related to their power of *reading*, both literally and metaphorically. Deciphering textual cues and reading people becomes part of the same activity. In fact, seeing and reading are frequently equated, and the notion of "seeing as reading" gains popularity in the context of both detective fiction and philosophies of seeing in the nineteenth century as "[t]he visible world [becomes] a text, the detective its astute observer and expert reader" (Smajić 2010, 71).[4] The dossier format in particular caters to this notion of seeing as reading. Made up of documents to be read and perused in order to be able to gain insight, the dossier arrangement places clues in sight of the reader and offers them the opportunity to take part in the act of detection themselves.

Henderson's opening implicitly promises that readers will be able to find all clues needed for solving his case within the texts he compiled. Furthermore, he frequently uses the second-person pronoun in statements that prompt both the reader and the addressee to take some kind of action, such as "[…] to which I beg to direct your most particular attention" (6) or "[…] to submit for your consideration the facts of the case" (7). He furthermore ends his letter with the words "[a]waiting the honour of your further commands" (10). This merges the roles of the real world reader and the fictional jury Henderson addresses and therefore encourages the reader to adopt the position of a member of the jury committee.[5] The reader is thus to take on the roles of detective and judge at the same time. Henderson's own failure to come to a clear conclusion ("I am constrained to confess my own inability, after long and careful study, to decide" (7)) further encourages readers to try their own hand at solving the case because it suggests that the text may not provide a satisfactory solution if readers do not arrive at one on their own. Already in his opening statement, Henderson thus defines the ideal reader for his dossier: the reader is expected to exercise the same kind of diligence and accuracy with which Henderson claims to have compiled the document, but is to go beyond this and eventually pass their verdict on the circumstances laid out before them. Henderson's dossier asks the reader to become actively involved in recreating the circumstances of the case. All it allegedly takes to come to the correct solution is exactitude and diligence.

Detection as a Process

The *Notting Hill Mystery* not only prompts the reader to act as a detective and investigate the clues; it also, through its formal setup, supplies strategies and devices that are designed to help readers to fulfill the role assigned to them. Interestingly, all these devices share an affinity to the form of the list. First and foremost, *The Notting Hill Mystery* displays detection as a process. In both *The Notting Hill Mystery* and the *Murder Dossiers* that will be discussed later in this chapter, the alternation of different document formats (reports followed by photographs followed by telegrams etc.) and especially the immediate recognizability that the document labels stipulate evoke the impression that the files are displayed according to the proceedings of the actual investigation and thus stress the aspect of processuality.

Wolfgang Iser describes reading as an event that happens in time and that is based on sequentiality. With every bit of new information that a text presents, readers may have to revise their previous assumptions in order to be able to integrate the new piece of information (see 1978, 128–129). The relation between text and reader is thus imagined as an ongoing process of meaning creation and modification. The event-like character of a fictional text allots each situation in a text concrete meaning but at the same time leaves it susceptible to later revision (see ibid., 67). A document that contains additional information can thus shine new light on a fact already known to the reader or highlight the importance of a detail that previously appeared meaningless.

In the context of *The Notting Hill Mystery*, this means that each additional document Henderson collects illustrates a step in his reasoning process that either corroborates previous findings or casts a different light on former statements. The processual character of Henderson's dossier as a whole is essential in rendering the individual steps in his reasoning transparent to the reader and one document becomes the basis upon which another can fully unfold its meaning. This process of creating meaning is not necessarily linear and often involves going back to different places in the dossier to compare statements before the investigation can proceed.

In lists, the processual character of meaning creation becomes especially apparent. Lists are capable of "arrang[ing] space and time by positioning selected components in a particular order in which sequence creates meaning" (Belknap 2004, 108), and because of the loose syntactical connections between their individual items, lists make particularly apparent how a change in the sequence of presentation or supplementing an additional item may result in an altered meaning:

> Because speech and writing are sequential, units heard or read in a list are comprehended first as having individual, discrete meaning, and then as having significance determined by relations to the preceding units. Furthermore, the dynamics and balance of lists adjust and shift as subsequent units are added. (Belknap 2004, 16)

The serial publication format of *The Notting Hill Mystery* can itself be considered list-like. With time passing between the publication of individual installments of the text, readers have no choice but to process each unit of the story sequentially. The text's separation into individual components thus not only takes place on the conceptual level but is also anchored in the material reality of physically distinct volumes.

Within individual sections, list-like devices such as Henderson's footnotes highlight places where new information impacts circumstances that have been previously mentioned, and they serve as a finding aid that helps to draw such connections. Henderson's use of footnotes emphasizes specific connecting points between (scattered) bits of information and accentuates the importance of exactitude in the process of compiling evidence; furthermore, his notes frequently comment on the process of the dossier's creation.

Only an exact reconstruction of events that misses none of the connections between statements can create an unassailable chain of evidence, and for such a reconstruction to be exact, it is necessary that many fragments of evidence be compared and placed in relation to one another. Henderson even warns that a piece of evidence on its own can never be considered entirely reliable:

> Mr. Aldrige's statements are also to a certain extent supported by those of two other witnesses; but, unfortunately, there are, as will be seen, circumstances that throw considerable doubt upon the whole of this evidence and especially on that of Mr. Aldrige [...] however, in conjunction with other circumstances, I learned enough to induce me to extend my researches. (4–5)

His concern illustrates that exactitude can be achieved only if relations between separate items or documents can be established and thus points out the processual nature of exactitude.

If the case is to be solved, Henderson's use of referencing systems suggests, an exact step-by-step comparison of all the documents is required. There is no single document or clue that conclusively proves Baron R.'s guilt. Instead, *The Notting Hill Mystery* presents detection as a process, in which each step is equally important. The dossier format relies on the representation of multiple perspectives and independent sources in order to fill the blanks left in one document with information provided elsewhere; the bigger picture only unfolds if all the pieces are viewed in conjunction. Since joining the pieces of information contained in the documents can only proceed step by step, a perusal of Henderson's files (i.e., the act of reading) reproduces the way in which each step of an investigation draws on previous steps and constitutes the basis for new insights.

Henderson asks his addressee (the insurance company committee in charge of deciding how to proceed with his findings) to verify that his reasoning steps meet the high standard of exactitude he sets for himself, and the dossier assigns readers the same role by making available to them the same listing mechanisms that Henderson relies on for cross-referencing his documents. The dossier offers the reader a position similar to that of an archivist trying to extract information from a compilation of documents,[6] and it supplies the tools that enable even an amateur to handle the material (see Codebò 2007, n.p.). Through its abundant use of list-like referencing devices, *The Notting Hill Mystery* encourages readers to reproduce each of Henderson's reasoning steps and thus merges the reader's role with that of the addressee of the text.

Processes of Exactitude: Footnotes and Cross-referencing

The Notting Hill Mystery employs a number of list-like devices to enable the reader to take part in the process of detection. Compared to other novel formats, dossier novels typically "present readers with a richer apparatus of 'finding aids,' or the instruments used by archivists to facilitate the retrieval of records, such as indexes, tables, calendars, and cross-reference guides" (Codebò 2007, n.p.). Dossier novels thus enable the reader to navigate the text and jump back and forth between passages that do not chronologically follow one another. Codebò's "finding aids" facilitate processes aimed at establishing relations between different points of data or information, narrow down possibilities, and are designed to eventually lead to an exact result.

In an attempt to define exactitude, Markus Krajewski views it as relational and as depending on certain practices. He argues that exactitude can only come into existence when nonidentical sources are viewed in relation to one another. Exactitude, thus, is related to comparability. This means that the greater the abundance of material, the greater the degree of exactitude that can potentially be achieved (2016, 213–214). In the case of *The Notting Hill Mystery*, every new perspective, and every additional witness statement Henderson adds has the potential to make his report more exact, be it by adding something new or by verifying information already known.

Krajewski enumerates several examples for what he considers to be processes that can be employed to achieve exactitude in a text, among them classifying, structuring, defining, quoting, referencing, and researching (see ibid., 224). All of these play a role in the *Notting Hill Mystery*. Strikingly, in both their form and their mechanics, Krajewski's processes of exactitude are closely related to the form of the list, as are Codebò's "finding aids" mentioned above. This clearly showcases the form's aptitude as an organizing tool and its ubiquity as a structuring device. Due to their brevity and function to condense information, lists make an abundance of content quickly accessible. The lack of context such condensation necessitates makes for quick access to and maximum variability in structuring and restructuring the information thus arranged. The list's reduced degree of mediation allows for different connections to be drawn based on the needs of any specific situation. The list form easily adapts to renegotiations of the reader's needs at different points in time, whereas a text with full syntax tends to link the content items in a specific way, be it causal or thematic or otherwise. Lists by definition separate the items on them; they thus make it considerably easier to restructure the information they contain and fit it to changing demands.

Right from the beginning of *The Notting Hill Mystery*, Henderson makes clear by his attention to detail and repeated emphasis on the "accuracy and completeness" (2) of his work that exactitude and the processes associated with it will be crucial for the investigative work to be performed. His careful compilation and cross-referencing of his source material encourages readers to apply exactly those techniques that Krajewski labels as processes of exactitude in their reading of the novel. Similar to Krajewski's approach, Henderson's investigative method relies on relationality. Instead of starting from a fixed number of reference points or a set of assumptions to be verified, Henderson's case, apart from his central aim to verify whether the life insurance claim made by Baron R. was justified, relies on a network of reference points that develops gradually as certain practices of exactitude are being applied to his collected materials.

Practices such as cross-referencing can generate reference points as they are being applied and thus contribute to organizing material in a relational way (see Krajewski 2016, 224). It is the combination of several such practices that can help the reader to work out the solution for the mystery presented. Henderson's evidence is circumstantial and only makes sense if his witness statements are compared with and related to one another. To turn his dossier into an unassailable chain of evidence, it is necessary to draw out connections between the individual statements that are not immediately apparent.

One means Henderson employs to make these connections visible and accessible to the reader is his use of footnotes to cross-reference statements. The footnotes supply explanations for unclear terms or items, and they help to bridge the gaps between his witnesses' different perspectives by providing cross-references between sections. Such references always go back to earlier sections of the case file and, for example, draw attention to several events that initially seem unrelated but occurred on the same date. The footnotes highlight events that might otherwise have been dismissed as coincidences, and through them, Henderson sketches out logical connections without making them explicit. Readers who are willing to follow the footnotes and skip back and forth between sections, for example, are much more likely to notice that Mrs. Anderton and Madame R. fall sick on the same day with the same symptoms (see 109). The serial publication format in which *The Notting Hill Mystery* first appeared further encourages such reading practices. With time passing between individual installments, Henderson's references also offer themselves for being used by readers as a memory aid in addition to a means of verifying the exactitude of his collected material.

Krajewski argues that simple acts of compilation can render an exact result if they are used to systematically generate an overall picture (see 2016, 214). Henderson's "descriptive strategy" (ibid., my translation)[7] leaves it up to the reader to go back and compare contrasting or complementary representations of events. The footnotes serve as a lead as to where such points of contrast or comparison can be found, but they leave it to the reader to spell out the conclusions to be drawn from those comparisons. The footnote hinting at the coincidence of dates for Mrs. Anderton's and Madame R.'s illness, for example, reads "Compare Mrs. Anderton's journal, December 9, p. 80" (109), thus pointing out to the reader where to look but leaving implicit the conclusions to be drawn. Later footnotes are even less explicit and only give references to other sections of the dossier to be consulted for reference, such as "Compare Section III., 3 &c" (170) or "Vide Section V., 5" (175).

Only by establishing relations between material that initially seems unrelated does Henderson (and can the reader) manage to uncover the hidden links between the collected documents. By structuring and cross-referencing his material, Henderson is able to access knowledge that he could not have gained through even the minutest examination of a single source (see Oertzen 2017, 427).[8]

Cross-referencing is, however, not the only use Henderson puts his footnotes to. He also uses them to comment on the quality of documents or the truth value of statements, for example, by listing further witnesses who can corroborate a statement or quoting from actual nineteenth-century state-of-the-art medico-legal specialist literature (see 263).[9] Statements such as "[t]he housemaid's deposition corroborates this part of the evidence" (201) or "[t]his I find to be the case.—R.H." (220) furnish Henderson's case file with a semblance of objectivity because they give the impression that only statements that have been verified are included in the file or that doubtful sources will be marked as such in the footnotes. This meticulousness greatly contributes to awarding reliability to the collected statements and makes even incomplete statements that leave open questions usable. The use of medical and technical terms[10] further contributes to the impression of reliability and objectivity and at the same time actuates another of Krajewski's processes of exactitude and incorporates it in the presentation of the novel: quoting. The most striking and innovative way, however, in which Henderson uses processes of exactitude becomes apparent from a look at how he uses structuring and restructuring as a tool to guide the reader and arrange and rearrange information.

Processes of Exactitude: Structuring
Henderson's notes that provide a commentary for the evidence he collected constitute the frame story of the novel, and they are an ideal and obvious starting point for examining the effects of structuring and restructuring in the text. Henderson's memoranda are uniquely fit for this purpose because in them, he explains in detail how he arranged his material according to a self-chosen structuring principle. These explanations provide insight into how his categorizing system works and why it was done that way. Henderson explains that "[t]he length to which these depositions have run has obliged me to divide them into distinct sections, each of which should bear more directly upon some particular phase of the case" (133). One of these sections, for example, is concerned with the first illness of Mrs. Anderton and her husband's death, and another one is concerned with the illness of Madame R.

Henderson chooses to arrange his evidence by topic rather than sticking to a strictly chronological sequence in order to give his readers the opportunity to consider each case separately and draw their own conclusions about the connections between the sections. In one of his frame story memoranda, he explicitly comments on his choices for arranging his material:

> I had at first proposed to submit to you in a tabular form the singular coincidences to which I allude; but, on reflection, such a course appeared objectionable, as tending to place too strongly before you a view of the subject with which I must confess myself thoroughly dissatisfied. I have, therefore, preferred leaving entirely to yourselves the comparison of the various dates, &c., limiting myself strictly to a verification of their accuracy. (136)

That the seemingly unmediated and list-like form of the table is considered to produce too biased a view of the case is curious but becomes logical when Henderson's preferred method of investigation is taken into account. Since he considers detection to be a process in which exactitude is based on comparing various materials, a compilation of evidence in a table would compress his findings into a single source, and he seems keenly aware that every act of reduction—which becomes inevitable when fitting things into a table—takes facts out of their context and thus already constitutes an act of interpretation. Thus, it is not only the comparison of dates on which his case rests but also the background information about characters and circumstances. Henderson's use of footnotes and cross-referencing proves that he is aware of the potential multirelationality of list-like forms and that their capability for grouping and rearranging information can be both an advantage and a setback. Henderson's dossier is an attempt to use the advantages and circumvent the setbacks by proposing multiple ordering systems and thus viewpoints from which to consider the case.

That the success of such processes of comparison crucially depends on the order in which documents are arranged becomes especially clear when Henderson rearranges the information from his sections in his concluding note to the case to better illuminate his suspect's motives and actions. In his summary, he changes the order of events to foreground a chain of causation rather than focusing his attention around certain topics, persons, or around temporal sequence (see 277). These changes of order are explicitly marked as such, with the original section numbering from his file sections placed next to each successive argument to highlight exactly in what way his material has been rearranged. By systematically arranging and rearranging evidence without entirely uncoupling it from its original context, he utilizes the very fragmentary form of the list to bridge the gap between pieces of evidence that initially seem fragmented and incoherent. Krajewski emphasizes the crucial importance of such a systematical approach to one's material if exactitude is to be achieved (see 2016, 214).

Another interesting effect of Henderson commenting on his structuring system is that it makes the novel's table of contents part of the story world rather than a paratextual device. Henderson's table of contents thus goes beyond the "basically functional nature of the paratext" (Genette 1997, 7). For Henderson's addressee, the table of contents remains paratext, the function of which is to present the text to potential recipients (see ibid., 1); for the reader, however, it becomes part of the story world. Since upon opening the book, the reader shares the addressee's perspective, the table of contents clouds the difference between the factual and the fictional world and thus creates an additional means of immersion. In his function as narrator, Henderson explicitly references his dossier's table of contents and refers to the captions used therein in his footnotes (see e.g. 38). This prompts the conclusion that the table of contents is included in Henderson's report as a reference and orientation point for the jury the case is presented to. By perusing the table of contents, the reader thus already takes on the role of a member of the jury and becomes an independent examiner of the facts of the case even before engaging with Henderson's documents.

Furthermore, the indication that the table of contents was created by Henderson and is part of his case file marks the order in which the documents are presented as deliberate and significant. It prompts the reader to watch out for connections between documents placed next to one another. Through such acts—or processes—of comparison, reference points for the case are generated and can then help to assess and place documents presented later in the file. That the witness statements are presented in writing rather than a court room setting is essential for how Henderson's dossier works because "the materialization of the speech act in writing enables it to be inspected, manipulated and re-ordered in a variety of ways" (Goody 1978, 76).[11]

Henderson carefully classifies each document included in his case file according to its genre as letter, statement, diary entry, or copy of official records. These labels are displayed right at the beginning in the table of contents. Through his choice of label, Henderson not only stabilizes his ordering system but also assigns an implicit value of reliability to the various documents. The mere fact that a statement was written down, Lisa Gitelman suggests, awards it a degree of implied reliability (or value) that depends on its visibility. "Documents are epistemic objects," she argues, and the knowledge they contain and convey depends on being displayed (2014, 1). The knowledge documents disclose is based on "an implied self-evidence that is intrinsically rhetorical" (ibid., 2), which Gitelman calls the "know-show function" (ibid., 1).

Henderson indeed gives a lot of thought to the way in which his evidence is to be presented as he is apparently aware that the form of presentation will influence the reception of the information. In section five, in his memorandum, he justifies why he opted for the full witness report rather than the table of dates he originally intended.

An excerpt from the table Henderson describes (and which is not included in his files) would look something like this:

Date	Mrs. A.	Madame R.	Baron R.
Oct. 14, 1854			Learns of Mr. W.'s will, which leaves money to his female heirs or, in case of their death, their husbands
Nov. 7, 1854			Marries Madame R.
Dec. 9, 1854	Falls sick the first time. Symptoms of antimony poisoning	Falls sick, treated for antimony poisoning	
Nov. 1, 1855–Feb. 5, 1856			Takes out various life insurance policies for his wife
Oct. 12, 1856	Dies, symptoms of antimony poisoning, but no evidence		
Oct. 1856	Husband commits suicide (with prussic acid from the Baron's medicine chest)		
Mar. 15, 1857		Dies, antimony poisoning	

The table as a form of presentation makes clear at first glance the parallel dates and symptoms between Mrs. Anderton's and Madame R.'s fits of illness, and the proximity of dates between Baron R.'s gaining knowledge of the fortune Madame R. is to inherit, their wedding date, and her first sickness. It furthermore makes apparent the relatively but not conspicuously short interval between the Baron insuring his wife's life and her death, and thus throws immediate suspicion on the Baron. However, it gives Henderson no feasible way to highlight the facts that cast doubt on the idea that the Baron may have arranged the three deaths, and it leaves no possibility to elaborate on what makes the case such a complex one. While the table can be seen as the final result of the processes of comparison Henderson employs to reach his conclusion, it takes away transparency and reproducibility. Since it cannot replace the judgment, doubt, and interpretation necessary to reach a conclusion, it ultimately has much less evidentiary force than Henderson's collected documents.

The Notting Hill Mystery presents the findings of Henderson's investigation not as depending on or relatable to a given constant that can be achieved by following a fixed set of rules (such as filling in dates in a table), but rather as the endpoint of a process during which gaps can only be filled in gradually, through acts of comparison. Reliable points of reference can be determined only through active engagement with the material.

The Evidentiary Force of Authenticity

The evidentiary force of Henderson's material has a twofold origin: one factor Henderson himself stresses is the form of presentation that enables the jurors (and the reader) to form an informed yet unbiased opinion of the documents laid before them. The second factor is related but different: the reliability and authenticity of the materials Henderson presents. The concept of authenticity that, in the nineteenth century, is closely tied to a non-biased and objective presentation of facts (both in detective fiction as in science) is closely linked with positivist beliefs common especially in the second half of the nineteenth century.[12]

Much of the nineteenth century's fascination with detection and detectives sparked from the idea that detection is based on scientific methods and logical reasoning and that those tools could potentially enable anyone to reach conclusions that initially seem nothing short of magical. In *The Notting Hill Mystery*, Henderson tries to strengthen this impression of detection as an exact science when he speaks of his investigation as "minute" and "laborious" and guarantees for the "accuracy" and "completeness" of his documents (1–2). These words not only emphasize the process-oriented nature of detective work but are also designed to evoke connotations of exactitude and verifiable scientific procedures. Henderson's introduction encourages readers to verify his claims about completeness and exactitude. This approach both serves as a confirmation for positivist beliefs and awards the reader the power detectives supposedly held at the time of the novel's publication—to be able to verify the facts of the case posed before them and to identify and correct possible flaws in his logic.

Since exactitude is of such paramount importance when working with the documents Henderson presents, it becomes only logical why he places great emphasis on posing his case in as unbiased a way as possible. The emphasis on exactitude also explains why the reader finds supposedly authentic documents such as a marriage certificate (101) or a copy of a handwritten letter (239) included in the dossier. In fact,

[r]ealist writers relied heavily on the archives of courts of law as sources for creating characters and crafting stories. Quite often, their works imitated legal discourse by proving the authenticity of wills, dowry contracts, deeds, or purchase agreements. (Codebò 2007, n.p)

This practice shows the fascination with and importance of authenticity in relation to objectivity at that time. The rhetorical technique of visualization has been employed to convey knowledge since baroque times (see Vissmann 2000, 211), and the feel of authenticity that supposedly original documents (as included in Henderson's dossier) evoke makes them appear to be objective and unbiased evidence, mechanically reproduced without human intervention. According to Lorraine Daston and Peter Galison, the absence of human intervention and the mechanical reproduction of observations are central to the understanding of objectivity most prevalent in the mid-nineteenth century. Thus, "mechanical objectivity," as Daston and Galison dub it, is the "attempt to capture nature with as little human intervention as possible" (20). Daston and Galison describe the scientist, or the detective—*The Notting Hill Mystery* does portray detection as a scientific process—in the age of mechanical objectivity as someone in possession of diligence and self-restraint but with as little capacity or tendency for interpretation as possible (see Daston and Galison 2007, 128). [13]

Henderson's approach to detection accords with this principle of not interfering with what is directly presented to the eye. He only compiles data and largely leaves the task of interpretation to his addressee (and, hence, to the reader). Even when he rearranges his reports in the last section to highlight causal connections, he merely changes the ordering system of what was already presented and thus sticks with the minimum level of interpretation that any form of processing or presentation entails. Henderson's aim is to create a reflection of the facts as they are without imposing his own opinion on them.

At a first glance, the list's lack of mediation, seeming removal of an interpretative instance, and its short, concise rendition of data points may seem the tool of objectivity par excellence; yet Henderson rejects the table as a suitable form of presenting his evidence. This reveals a curious contradiction: on the one hand, his rejection of the table form shows he is aware of the authenticating effects of form (especially the representational form of the dossier) he is apparently trying to avoid,[14] and on the other hand, he heavily relies on techniques and practices such as listing and cross-referencing to achieve a degree of detachment and to try and convey an objective unbiased impression of the facts of the case.

The relation of fact and form in the dossier format is worth exploring in more detail. In nineteenth-century print culture, the majority of print products were functional rather than literary texts (see Gitelman 2014, 12). For functional texts such as fill-in-the-blanks forms, their formatting was central to how they conveyed meaning. Lisa Gitelman dubs this the "know-show function" and argues that such forms—the name itself is telling—"helped to shape and enable, to define and delimit, the transactions in which they were deployed" (ibid.). Form can thus express purpose even before the content of any given document is known to a reader. Henderson compiles his documents in the form of a dossier to signal to his addressee (the role of whom the reader is to take on) as soon as they open the table of contents that his documents are to serve as evidence and that they have been purposefully structured into distinct sections to support an argument.

Cornelia Vismann argues that lists do not communicate directly, but that, rather, they control what is being communicated (see 2000, 20). Henderson's table of contents is a case in point, and the footnotes in the dossier fulfill a similar function. Footnotes provide additional information or evidence that supports arguments made in the text, and their mere presence in the dossier, regardless of their content, signals to Henderson's addressee that he is trustworthy and meticulous, and that his exactitude can be relied upon. In the context of the dossier form, where exactitude holds such a high value, even the mere wealth of documents Henderson has collected makes him appear as a competent investigator. The quantity of the statements and documents included in his dossier is turned into a signifier for the quality of Henderson's research through the format of their presentation alone.

Mesmerism, Lists, and Science

There is, however, a twist to Henderson's meticulous presentation of his conclusions to the case. According to Henderson himself, the conclusions his documents suggest are "so at variance with all the most firmly established laws of nature" (6) that he would rather "ignore a chain of circumstantial evidence so complete and close-fitting in every respect, as it seems almost impossible to disregard" (6) than accept what his own investigation indubitably points to: that mesmerism is real, meaning that people can be manipulated to act against their own will through a kind of unde-tectable psychic force.

This seems so shattering and shocking to this story world because it invalidates the foundation that (positivist) scientific thinking is based on, namely that any perceptible event can be explained with logic and reason, and that whatever claims the status of truth must be verifiable. Both pos-sible solutions to Henderson's dilemma—that either mesmerism is real or that his logic is flawed—seem equally implausible and equally unacceptable.

This leaves readers with a paradox: they can follow the process through which Henderson arrived at his conclusions, and they can testify to the flawlessness of his logic. But the only possible inference this allows for invalidates the method by which readers have come to it. The practices of exactitude which a reader of this dossier must follow to ascertain verifiable results lead to mesmerism as an explanation—a phenomenon so inherently *un*verifiable that Henderson wonders if crimes of such a kind can even be prosecuted (see 284). These two dominant forces are diametrically opposed to one another and hence incompatible in Henderson's understanding.

Although mesmerism was initially advertised as a science when it gained rapid popularity in the 1840s (see Willis and Wynne 2006, 2), by the time *The Notting Hill Mystery* was published, mesmeric experiments were dis-reputable within the scientific community (see Karpenko 2017, 148–149). Even though mesmerism had a profound impact on Victorian culture, it was generally considered a pseudoscience (see ibid., 6), and especially toward the end of the nineteenth century, the practice carried a "whiff of fraudulence or charlatanism" that even spread its taint to its more legiti-mate relative hypnotism (Leighton 2006, 207).

Since the reader of *The Notting Hill Mystery* is encouraged to share Henderson's role as investigator and verify the steps of his reasoning, it stands to reason to assume that readers will accept the Baron's mesmeric abilities as a given rather than question their own judgment. Lara Karpenko, in her essay on mesmerism and sympathetic identification in *The Notting Hill Mystery*, does not even consider the possibility that Henderson's reasoning might be flawed and states that from Henderson's investigation, "it is clear that the Baron committed the murders" (2017, 159) and that, hence, the Baron's mesmeric powers are a fact of the story world. Henderson's clearly voiced reluctance to believe what his investiga-tion seems to point to draws attention to the stark contrast between the positivist methods he employs and the belief in the objectivity of reasoning on the one hand and the lack of verifiable proof that makes it impossible to see the Baron punished for his crimes on the other hand. *The Notting Hill Mystery* thus seizes on the fear that the Victorian belief in science as a universal instigator of progress and way of explaining the world might not live up to expectations. The novel's innovative form and emphasis on exactitude as the foundation of scientific investigation testifies to a strong belief in positivist thinking and methodology as capable of producing universally valid explanations, but the success of its villain at the same time draws that belief into question and makes apparent the tensions inherent in it. The reader is left with the uncomfortable realization that even if Henderson's methodology can validly identify the Baron as the guilty party, it leaves the authorities incapable of convicting him of the crime. It is left to the reader to resolve this paradox.

DETECTION AS A GAME: *THE MURDER DOSSIERS*

Like *The Notting Hill Mystery*, the *Murder Dossiers*, written by Dennis Wheatley and planned by Joe Links, are arranged in the form of a dossier. On the cover for *Murder off Miami* (1936), the first of four of these crime dossiers that were published between 1936 and 1939, Wheatley and Links announced that their creation would introduce "a new era in crime fiction." The main innovation Wheatley and Links introduce is that the dossiers contain actual physical objects such as bloodstained cloth or (allegedly) human hair that serve as evidence and can be examined by the reader. As a consequence, "[r]eaders could have the satisfaction of solving the mystery by examining the same clues, in a physical sense, as the detective" (Cox 1989, 320). The possibility to physically handle material clues rather than just follow a text that describes these clues invites the reader to slip into the role of detective and takes reader engagement yet one step further than *The Notting Hill Mystery*.

Wheatley and Links, in their author's note preceding the first volume, emphasize their authentic presentation of the crime "in exactly the same sequence as that in which it was unravelled by the investigating officer" (n.p.) and promise their readers they will respect the fair play principle of Golden Age detective fiction and not make use of "any extraneous or misleading matter," thus setting their dossiers apart from other novels of the era that have disappointed their readers by disobeying the fair play principle.[15] The *Murder Dossiers*' innovative approach to the genre, together with Wheatley's renown as a writer[16] and the affordable price of three shillings and six pennies the dossiers were sold at, all contributed to the success and popularity of the *Murder Dossiers*—the first volume sold over 100,000 copies.

The clearly defined fair play rules hotly discussed and mostly observed in the 1920s and 1930s hint to a readership that appreciated the opportunity to get involved in the act of detection and guess along to a certain degree, and the *Murder Dossiers* cater to that wish in a special way. Both dossiers discussed in this section merge the role of reader and detective, but they do so in very different ways. While *Murder off Miami*, the first dossier, almost painstakingly attempts to emulate the presentation and proceedings of an actual police investigation, the fourth and last dossier, *Herewith the Clues* (1939), presents itself as a game that engages the reader by awarding points on a score sheet for the correct interpretation of the pieces of evidence it contains. The remainder of this chapter will juxtapose the two dossiers and trace the development from police file to game by looking at the way these dossiers employ lists and list-like elements to involve their readers in the act of detection.

Murder Off Miami: *The Case File*

Murder off Miami includes a paratextual author's note printed on the inside cover of the dossier that introduces readers to the new format and gives the authors the opportunity to explicitly praise the merits of their creation. The author's note teems with words from the semantic field of authenticity: it promises readers "original handwritten documents," "actual clues," and a presentation of facts in "correct order," which, together, make up "the complete Dossier of a crime" (n.p.). This focus on authenticity casts the reader in the role of detective: if the document constitutes the collected evidence of a crime, then the person to whom it is addressed and who engages with it must be the one who is meant to solve the crime.

As a means to convey objectivity and authenticity, the list makes its first appearance even before the reader enters the story world. Already in its second paragraph, the author's note lists the variety of documents and constitutive parts of the dossier. The cumulative mention of "[c]ablegrams, original handwritten documents, photographs, police reports, criminal records" (ibid.), and many more items function to convince the reader of the originality of the *Murder Dossiers'* format. By including an abundance of elements that are tied to factuality and bureaucracy in the real world, this enumeration conjures up the illusion that the *Murder Dossiers* contain or at least accurately represent the kind of documentary evidence that would make up an actual police investigation file.

The instructions in the author's note emphasize that the crime can be solved by someone "who has never seen any of the people concerned, but reaches the correct solution of the mystery solely upon the evidence in Dossier form, exactly as it is presented to you [the reader]" (ibid.). These words are underlined in the author's note to stress both the authentic character of the collected documents and the reader's intended role as the investigating officer's superior. The reader is supposed to take the position the story world assigns to the character who signs the document with the solution and warrant concealed in the sealed section at the end. Furthermore, by asking the reader to decide "who *you* will arrest" (ibid., emphasis in original), the author's note not only imparts on them the viewpoint and role of investigator, but also implies that the reader now holds the responsibility of a detective to punish the guilty and protect the innocent; in addition, the wording implies that in their role as detective, readers will also have the power to do so. This implied investigative authority strongly contributes to fostering reader engagement.

Despite their innovative form and high potential for reader engagement, however, Wheatley's dossiers are still novels of the detective genre and as such could hardly function without providing closure. Accordingly, the dossiers also contain the solutions to the crimes they pose. The solution to *Murder off Miami* is presented as a police report that matches the documentary style of the case file-based story and thus seamlessly blends in with the other documents in the collection. However, this section of the dossier is sealed with a piece of paper that is glued to the back cover. The paper presents a physical obstacle that has to be removed before the solution is revealed and thus institutes an additional means of involving the reader: the forced stop in the reading process functions to give the reader pause to think about the correct solution themselves before they read on. Unlike texts that only engage readers intellectually, the dossier's sealed solution section prompts interaction with the dossier as a physical entity.

In accordance with the dossier's formal structure, the physical shape of Wheatley's novel, too, is designed to resemble a case file rather than a work of fiction. All pages are only printed on one side, punched, and held together by a piece of strand threaded through the punched holes (see Fig. 3.1). The table of contents typically found in novels is omitted entirely,

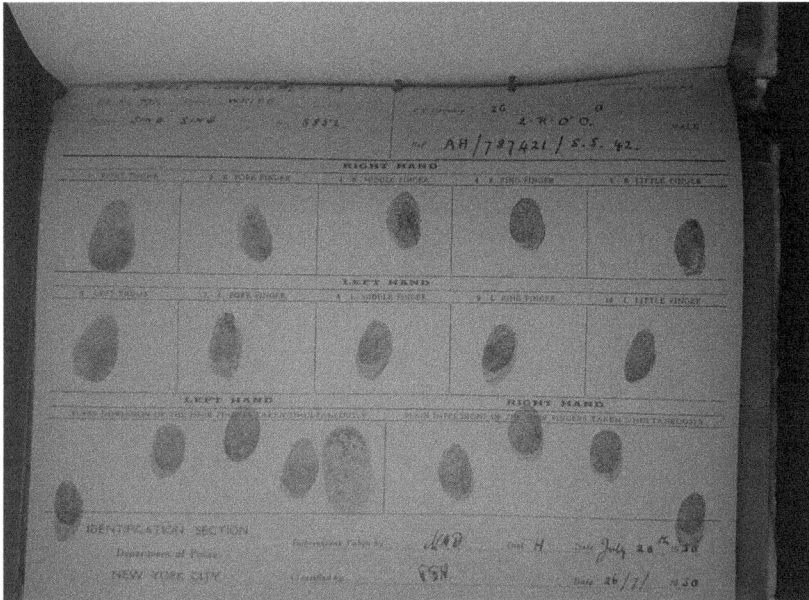

Fig. 3.1 Dossier format with punched holes

which implies an uncertain progression and outcome of the investigation to be conducted and points to the possibility that a failure to resolve the case may result in a lack of closure. The absence of a table of contents suggests the reader is expected to become active as a detective to prevent such a lack of closure. Even the bibliographical information that is usually printed on an extra page or on the inside of the front cover is, in this case, printed on the inside of the back cover and can thus only be accessed once the seal to the section with the solution is broken. If the jacket were removed, the dossier would appear like a loose collection of documents taken out of a folder.

The reports are printed in typescript, which, in the 1930s, was very much part of the "aesthetic ideologies" of "business, journalism, corporate and state bureaucracy, education, and scholarship" (Gitelman 2014, 13) and thus awards Wheatley's collection of documents an official character. The typescript font in the reports is clearly distinct from the font in which the author's note preceding the dossier is printed, and the change of font indicates a shift of focus from literary entertainment to administration matters. According to Lisa Gitelman, the look of type-scripts was associated with office environments and "secretarial production" during the 1930s (ibid., 56), and *Murder off Miami* evokes those contexts to create the illusion that the reader is perusing a file produced for the administrative purposes of a police station rather than for private entertainment.

Furthermore, the documents display file and form numbers that mix letters and numbers in the top outside corner of the page where one would expect to find page numbers in a novel. The actual page numbers are printed on the top inside corner, close to the inner margin, and become almost invisible once the first couple of pages are turned. Moreover, only those pages that the form numbers classify as report carry page numbers at all. Page numbers are omitted from documents the file classifies as photographs, telegrams, and other document types. By seemingly replacing the consecutive numbering of pages as an ordering system for the content of a book with the file and form numbers that designate different types of documents in bureaucratic procedures, *Murder off Miami* emulates the formal setup of real-world documents or police files and thus contributes to evoking an impression of authenticity—"Form RL/2120/C.7" (1), for example, designates a report, "Form GO/7431/N 58" (following page 13) is a memo, and "Form IS/828/P7" (following page 58) denominates a criminal record, with the letters determining the document type.

Besides the paratextual clues that directly address the reader, it is these structural alterations that signal to the reader they are dealing with a police file rather than a novel. The way these different signifying systems structure and categorize is inextricably linked to the form of the list. The form and file codes listed at the top of each page classify and thus prestructure the documents in the dossier according to its source: the classification code for report, for example, signals that the document will contain first-hand observations and deductions, and the form that marks the criminal records documents conveys the implicit assurance that the information it contains is verified by an official government agency. The file code thus gives hints as to which kind of clue may be found in the document and additionally indicates how reliable the information thus gained is likely to be. It is the list's exceptional power of condensing information that makes this possible. By listing each form code with its designated document type or function, the reader detective can gain an enormous amount of information on a meta-data level even before engaging with the content of any individual document.

The continuous labeling of documents with form numbers creates coherence that is situated on the level of formal presentation but takes on functions typically ascribed to the level of plot. The coherence that the form numbers create thus goes beyond the function of page numbers as indicators of sequence in regular novels because it provides additional information such as the source of a document, its origin and channels of distribution, and its reliability—factors that affect the level of plot. It is a typical strategy for dossier novels to "imitate the most commonly accepted procedures for establishing truth in [the] certain cultural context" in which they are situated (Codebò 2007, n.p.). The listing of form numbers at the top corner of the documents in the dossier thus situates the individual documents within the context of police procedures and serves to indirectly vouch for their authenticity. Authenticity in *Murder off Miami*, thus, operates on two distinct but mutually reinforcing levels: the author's note promises the reader a fair reading experience with access to all the necessary clues and no misleading strategies, and the formal setup of the text promises that the reader detective will be working with documents the reliability of which meets the standards of official police investigations.

Another factor that contributes to the *Murder Dossiers'* authenticity is that they include handwritten letters and other pieces of material evidence glued onto the pages in plastic or paper bags. The inclusion of actual objects bypasses the mediating instance that even the most objectively minded description of an object cannot go without and leaves it entirely up to the reader how much attention they want to bestow upon any individual item included. Through these objects that readers have to physically manipulate to be able to interpret the clues they contain—for example, by opening a sealed letter—the *Murder Dossiers* offer their readers an experiential dimension in the direct sense of "involv[ing] sensorimotor patterns" (Caracciolo 2014, 59–60) that are the basis of our ability to perceive and interact with the world around us.[17] The dossiers thus engage readers on a basic phenomenological level. Caracciolo argues that an experiential text "activates something akin to actual memories" and "triggers the sensory residue left by a large number of past occurrences" (ibid., 46); by bypassing the mediating instance that usually facilitates such trigger moments, the *Murder Dossiers* provide direct sensory input rather than activating memories of it and thus offer readers an exceptional degree of immersion that is based on direct sensory experience and plays into the texts' claims to authenticity.

Not all of these extra items yield relevant information, and some (such as the bloodstained piece of curtain on page 15a) are included only for the sensational effect. Others, however, feature clues that are vital to the solution, and those objects thus directly engage the reader in solving the puzzle. The lack of mediation that the inclusion of these objects allows for creates the illusion that the reader is working an authentic case in which material pieces of evidence play a central role in convicting a suspect.

As is the case with the photographs in the dossier, the pages with the material evidence pieces are excluded from the consecutive page numbering that the novel as a whole provides. They are either placed in between two consecutively numbered pages, or with some document types, a letter is added to the previous page number to create a loose tie to the more narrative context of the report in which the piece of evidence is mentioned (see Fig. 3.2). Thus the formal division between, for example, pages 15 and 15A to a degree also separates the material clues from the story(-events) described in the investigating officer's report, the pages of which are consecutively numbered. Even though only three of these alternatively numbered pages exist, this formal separation has several implications for

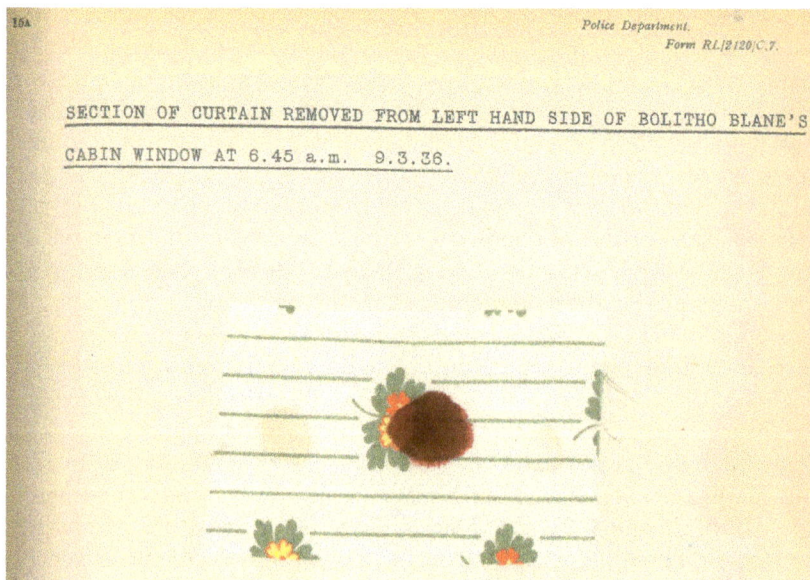

Fig. 3.2 Evidence page

how the text can be read. The list-like setup of these alternatively numbered pages creates a second-order classification system that allows the reader to go through the dossier and only consider and compare certain types of evidence, such as the consecutively numbered reports, the material evidence with alternative numbering, or the photographs, which are printed on a different kind of paper and can thus be easily picked out. The alternative ordering systems that are independent of consecutive page numbering make these pages instantly recognizable and allow for easier navigation and thus for reader engagement.

The pages with alternative numbering are further held together by an ever unvarying caption that labels the piece of evidence and then explains where and when it was found, for instance, "section of curtain removed from left hand side of Bolitho Blane's cabin window at 6.45. a.m. 9.3.36" (15A).

The captions in these alternatively numbered pages always follow the same pattern and provide a kind of title or overarching category (material evidence found) that holds the material clues together. The brevity that this list form of presentation enforces in this case also suggests the relevance of the items presented this way. Lists can reduce content to an informational core and thus suggest the little that remains is imbued with heightened importance. There are three of these pages in the dossier, and though they are scattered widely, the alternative numbering and repeating captions allow reader to view them as a list. If they are put together and read as a list, each alternatively numbered page, like a bullet point, encapsulates a different development stage of the case. The first piece of evidence provides a reason why the dead person may have committed suicide, the second page proves that the dead man was actually murdered, and the third and last page, which includes three separate pieces of evidence, displays objects that incriminate some suspects and exculpate others, thus mirroring the different stages the investigation takes.

Page numbering and the capitalized and underscored letters set these pages apart from the rest of the text and accentuate their special status. Those devices frame these pages as possible benchmarks that subdivide the dossier, not unlike a table of contents, the purpose of which is to divide a larger text into distinct sections. Similarly, the alternatively numbered pages divide the dossier into stages in a case. The form of the list is essential to setting up such a reading experience because it affords the condensation of information to an informational core and the loose links (in this case given through the special numbering and unvarying caption system) that allow for an overview and easy restructuring.

Reading Strategies

Murder off Miami makes ample use of lists and their affordances to encourage specific reading strategies, which differ considerably from those that readers of *The Notting Hill Mystery* have to apply to successfully assemble useful information. While *The Notting Hill Mystery* requires readers to carefully extract information through processes of exactitude, *Murder off Miami* takes care of this for the reader. A reader taking careful notes of the times for which each suspect mentioned in the police report has an alibi will find the result of their efforts presented neatly summarized in list form on page 49. The list is captioned "times accounted for by presence in the lounge," followed by a brief explanation and an enumeration of the names of people present at a location that gives them an alibi for the murder, with the names sorted into relevant time slots. This list summarizes, for the convenience of the reader, information that could have been collected from the previous reports and thus already fulfills the main task that *The Notting Hill Mystery* poses to the reader as a detective. The list of times accounted for is followed by another list of "unvouched for times" (50), which assembles under the name of each suspect all the time slots unaccounted for so far. This list is followed by yet another list titled "possible motives" (51). Curiously, this list enumerates all the suspects, including those with no discernible motive at this point in the investigation. Entries for suspects without a motive are made in the manner of "Mrs. Jocelyn. Nil, as far as known at the moment" (51), and this statement is repeated for several suspects. The inclusion of seemingly superfluous or self-evident information, such as that no motive is known at the moment, creates an impression of completeness and thoroughness.

These three consecutive lists provide summaries of the facts known so far and thus hint to the kind of role the reader is supposed to take on in this dossier (which differs from the reader's role in *The Notting Hill Mystery*). By presenting to the reader all the information available so far from the written reports, the text aims to put them in the position of the investigating officer's superior to whom the reports are addressed. It becomes apparent that the two positions of investigating officer (that the reader takes in *The Notting Hill Mystery*) and superior (which the reader is supposed to take in *Murder off Miami*) have very different implications: the officer's task is to collect, cross-reference, and summarize information, a duty that requires diligence but (only) routine skills. The superior, on the other hand, is required to interpret the collected data and spot the gaps in the seemingly all-encompassing information.[18]

Wheatley's dossier asks the reader to identify the odd detail in a given array of information rather than assemble said information, and the inclusion of the letters, memos, and other material pieces of evidence provides a unique opportunity to do so. Three crucial details—an ill-fitting suit, a razor cut, and a peculiar tooth brush—are to be spotted in the photographs the dossier includes and are not mentioned at all in the investigating officer's meticulous reconstruction of timelines and motives. The reading strategy that leads to success here, the readily included complete timelines suggest, is not to pick out and cross-reference details, but to spot anomalies in the details which are already arranged into a convenient and seemingly clear shape of presentation. The list is the ideal format for this modus operandi because it affords reduction, brevity, easy comparability, and overview.

The lists of timelines and motives in *Murder off Miami* are followed by yet another list titled "inventory of the late Bolitho Blane's property found in 'c' suite of S.Y. Golden Gull" (52), subdivided into the objects contained in each of the deceased's suitcases. Contrary to the three previous lists, this one contains new information not mentioned or discussed before. Hidden amid all the objects enumerated as contents of suitcase number four, readers can spot the item "1. Bottle Gum Tragacanth" (53), an adhesive that strongly hints the deceased must have had false teeth. Put into context with the conversations recorded in the reports, which reveal that one of the suspects has false teeth, this piece of information hints to the identity theft at the core of this murder mystery.

The structural setup of the novel, however, has three lists that only contain summaries of already known and irrelevant information immediately preceding the list which does contain a clue. Even though readers may deduce the spot-the-odd-item reading strategy from the presence of the previous lists, the inventory tricks them into studying it with as little attention as the already known information preceding it. Even an attentive reader, thus, is unlikely to remember the gum tragacanth from the inventory list eleven pages later when the subsequent report mentions false teeth in connection with one of the suspects who later proves to be the presumed dead person in disguise.

The formal presentation of lists with different functions following one another directly manipulates the reader into inattention. Lists, Jack Goody claims, "must be processed in a different way not only from normal speech but from other ways of writing" (1978, 81). Because they usually lack syntactic context, they depend on practices that imbue them with meaning (see Mainberger 2003, 12). Such practices depend on the context in which the list appears. In detective fiction, the appropriate practice is frequently demonstrated by the detective figure and usually involves finding the common denominator among a number of items or recognizing the metonymical significance of a detail that stands for something else, such as the gum tragacanth that can alert a reader to the fact that the deceased must have had false teeth. By merging the roles of reader and detective, *Murder off Miami* equates the observational skills tied to perception with the interpretational skills needed to recognize patterns and allusions in a text and thus constructs "the ideal observer as an ideal reader" (Smajić 2010, 72).

Imagining the ideal observer as ideal reader, as Smajić suggests, has implications for how storytelling works in this text and (partly) explains the prominent role of lists in Wheatley's dossiers. In *Murder off Miami*, and frequently in detective fiction in general, the ability to categorize—be it top-down, bottom-up, or along a uniformly horizontal level—is equated with the capability to generate meaning. The strategies that enable readers to connect the items on a list and fill the gaps to create meaning from fragmentation thus become the dominant meaning-making strategies within the framework of detective fiction. Equating sense-making with categorization has profound influences on the approach to storytelling that detective fiction takes, as well as on the worldview it propagates. It implies, first and foremost, that everything can be sorted into distinct categories, that category boundaries are stable, and, implicitly, that there is such a thing as objective truth. This view, advocated, for example, in the anthropomorphical measurements the Bertillon system used to identify criminals or in Cesare Lombroso's (1835–1909) considerations on the science of criminal anthropology, is profoundly positivist—as is the genre of detective fiction as a whole. A reader can only take on the role of detective in a story if the assumption holds that there is an objective truth that can be uncovered via observation and rational thought.

The solution to *Murder off Miami*, in fact, takes great pains to convey such a positivist worldview and implies that there is exactly one solution to the facts presented and that this one solution must be obvious to anyone who is able to make rational conclusions. This becomes apparent from the language used to present the solution. At the beginning of the sealed section, the investigating officer's superior, whose role the reader takes on, opens his final statement with a memo reading "Solution of murder perfectly clear on evidence admitted" (n.p.), thus embarrassing readers who have not come to a perfectly clear solution yet. The language in the solution section is dominated by expressions such as "there can be no doubt" (132), "it is obvious," "always" (133), and "it is clear" (134), and thus suggests that the conclusion presented here is inevitable and plainly outlined in the evidence presented. "[D]etective fiction does not permit alternative readings" (1988, 144), as Franco Moretti phrases it.

The list form, in which the most important clues are summarized and recapitulated, reinforces this impression. The section with the solution is titled "lieutenant Schwab's analysis of the foregoing evidence" (132) and therefore already announces that all evidence necessary to come to this conclusion has been presented in the dossier. That Schwab's interpretation of the evidence is called "analysis" implies the rational and scientific thought process that stands behind his solution and forestalls objections about arbitrariness or guessing that the reader might bring up against it. Despite these efforts, it is highly questionable whether the clues are as unambiguous and conclusive as the solution tries to make the reader believe, starting with the blurry quality of the photographs that make it hard to even identify the telltale razor cut on the murderer's face. Yet, the simple mechanics of numbering Schwab's analytical conclusions (and thus turning them into a list) awards them an air of scientificity that links them to the world of mathematics and deontic logic, where elements can be put together according to principles that render the conclusions achieved inevitable.

Toward the end of his file, the investigating officer presents a list of alibis that excludes every single person on the boat as a murder suspect (129–131). Similar to when the investigating officer presents his first list of alibis and unvouched for times, this list summarizes the information previously revealed in the reports and witness interviews. It presents names and time slots accounted for, and thus provides a reliable alibi for everyone for the time the murder was committed. The list format's seeming lack of mediation and presentation of objective facts (the accounting for time slots exact to the minute especially helps with this) is of central importance in conveying this impression. Once again, the most promising reading strategy is not to remember and put together details but to spot the gaps in the seemingly gapless weave of evidence. According to Wolfgang Iser, gaps in a text stimulate the "constitutive activity of the reader, who cannot

help but try and supply the missing links" (1978, 186). In detective fiction, filling those gaps often resembles an act of investigation, and texts
such as *Murder off Miami* actively encourage readers to become involved
in identifying and filling the gaps the text presents.

The conclusion to be drawn from this list of facts is to think outside the
box: if nobody on the list committed the crime, it must be somebody not
on the list. The only person this leaves is the supposed murder victim, who
indeed turns out to have murdered his secretary in his stead and taken his
place as impostor, which makes the entire carefully established timeline
invalid. The list that presents the alibis frames and preselects evidence, and
determines a priori what readers will most likely consider relevant. It functions to present a time structure as linear and complete that is in fact missing relevant pieces of information and thus invites readers to assume a
focus that entails misguided conclusions—a strategy that will be elaborated on in my chapter on Agatha Christie.

Herewith the Clues: *The (Detection) Game*

Across the four volumes of the *Murder Dossiers*, their focus shifts decidedly
from trying to accurately imitate a real-world police file and investigation
to turning the acts of identifying and interpreting evidence they ask for
into a game. The second dossier already is less meticulously about the file
format that the first dossier relies on to convey authenticity. *Who Killed
Robert Prentice?* opens with an explanatory newspaper clipping that
informs the reader why the detective they encountered in Miami in the last
volume is now in London (see 1). As a piece of evidence, it has no value
and therefore no place in a police file. Even if readers accept the dossier's
later claim to be detective Schwab's personal collection of evidence, its
compilation exhibits stark continuity and plausibility errors and appears
less coherent in its design than the first volume.

These errors do not concern the level of story (fabula) but its presentation (suzhet) as a case file.[19] The volume still plausibly explains how
Schwab could have access to the material collected, but its presentation as
a police file—with its pages punched and held together by a piece of thread
and with material pieces of evidence from the official police investigation
included—does not withstand even superficial scrutiny. Although Schwab
might plausibly have access to police evidence (see 46), it makes no sense
for these objects to be included in his private dossier (there are, e.g.,

obvious problems with police procedures such as observing the chain of custody).

The author's note printed on the inside cover of the second volume, in fact, announces that the second dossier is "not like a straight police investigation at all" (n.p.). The authors' aspirations, this suggests, have changed. The documents compiled in the second dossier constantly remind the reader of their position as the reader of a piece of fiction rather than try to conceal it from them. One consequence of this is that the merging of the roles of reader and detective is much weaker in this volume. This already becomes evident from a look at the jackets of the dossiers: while the first dossier asks the reader to "[b]e your own detective" and thus emphasizes the role the reader is supposed to take, the jacket of the second dossier prompts to "[t]est your powers of deduction," which also demands a high level of engagement but turns the putting together of clues into a personal intellectual challenge, eschewing the connotations of responsibility that resonate with the first dossier and also with *The Notting Hill Mystery*.

Over the course of the volumes, the clues become more playful and less oriented toward authentically representing a police investigation. The newspaper the second volume includes after page 52, though it features a report of court proceedings that contains information relevant to the plot, also comprises a clearly ludic element: page 6 of the newspaper includes an article titled "Writer Who Made 'Murder Fiction' History Living near Scene of Crime: Famous Authors [sic] Views on Sussex Mystery," in which Wheatley and Links speculate about who the killer might be (both express contesting views and both suspect the wrong person).[20] As does *Murder off Miami*, *Who Killed Robert Prentice?* attempts to merge elements of the story world with the real world. Instead of positioning the reader as the investigator of a real case, though, in this case the authors purport to have performed a metaleptic crossing of diegetic levels. This is a more playful but less subtle variation on the first dossier's blurring of diegetic levels.

These experimentations attest to the ludic quality that has been ascribed to detective fiction by several scholars. George Dove, when trying to establish elements of a "detection formula," argues that one of the two basic ingredients of detective fiction is that it invites the reader "to participate in a game that carries its own special rules and conventions" (1990, 29),[21] and in a later volume he argues for "the primacy of the play mode in detective fiction" (1997, 13). Carl Lovitt further contends that the fair play tradition that British writers in the Golden Age of detective fiction adhered to is rooted in "a distinctly bourgeois conception of gamesmanship" and thus caters to a "readership that appreciated refined and highly civilized forms of play" (1990, 68).[22]

The *Murder Dossiers'* shifting focus from authenticity to play illustrates an interesting tension inherent in the ideology of the Golden Age detective novel. In aiming for a maximum degree of realism, Julian Symons argues, *Murder off Miami* achieved the contrary and instead "blew the gaff on the artificial nature of the Golden Age story" (1985, 120). By placing such a high value on imitating a real case file, it not only exposed its own artificiality but also drew attention to the highly constructed nature of other Golden Age novels. Yet, in making the novel appear in the shape of an actual case file, *Murder off Miami* appears to be the ultimate unison of the Golden Age principle of fairness and Wheatley's claims for authenticity—the opposite of artificiality.

A closer look, however, reveals that Wheatley's aspirations to authenticity and the Golden Age principle of fairness, which necessitates the artificial and constructed nature of detective fiction to disperse clues throughout the text, are quite at odds with one another. Crime is rarely fair, and criminals tend to try and conceal hints to their identity rather than give the detective a fair chance. The ideal that all the clues necessary to solve a case should be accessible to the reader and the premise that the crime must be solved in the end are ideological demands that clash with the realistic representation that Wheatley's first dossier aspires to.[23]

Somewhat ironically, the authors' attempt at creating a realistic detective experience by presenting their story as objective case data triggered criticism about both the first dossier's artificiality and its lack of characterization—and thus a lack of attributes that characterizes fictional texts. Roughly fifty years after the crime dossiers first appeared, Symons picks up on these original points of critique when he surmises why the later volumes of the *Murder Dossiers* were less successful than *Murder off Miami*. Symons writes that after the novelty of including real clues had worn off, people were put off by the circumstance that:

> it was very nearly impossible actually to read them [the dossiers]. There was in the nature of things no characterization of any kind, and interest rested solely in the comparison of the texts with the visible clues in an attempt to discover discrepancies. (1985, 120)

Symons rightly points out the necessarily artificial nature of *Murder off Miami* that results from this tension between fairness and authenticity.

He, however, does not discuss how the later volumes' deliberate shift of focus toward more playfulness affects both their target audience and their formal design and thus makes the dossiers interesting case studies despite their dwindling commercial success.

The fourth dossier, *Herewith the Clues*, takes the ludic elements to an extreme and embeds them on the level of form as well as on the level of content. It signposts to its readers, for example, by including a score sheet on which readers can award themselves points for correct guesses, that it is to be considered as a narrative game rather than a typical detective novel.[24] This shift of focus already becomes apparent from the title, which flaunts the physical objects included that make the dossiers unique and showcases their importance to the reading experience. Above the title, the cover additionally advertises in bold print "five times as many clues as in any of the previous dossiers" to alert readers to its main selling point. The earlier dossiers feature more sensational titles that contain genre-typical keywords such as "murder," "killed," and "massacre."[25]

Games demand and create a different kind of immersion than fictional narratives, and the role they assign to players differs from the role fiction assigns to its readers. Two central qualities of games are that they have great interactive potential because they "have to be actively (and often physically) interacted with in order to 'work'" (Schubert 2019, 116) and that they often follow a non-linear structure because players have the agency to make choices from a number of options the game provides, which "can lead to different experiences and outcomes" (Schubert 2019, 117). This runs counter to the "focus on 'linearity' in representing [textual] events" that is usually considered a key feature of narrative (see ibid., 116).[26] The remainder of this chapter will explore how *Herewith the Clues* negotiates the tension between narrative and play and situates itself at the intersection of both. The form of the list plays a central role in making the play-like qualities of this dossier possible, and the shared affordances of narrative and play (such as coherence and involvement) enable the dossier's liminal position.

Interestingly, it is the very same features that the first murder dossier uses to assert its authenticity that now take on the function of turning the fourth dossier into something like a game: the material clues. Across the volumes, the reader's engagement with those clues demands more and more interaction. The second volume, for example, includes two sheets of letter paper that smell of the same perfume and therefore indicate they were written by the same person. Even the first volume only contains one text-based clue, but having its readers spot objects in a photograph at least sticks to seeing as a mode of perception. Asking the reader to use an organ of perception other than their eyes requires interaction with the book as a physical entity that goes far beyond turning pages.

The fourth volume takes the interaction required by the reader to yet another level: it contains a secret note, the invisible writing on which becomes visible only if the paper is dipped in water and thus requires the involvement of material that is not part of the dossier. This kind of manipulation goes far beyond the role of the attentive reader a more conventional detective story calls for, and the degree of interactivity required to reach the desired goal is much more typical of games than of stories.

That *Herewith the Clues* is meant to be considered at least partly as a game becomes particularly clear from the score sheet included before the sealed section with the solution (see Fig. 3.3). The score sheet is accompanied by an author's note that instructs the reader on how to fill it in and on how to award points for each suspect correctly eliminated. This paratextual note bears great resemblance to game manuals that aim to introduce players to the rules of boardgames, and the fact that several score sheets are included suggests that this game of detection is meant to be played by more than one player. The author's note explicitly states that "[e]ight solution sheets are provided so that each member of the family may fill one up" (53) and even warns against cheating: "[n]o peeping, now!" (53). Cheating, of course, is only possible if we assume that the reader's job is not to merely follow the story and read through the solution, but to engage with the material included in the volume in a way that will enable them to score the points that the score sheet promises as a reward for such engagement.

Furthermore, for cheating, there need to be agreed-upon rules which can be broken by the recipient, which is another feature of games rather than narratives. In *The Reader and the Detective Story*, George Dove posits detective fiction as a kind of game with agreed-upon rules between author and reader when he writes that "the rules of the tale of detection are the rules of organized play; they exist only to make possible the playing of the game" (1997, 11). Dove's conception of "game" is based on genre conventions and the assumption that detective fiction, more so than other fiction, facilitates a "hermeneutic impulse that acts as a structuring force" (ibid., 21), meaning a desire to become actively involved in solving the problem. The rules Dove speaks of are the unspoken rules of fair play that dominate the detective fiction of the Golden Age. They are directed toward the authors rather than the readers of detective fiction. The rules

READER'S MARK SHEET

(See Authors' note on last page before Solution)

I eliminate the following suspects for the reasons stated below :
(Use two lines only in cases where you have more than one reason for eliminating a suspect.)

(1) ....

(2) ....

(3) ....

(4) ....

(5) ....

(6) ....

(7) ....

(8) (a) ....

(b) ....

(9) (a) ....

(b) ....

(10) (a) ....

(b) ....

(11) (a) ....

(b) ....

(12) (a) ....

(b) ....

(13) (a) ....

(b) ....

(14) (a) ....

(b) ....

I identify Orloff's murderer as..

NOW REFER TO SOLUTION

Score **two** points for each suspect correctly eliminated by either one full or two partial reasons.
Score **one** point for each suspect only partially eliminated by one correct reason.

Score ....

If the murderer is correctly identified add five points to score.
If score now totals maximum (33 points) add further seven points to form Grand Total (40 points). *Grand Total* ....

(Signed)..

Fig. 3.3 Score sheet

in the fourth dossier (that the "[n]o peeping, now!" admonition implies might be broken), however, are directed to the recipient. They, for example, include the number of points awarded for each correctly interpreted clue and the instruction that the reader/player's suspicions must be entered on the score sheet before the sealed section is opened. Furthermore, they only apply to the very specific volume within which they are printed rather than to detective fiction as a whole and, therefore, are closer to the set of rules included in a boardgame than to the generally applicable genre rules that Dove discusses.

Another feature that *Herewith the Clues* shares with many games is that it promotes competition between several players/readers who are encouraged to try their hand at solving the murder case presented simultaneously. The inclusion of not one but eight score sheets attests to that, as does the awarding of points for correct interpretation of the evidence. The purpose of awarding points is to make individual approaches comparable and to let the player who scores the most points emerge as the winner of the activity.

Last but not least, iteration can be named as a defining characteristic of play as a symbolic form, as discussed by Stefan Schubert.[27] According to Schubert, games "encourage repeated playthroughs or repetitions of individual sequences" (Schubert 2019, 117) and thus award play an iterative nature. If the reader wants to successfully attribute each exculpatory piece of evidence to the correct suspect, they will have to go through the material presented multiple times, each time with their efforts focused on a different suspect. This clearly iterative reading process deviates significantly from reading processes in conventional fiction, where the reader always starts at the beginning, follows along the numbered pages, and when s/he finishes does not need to start again to get the full experience the novel provides.

Iteration, interactive engagement with the material, being able to compare one's performance to that of other participants in an activity, and the element of competition are highly unusual elements for storytelling but standard features of competitive games such as Cluedo (1949),[28] in which players also have to solve a murder case by eliminating suspects and possible murder locations and weapons. The difference between the dossier and the game is more one of degree and presentation than one of kind. By showcasing its ludic elements and deemphasizing its (undeniably) narrative core, *Herewith the Clues* blurs the boundaries between narrative and play.

With this altered orientation, the structure of the dossier also changes significantly: the individual parts of the dossier become clearly divided into separate sections, and each section becomes increasingly list-like. The dossier starts out in the by-now-familiar format of reports narrated by an officer who was present at the crime scene, from which the reader learns that a murder was committed at the so-called Milky Way Club. The suspects are the members of a criminal organization using the club as a meeting place. In addition to the page numbers, which stay located at the upper inside corner of the pages where they are nearly invisible, these documents no longer display file numbers but instead show dates followed by page numbers within each specific report.

Rather than have the pieces of material evidence scattered through the text according to when and where they were found, this dossier opts for collecting them all in the same place and having them form a separate section following the reports. A list of handwritten signatures is followed by another list of material objects contained in semitransparent paper bags glued to the page. Each piece of evidence is labeled and listed as "Exhibit A," "Exhibit B," and so on, alphabetically sorted, all the way to P (see Fig. 3.4). The material evidence section is followed by another section consisting entirely of photographs of each suspect taken the night of the crime. The objects and photographs are, again, not included in the consecutive page numbering, but the photos are easily identifiable even without page numbers because they are printed on different, thicker paper. The photos, in turn, are followed by a one-page profile and mini biography of each suspect. The profile comes in list form and gives information about age, height, build, eye color, and so on, and the biography is written in paratactical style, dominated by main clauses. At the end of the volume, we find the score sheets—easy to locate because they are printed on yellow paper—included before the sealed section with the solution.

The list format, both on the level of structuring the different story elements into distinct sections and also within each section, plays a central role in organizing the content. It is no coincidence that both the game Clue and Wheatley's dossier use list-based score sheets to track the progress of the players'/readers' investigations. Lists afford order and are apt to provide a (structured) overview over large quantities of data. The score sheet achieves this same function in providing the reader with a prestructured grid for note taking. The number of available lines in the grid already reveals that fourteen suspects can be eliminated and that only seven of them can be eliminated by a single piece of evidence. For the other seven suspects, the score sheet subdivides the lines to be filled in into "a)" and "b)" (see Fig. 3.3). This prestructuring through the form of the list not only tells the reader how to collect evidence but also ensures efficiency of note taking by exactly indicating and limiting the space available for comments on each suspect. Additionally, the limited space provided for the

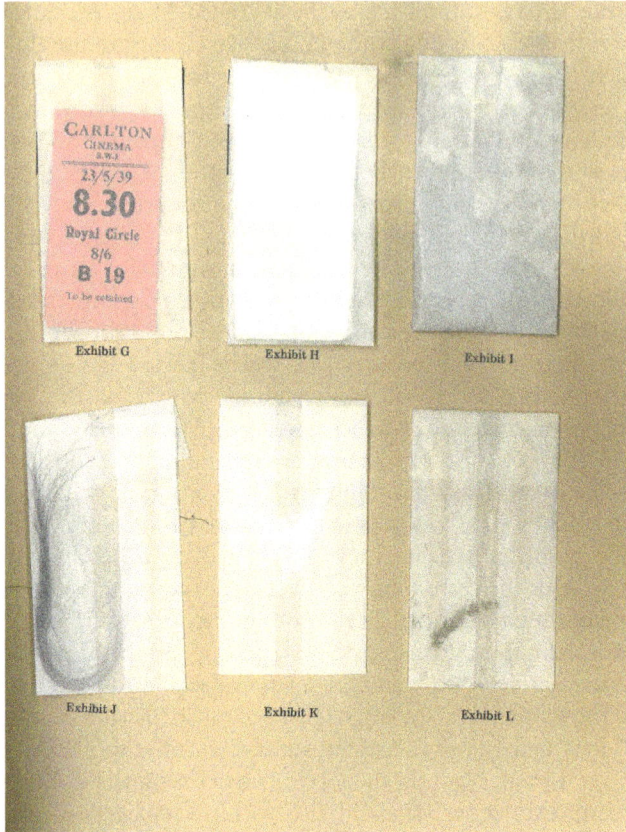

Fig. 3.4 List of pieces of evidence

notes assures a degree of clarity and overview because prestructuring the page into sections for each suspect ensures that all the notes can be reviewed within the space of one sheet.

Furthermore, alphabetically labeling the material pieces of evidence as exhibit A to P already constitutes an act of classification and ordering on several levels: having separate and labeled items makes it clear from the beginning that each object the reader can engage with has a clear purpose (for the game or the story), one that is directly tied to incriminating or exculpating a suspect. Moreover, the labels determine what kinds of objects can count as evidence. The structured labeling imbues each object with importance and relevance, and thus with the potential to change the investigation (i.e., by exculpating or incriminating suspects). At the same time, the concise list structure situates the dossier within a positivist system of belief in which a single objective truth is possible and desirable. The list structure thus places this dossier in the tradition of the positivist ideology of detective fiction.

In its function to organize and categorize knowledge, the list also plays a role in forming the structure of this dossier as a whole. The distinct sections that present content in a list-like way, pre-sorted into categories, encourage an engagement with the text that is inherently non-linear. The sectioned list format makes it extremely easy for the reader to navigate between photos, reports, and pieces of evidence without losing time locating items. It thus affords easy comparability and cross-referencing between the individual types of evidence. Such a non-chronological engagement with the material can forge connections that lead to uncovering the guilty person.

The non-linear reading strategy this format demands seems to run counter to linearity as a key feature of narrative. Regardless of the presentation order of events, which can skip back and forth in time, at least on the reception end, stories are marked by a clear and unalterable progression from beginning to end, as indicated by the consecutive numbering of pages. The missing page numbers from the evidence and photo sections are a strong indication that these sections are not meant to be read in the sequence in which they are presented but instead are intended for browsing, depending on which suspect the reader is investigating at the moment. If page numbering is read as a list that dictates sequence and linear order, the absence of this elsewhere ubiquitous structuring device can be considered as another indicator that the dossier is to be located more in the realm of games than that of stories. On the fabula level, all these sections are part of the story world, but the arrangement into separate parts has them appear as more of an appendix, to be consulted as necessary, and separate from the more narrative and linearized crime scene reports. This gap arises from the different ways in which stories and games work. While a narrative is best experienced in the sequential order of its presentation, games typically require the kind of targeted interaction that the dossier's sections seem tailor-made for.

Another ludic element (though one that is also frequently found in fiction) that the fourth dossier features is the breaking of the fourth wall in the section with the suspects' photographs.[29] Besides giving each suspect's name, the photographs are also captioned with disclaimer notes which read, for example, "[t]he particulars regarding 'Scab' Wilson and 'Mug' Masters which are given in the script have, of course, no reference whatever to Mr. Dennis Wheatley and Mr. J.G. Links, who posed for this photograph" (n.p.). Putting the real names of the people photographed next to those of their characters disrupts what Coleridge called "the willing suspension of disbelief" (2006, 478)—the reader's immersion in the fictional world—and thus emphasizes the dossier's fictionality.[30] The contrast to the first dossier, which emphatically tries to evoke the impression of being a real case file (and, e.g., only includes the fictional characters' names in the photographs), could hardly be greater.

Phil Baker derisively comments that the volume used the minor celebrity photos to advertise its merits "as if this was another technical innovation" (2009, 274). If the altered purpose and target audience of the fourth dossier is taken into account, however, this advertising strategy makes sense. The clues, advertised as a technical innovation that enables heightened immersion and authenticity in the first volume, in *Herewith the Clues* serve a different function, one that is perfectly compatible with using celebrity photos to advertise: the volume aims to include the reader not in an authentic investigation, but into a circle of people who enjoy playing the same kind of game for intellectual entertainment. In playfully featuring celebrity photos in the guise of characters, *Herewith the Clues* pretends to establish a group relation between the reader and these celebrities, who handle the same objects as suspects that the reader is presented to interact with as investigator.

One might ask whether *Herewith the Clues* can be considered a novel despite the predominance it gives to its ludic and interactive elements. The dossier certainly takes the engaging and non-linear features which already emerge in *The Notting Hill Mystery* to an extreme and has to be situated at the intersection of narrative and play. The lists that dominate the structure of this dossier frequently have a dual purpose: by engaging the reader in the act of detection, they further both ludic and narrative elements. Lists that serve a primarily ludic function generally also manifest a narrative dimension. The lists of personal belongings of the murder victim that the first murder dossier includes, for instance, not only provide the reader with the possibility to spot the item that is odd but also characterize the victim; even the fourth dossier's list of material clues that is presented in no narrative context whatsoever relies on readers making judgments on a suspect's character traits or habits: one suspect, for example, is to be excluded because of her use of an extravagant hair pin "of such an unusual type that it is not even stocked by the majority of hairdressers," the solution suggests (59).

Lists offer great potential for immersion because of their appellative function that invites readers to fill the gaps left in the story. Wolfgang Iser's concept of textual gaps is based around how readers interact with texts to generate meaning and thus provides an explanatory model for how interruptions in the continuous flow of narration stimulate the "constitutive activity of the reader" (1978, 186). The lists in this chapter invite readers to fill the gaps they contain in varying degrees of direct appellation. Sometimes the invitation remains implicit, for example, by having characters (such as Henderson) try to piece the connections together along with the reader; sometimes the texts address the reader with direct prompts, as is the case with the score sheet in *Herewith the Clues*. In the latter case, asking the reader questions such as "can your powers of detection lead you to the murderer" on the jacket of the volume questions their role as mere observer and aims at involving them in the story as a surrogate protagonist or player in a game.

Dossier novels use list-based formats to draw readers in and facilitate easy access to the information they contain. The dossiers discussed in this chapter rely on the list form's capacity to track, organize, and restructure information efficiently, and devices such as the score sheet in *Herewith the Clues* or the table of contents in *The Notting Hill Mystery* become part of the investigative tools the reader has at their disposal. The formal properties of dossier novels thus encourage readers to track the clues they find scattered throughout the dossiers and reorganize them to reveal connections between them. The following chapter will discuss how the novels of Agatha Christie take these basic mechanisms of reader involvement as their starting point to manipulate reader expectations.

Notes

1. Arguably, prototypical detective fiction will both contain a detective character and illustrate the steps in a reasoning process that ends with the solution of the crime. Sweeney argues that Poe's "Murder in the Rue Morgue" (1841) is the first piece of writing that meets both definitions (see 1990, 13).

2. Wheatley was responsible for the content of the dossiers, Links for the planning stage, for example, for arranging the photos to be included. This is why my discussion will only refer to Wheatley as the author.
3. The kind of depersonalization that collecting large amounts of data leads to has been called a hallmark of efficient bureaucracy by sociologist Max Weber. He argues that bureaucracy "develops the more perfectly, the more it is 'dehumanized,' the more completely it succeeds in eliminating from official business love, hatred, and all purely personal, irrational, and emotional elements which escape calculation" (1978, 975). James Purdon further argues that such short paper note forms as Henderson uses are an important "part of the material culture of wartime" (2016, 60) because of their function to efficiently accumulate and at the same time depersonalize information.
4. Unless indicated otherwise, all emphases have been removed from quotations in this chapter for better readability.
5. In "How to Do Things with Words," J.L. Austin proposes a new grammatical class of words he titles "performative" (2004, 163). Performative statements differ from other statements in that they are neither true or false, but have (or at least aim at having) a direct effect. Performatives, Austin argues, are thus more closely related to actions than descriptions (see ibid., 162). Henderson's statement, in which he asks his addressee to assess his collected material, could be considered performative.
6. On practices of collecting, ordering, and archiving, which are closely intertwined with the form of the list, see the edited volume by Sarah Schmidt (2016).
7. "Beschreibungsstrategie."
8. Oertzen refers to this approach in general and does not relate it to *The Notting Hill Mystery*.
9. Henderson, for example, refers to Alfred Swaine Taylor's (1806–1880) *On Poisons, in Relation to Medical Jurisprudence* (1848) and quotes a specific edition and page number to corroborate his statement that the effects of antimony poisoning can vary dramatically depending on the idiosyncrasies of the poisoned person's constitution (see 263, compare Taylor 1859, 91; 101).
10. Interestingly, Henderson advises the general reader to skip these technical terms (81).
11. Presenting the witness testimonies as written documents also enables Henderson to use footnotes to comment on any particular witness's reliability. Such acts of classification—another process of exactitude listed by Krajewski—help both the reader and the addressee to evaluate and rank the material presented.

12. See, for example, Lorraine Daston and Peter Galison's work on objectivity: "[t]he history of scientific objectivity is surprisingly short. It first emerged in the mid-nineteenth century and in a matter of decades became established not only as a scientific norm but also as a set of practices" (2007, 27).

13. See also Codebò, who emphasizes that "documentation exists as an essentially anonymous activity" (2007, n.p.). Just as the scientist, the compiler of a dossier is supposed to present their material in a neutral way and refrain from interpretation.

14. For the authenticating function of files and the connection of truth and writing, see Vismann (2000, 11).

15. For a discussion of the fair play principle, see the chapters on the genre history of detective fiction and on and Agatha Christie.

16. In the 1930s, Wheatley was as well known as Agatha Christie (see Baker 2009, 11).

17. According to Marco Caracciolo, experientiality "refers to the capacity of a story to tap into—and have a feedback effect on—the background of different recipients" (2014, 50). Experiential texts thus prompt strong reactions that are based on sensory imagination, emotions, or shared socio-cultural backgrounds (see ibid., 51).

18. The reader in the *Notting Hill Mystery* is asked to fill the role of investigating officer and compile the information scattered throughout the dossier while reading the text, but Henderson's frame narrative at the same time asks the reader to interpret the evidence they collected and act as his addressee and jury. Consequently, the reader of *The Notting Hill Mystery* has to fulfill two roles alternately, whereas the *Murder Dossiers* only ask their reader to interpret and not to collect evidence.

19. Viktor Sklovskij defines fabula as the chronological sequence of events. Any individual representation of these events of a fabula is called suzhet. One fabula can generate many different suzhets (see 1991, 170).

20. Moreover, the newspaper contains real advertisements, for the inclusion of which Wheatley earned an extra 300 pounds (see Baker 2009, 359).

21. The second crucial element he mentions is "the assurance that the mystery will be resolved" (29).

22. Lovitt dates the Golden Age from 1918 to 1939.

23. On the ideology of Golden Age crime fiction, see Knight (1980, 107–134).

24. Wheatley and Links considered selling the fourth volume in a box rather than as a bound volume but abandoned the idea because that would have placed *Herewith the Clues* in the games department of stores rather than with the other books (see Humphreys 2002, n.p.). The consideration of this possibility, however, shows that *Herewith the Clues* was supposed to be framed differently than the other volumes.

25. When published in the US, the first two volumes appeared under different titles (*File on Bolitho Blane* and *File on Robert Prentice*) as part of a series including other authors who imitated Wheatley and Links's idea (see Humphreys 2002, n.p.).
26. On the role of linearity as a dominant characteristic of literary texts, see also Aarseth (1997, 41–42).
27. Schubert uses Lev Manovich's conception of symbolic form as a way of structuring experience through a specific poetics, aesthetics, and pattern of creating meaning to discuss the relation of the symbolic forms of play and narrative (see 2019, 114; see also Manovich 1999, 81). For a detailed discussion of the form of the list in relation to symbolic form, see Link 2022.
28. The title of the game appears to be a blend of the words "clue" and the Latin "ludo," which translates as "I play."
29. Contrary to the elements discussed so far, this one is situated on the level of content rather than referring to the formal and structural properties of games. The point still is worth dwelling upon because this element interlocks so well with the form-based ludic features.
30. By posing for the photographs themselves, Wheatley and Links foreground their position as authors. According to Phil Baker, this act borders on "self parody" (2009, 374).

CHAPTER 4

Manipulating Readers: The Novels of Agatha Christie

Agatha Christie (1890–1976) is one of the best known crime writers of (and beyond) the so-called Golden Age of detective fiction and has been labeled "one of the greatest reader-manipulators to be found in the various genres of fiction" (Alexander 2009, 25). Christie's novels, especially those about her two famous detectives Hercule Poirot and Miss Marple, continue to enjoy lasting popularity among readers, and her novel *The Murder of Roger Ackroyd* (1926) is ranked fifth among the *100 Top Crime Novels Selected by the Crime Writers' Association* (1990).

John Lanchester, in the *London Review of Books*, surmises that Christie's lasting popularity lies more in her mastery of form than in the literary qualities or the actual plots or outcomes of her novels (2018, n.p.).[1] He argues that Christie's "career amounts to a systematic exploration of formal devices and narrative structures" rather than an in-depth exploration of character psychology (ibid.). The form of the list features prominently in many of Christie's crime novels and frequently plays a central role in manipulating readers' attention and expectations.

While the previous chapter examined from the perspective of reception how readers interact with the lists featured in dossier novels, this chapter will take a closer look at the levels of narrative and character representation. The first part of this chapter discusses how the narrative structure of Christie's novels makes use of the affordances of the list form to manipulate reader attention and evoke patterns of thinking that invite readers to

© The Author(s) 2023
S. J. Link, *A Narratological Approach to Lists in Detective Fiction*,
Crime Files, https://doi.org/10.1007/978-3-031-33227-2_4

draw misleading conclusions. The surprise endings of *The Murder of Roger Ackroyd* and *Murder on the Orient Express* (1934) will serve as prominent examples of this strategy. Such manipulations of the reader will then be discussed in the context of the fair play principle that governs detective fiction from the Golden Age.

Christie, however, not only uses lists to manipulate her readers but also has her detectives frequently make and refer to lists as tools to structure their thoughts and to break down complex problems into compartmentalized and manageable parts. The second part of this chapter examines how Christie's investigators use the list form's fragmented structure. *Death in the Clouds* (1935), *A Murder Is Announced* (1950), and *Hickory Dickory Dock* (1955) all exemplify how Christie's detectives employ lists to either gain an overview over or impose their reflections on seemingly disparate pieces of evidence.

In their function as memory aid and notation system, these lists can also provide access to the detective's thoughts and serve as physical evidence of the detective's penetrating gaze and their capability to restore order to a seemingly chaotic world. Christie's later novels employ the same patterns of listing to self-referentially make fun of the genre's very obsession with classification, compartmentalization, and the reduction of complexity.

MANIPULATING THE READER: CREATING PATTERNS OF THINKING

"Form," according to Karin Kukkonen, "works as a pattern of thinking" (2013, 162). Such patterns, she argues in the tradition of New Formalism, are "produced by the text in the reading process" (ibid.). The form of the list, when encountered by readers in a text, evokes very specific patterns of thinking, as, for example, the assumption that relevance is a defining criterion for including something in a list. The analytical context that detective fiction situates itself in suggests that readers attempt to identify a common feature that the items assembled on a list share.

Common features such as *stolen goods* or *suspects*, or even something as broad as *evidence*, provide the reader with a caption for the list that allows them to contextualize it. If the text does not disclose such a feature or connecting principle, the list form invites readers to find a pattern which renders the items as a coherent set. Thus, the very simple form of the list, "paradoxically, requires highly complex decoding strategies" (von Contzen

2017, 232).[2] Many of Christie's novels rely on the complexity of such decoding mechanisms and employ the form of the list, in combination with carefully placed ambiguities that leave references and causalities undefined, to play with readers' expectations and invite them to make misleading assumptions. It is the contrast between the expectations thus raised and the stunningly unexpected solution to the mystery that creates the surprise effect for which many of Christie's novels have been praised.

Christie's crime novels make ample use of the list form and explore the manipulative potential of the gaps and loose syntactic connections that award the form of the list its "computationality," its ability to easily reorder and repurpose elements (Stäheli 2011, 92). Christie frequently employs lists to direct or misdirect her readers' attention and makes use of the reader's assumptions about relevance and categorization that lists usually afford to lead her readers astray. Such manipulations can take place on both the levels of fabula and suzhet.[3]

Form and Attention

The Murder of Roger Ackroyd is one of Christie's best known works and provides a number of examples of how form can (mis)direct attention and manipulate readers and characters alike. The novel is narrated by the local doctor, Dr. Sheppard, who also features as a character and takes on the role of detective Hercule Poirot's assistant during the murder investigation. The stunning conclusion to the novel unmasks Dr. Sheppard as the murderer. Sheppard, in his role as narrator, displays no signs of unreliability, and his story world position as detective Hercule Poirot's assistant gains him the reader's trust from the beginning. This ensures that the reader's analytical capacities and attention will be focused on other characters when looking for suspects. Sheppard's deceptions frequently rely on readers' assumptions about form and conventions, and the form of the list affords a particular manipulative potential through its capacities for omissions and summarizing.

Stephen Knight has pointed out that in the novels of Agatha Christie, "the cause of disorder […] is consistently a matter of major personal betrayal" (2004, 91). This is seldom truer than in the case of Ackroyd,[4] where this betrayal takes place on two levels simultaneously. On the level of the fabula, the village's trusted doctor and the detective's (seemingly) trusted assistant are responsible for the very disorder it is his responsibility to resolve. Furthermore, on the suzhet level, Sheppard betrays the reader's trust that a first-person narrator who displays no signs of unreliability will share their knowledge and observations (however limited) with the reader. Carl Lovitt even goes as far as to argue that besides undermining the trust of his community as a character, Dr. Sheppard as a detective fiction narrator "threaten[s] to undermine the conventions of the genre" (1990, 72). Indeed, by making a first-person narrator the murderer, Christie, breaks the first (and by implication most important) of the ten commandments Ronald Knox established in his "Detective Story Decalogue,"[5] which states that the criminal cannot be someone whose thoughts the reader has access to (see 1976, 194).

In chapter 23, toward the end of Ackroyd, Dr. Sheppard reveals that the novel the reader has been following is the written version of his personal notes regarding the investigation; this turns the entire novel into a diegetic text that exists as an object within the story world. This move strongly implies that the reader now knows (absolutely) everything Sheppard knows and considers as relevant to the investigation—an assumption which practically excludes him as a suspect. Moreover, such a "diegetization of the narrative" (Gibelli 1992, 390)[6] makes the table of contents part of the text rather than the paratext and implies that Sheppard is responsible for the labeling of chapter titles.[7] This works to justify the narrator's deception (of the reader) and marks it as a necessity of the plot (since detective Poirot has access to the manuscript and Sheppard needs to conceal his deeds). Furthermore, reading the novel as a manuscript composed by Sheppard functions to retrospectively characterize him and put on display Sheppard's arrogance and sense of superiority in assuming his involvement in the crime would go unnoticed by his narratee.

Even though Sheppard's deception is motivated by the plot, a first-person narrator who deceives the narratee—the reader of Sheppard's manuscript, in this case both the reader and detective Poirot—"violate[s] the cooperative principle of pragmatics," as Emanuela Gutkowski points out in her excellent article "An 'Investigation in Pragmatics': Agatha Christie's The Murder of Roger Ackroyd" (2011, 52). Gutkowski discusses how readers will assume a causal link between statements that directly follow one another. Her example is from chapter 18, where the reader is led to assume a direct connection between a detail of the investigation (regarding the character Charles Kent) which Dr. Sheppard expresses his confusion about and another detail (regarding the murder) that Poirot, who at this point already suspects Sheppard, has recently figured out. This leads readers to assume that the statements about Sheppard's confusion and

Poirot's musings both refer to Charles Kent and that Sheppard's confusion concerns the identity of the murderer (see 220). Thus, Sheppard
diverts the reader's attention from himself by means of omissions and
careful arrangement of the sequence of statements rather than direct lies.[8]
Though this specific example does not involve a list, the principle of association by proximity is fundamental to how lists work and create meaning,
and Sheppard is not the only character who uses this to his advantage.

Christie also has detective Poirot use this very principle of association
by proximity in a list to trick Dr. Sheppard (and the reader) by diverting
their attention—and thus their suspicions. Toward the end of the novel,
Poirot asks Sheppard to invite a number of suspects for a "little
conference":

> 'I have a commission for you, my friend,' he said at last. 'Tonight, at my
> house. I desire to have a little conference. You will attend, will you not?'
> 'Certainly,' I said.
> 'Good. I need also those in the house—that is to say: Mrs Ackroyd,
> Mademoiselle Flora, Major Blunt, Mr Raymond.' (249)

The reader (and also Dr. Sheppard, who is unaware Poirot already knows
of his guilt) automatically assumes that the four names that follow the
colon are those of the people to be considered suspects, especially because
they immediately follow the tag "those in the house" that additionally ties
them together as a group. Even though the previous sentence makes clear
that Poirot and Sheppard will also be present for this conversation ("You
will attend, will you not?"), they will likely not be considered suspects by
the reader. Sabine Mainberger points out that making something part of a
list is a binary yes/no decision because in a list, "there is no compromise
between inclusion and exclusion of an[y] element" (2003, 37).[9] Poirot's
trick, thus, depends on a mismatch between form and content, in which
the form of the list suggests a boundary that the content (i.e., the group
of suspects) disregards.

Christie plays with the reader's assumption that the list that follows the
colon and the tag "those in the house" is a self-contained entity independent of its immediate context. This passage relies on a (common) strategy
of reading that considers lists and list-like descriptions as relatively independent of the text that surrounds them (see, e.g., Mainberger 2003,
114) and counts on readers not connecting Sheppard's presence at the
"conference," which is clearly indicated in the sentence immediately

preceding the list, with Sheppard's inclusion in the circle of suspects. Therefore, the reader will likely be caught by surprise when the list of suspects Poirot presents to the assembled group a couple of pages later includes Sheppard (see 270).

Lists, Urs Stäheli argues, have a "naturalization effect"; we are inclined to accept the contents of a list without much questioning because a list "produces a reality of its own" (2016, 15). The form demands that we perceive this reality as a self-contained entity that can be considered and made sense of separately from its surroundings. Christie uses the reader's awareness of the list's properties and affordances (based on experience with the form in scientific and everyday contexts) to induce misleading assumptions about connections between the elements of her text.

This strategy can be observed not only when having a look at select passages that employ lists but also when considering the use of lists throughout the entire novel. "[D]evices such as notes, prefaces, and indexes," Edward Maloney writes in *Footnotes in Fiction*, "have all been used by writers to direct their readers towards particular interpretive strategies or conclusions" (2005, 20), and they thus draw attention to the close interconnection between certain forms and certain reading strategies. Christie's novels employ the reading strategies that lists elicit to cleverly manipulate her reader's attention. Lists function "as a cultural technique for creating clarity" (Stäheli 2011, 87),[10] and Christie's narrators and characters make use of this to misleadingly evoke the impression of such clarity while, in fact, omitting relevant items or placing them in the vicinity of the list instead of including them within the formal unit of the list itself.

The short, concise form and the easy overview that lists provide over the items they include invite the reader to compare and cross-reference their contents, especially if several lists concerning the same or similar topics are provided.[11] Ackroyd provides the reader with several lists of suspects over the course of the investigation, most of which do not feature Dr. Sheppard. He is not among the suspects inspector Raglan lists in chapter eight (97–98), nor is he among the people who will inherit enumerated in chapter ten (118), nor does he feature in the list of people who will profit from Ackroyd's death in chapter fifteen (182). Not only do those lists not make Dr. Sheppard visible as a suspect to the reader; they also (potentially) redirect the reader's attention to another name that does feature on all three of those lists: that of the housekeeper Miss Russell. The housekeeper moreover features as the last item on the list of people who visited Dr. Sheppard on the day of the murder (141), a position that draws particular attention, especially since none of the other names listed there have been mentioned previously.

Having a list item such as a suspect's name feature on several related lists in different places throughout the novel creates the impression of heightened relevance in the reader's mind. An item that comes up several times appears as a more reliable clue as well: the rhetorical force of repetition is frequently employed in lists to effect a "leveling of contrariness and incompatibility in the items enumerated" (Mainberger 2003, 28).[12] This strategy can also be observed in Hickory Dickory Dock (1955), where a list of questions starting with "Who" alternates with the repetition of the name of one suspect over and over again: "Nigel Chapman." The name is spelled out in full eleven times throughout the dialogue between Poirot and a police inspector on that page, and the parallel structure of the questions in the last paragraph even further amplifies the effect (see 229). The repetition of Nigel Chapman's name in between the parallelistic questions directs attention away from details that do not fit the theory that he should be the killer by signposting that several suspicious instances do connect with that name. The formal structure of repetition veils inconsistencies by suggesting that Nigel Chapman is not only the obvious answer to the questions asked but also the only possible answer. Since rhetorical strategies suggest that frequency correlates with importance, the repetitions that draw attention to Miss Russell in Ackroyd and Nigel Chapman in Hickory deflect attention from incongruities and other suspects (such as Sheppard) that might otherwise draw the reader's interest.[13]

Relevance and Visibility

Dr. Sheppard's (non-)appearance on Ackroyd's suspect lists (as well as the repetition of Nigel Chapman's name in Hickory) shows that the criterion of visibility is inseparable from the form of the list and offers itself as a strategy for reader manipulation. Urs Stäheli argues that lists, through the process of selection that is inextricable from them, set certain items apart from their contexts in order to highlight them and therefore determine what is made visible.[14] This "constitutive function of list" ensures that what is listed is automatically considered relevant (Stäheli 2017, 364). Because of this equation of visibility with relevance and its affordance to represent information (seemingly) objectively and concisely, the form of the list offers itself as a means of conveying false clues. These, for example, invite readers to ascribe high relevance to details which ultimately turn out not to be related to the main investigation.

This is, for example, the case in *Death in the Clouds* (1935), where Poirot gains possession of a victim's notebook, which seems connected to several suspects' activities. The lists of encrypted names contained therein and printed in the book for the reader to inspect, however, provide no hint to the identity of the murderer, even if it is possible for the reader to decrypt large parts of the list and match the entries with suspect names:

CL52. English Peeress. Husband.
RT362. Doctor. Harley Street.
MR 24. Forged Antiquities.
XVB 724. English. Embezzlement.
GF 45. Attempted Murder. English. (113)[15]

The entry for attempted murder, however, which seems to hold the most relevance for the investigation, cannot clearly be matched with any of the suspects. This list plays with the reader's assumption that the information provided in lists is relevant and that, hence, it should be possible to match the suspects with the entries in the notebook. When Poirot resolves the case, he makes no reference back to the unmatched notebook entry and thus leaves open the question of whether the attempted murder entry in the notebook can be attributed to any of the suspects. The listed information turns out to be irrelevant.

In a similar manner, both *Orient Express* and *Ackroyd* feature tabular lists drawn up by detective characters, which elucidate the whereabouts of certain persons around the time the crime was supposedly committed. Since these lists are visually set apart from the continuous text around them and thus highly visible, they invite readers to consider them as summaries of relevant information that a (proficient) reader will be able to make sense of and draw conclusions from. List items thus presented are likely to be understood as "building blocks for a coherent and meaningful narrative" (see von Contzen 2017, 236),[16] and readers will try to detect meaning and construct such a narrative around the supposed clues thus assembled.

The tabular lists in *Ackroyd* and *Orient Express*, however, flout these expectations. Both lists appear as summaries of hitherto known clues assumed to be relevant to the solution of the crime, but the *Ackroyd* list does not even include the guilty party in its account of whereabouts (see

97–98), and the *Orient Express* list presents a temporal succession of events that ends almost an hour before the crime was actually committed (see 111; 265). As was the case with Poirot's enumeration of suspects in *Ackroyd* discussed above, these lists invite the reader to be "distracted by content and [...] not question the logic of the list—how it frames their thinking" (Young 2017, 63), in this case by making readers take for granted the relevance of the information provided. In the *Orient Express* list, the impression of relevance is reinforced by a character commenting on the list with the words "[t]hat is very clear" (111), which implies the list has provided him with new information or a new angle on the information presented that he can make sense of. In the case of *Ackroyd*, the physical space on the page between the list and the continuous text is turned into conceptual space between the list's content and the surrounding passages that functions to distract readers from the presence and naming of the actual murderer in this scene.

Categorization

While the previously discussed examples invite readers to engage with details or draw conclusions which turn out to be irrelevant to the context of the list, my next example is concerned with framing and focus as created by categorization. The third and last section of *Orient Express* features profiles of all passengers who traveled on the train coach in which the murder was committed (see 205–208). Those profiles list the passenger's name, country of origin, berth number, and traveling class, followed by the categories "Motive"—which is left blank for almost all of the suspects—"Alibi," and, in most cases, "Evidence Against Him [/Her] or Suspicious Circumstances" (205–208):

> Mary Debenham—British subject. Berth No. 11. Second Class.
> Motive: None.
> Alibi: Midnight to 2 a.m. (Vouched for by Greta Ohlsson.)
> Evidence Against Her or Suspicious Circumstances: Conversation overheard
>   by H.P. and her refusal to explain same. (208)

This setup invites readers to compare the passengers' profiles with regard to the listed categories in order to spot the detail that is odd and thus gives away the correct suspect.

These profiles give the appearance of working like an index that the reader can go back to in order to locate pointers to relevant pieces of information. According to Urs Stäheli, an index "provides signposts" to the reader and "points out what is worth seeing/reading" (2016, 17). The items that the index renders visible suggest that the relevant clue is to be found among the categories of "Motive, Alibi, or Evidence" that detective Poirot, the list-maker, deemed worth including for each suspect. By highlighting these three categories, Christie's novel plays with the reader's expectations of and experiences with identifying the correct suspect in detective novels. However, here, the category of motive is left blank for almost all suspects, and the categories of alibi and evidence do not contain relevant information, so a perusal of Poirot's profiles cannot single anyone out. The sober and seemingly businesslike enumerations seem to "say everything without meaning anything" (Mainberger 2003, 118)[17] because the list form's association with facticity and clarity veils the lack of interpretable content.

Since the twist of *Orient Express* reveals that *all* the suspects are guilty and have committed the crime collaboratively, the only reading strategy that can lead to success is finding out what connects all these profiles. But gaining relevant information from the profiles is doubly impossible for the reader: first, because the information on motives and others they promise to provide is incomplete and, second, because genre expectations prompt readers to look for one suspect who can be identified through singling out one detail, rather than finding out what all suspects have in common.[18] A successful reading necessitates a re-framing of the information and a different approach to processing data that is geared toward combination rather than selection.

That the meaning of a text is not fixed but at least partly depends on the reader's expectations is a basic premise of Wolfgang Iser's aesthetics of reception. Iser sees the meaning of a text as the product of an interaction between text and reader rather than a text-inherent property. According to Iser, (literary) texts consist of a number of narrative schemata that constitute a primary code, on the basis of which readers fill in the blanks left in the text with their horizon of expectations to create a secondary code (see 1978, 93). Iser even argues that a text can only have an impact on readers if it is not identical with their horizon of expectations (see ibid., 43). The way recipients make sense of a text is thus crucial to its meaning. Genre conventions, such as the idea that there is usually only one perpetrator in a detective novel, form an integral part of a reader's horizon of expectations (see Jauss 2004, 1241) and therefore constitute an ideal leverage point for manipulating readers.

Orient Express relies on categorization-related manipulative strategies to highlight the diversity of the suspects and thus invites readers to consider them individually rather than as a group. The list of profiles discussed above highlights the passengers' different nationalities in the profiles' headings: "Hector MacQueen—American subject […] Conductor—Pierre Michel—French subject," and so on (205). The list points out the passenger's various nationalities and origins in close succession in order to emphasize their apparent differences over their possible similarities, and thus discourages the idea that they might be connected in any way but through the physical space of the train coach they share. This perceived difference also functions to strengthen the alibis they give to one another: "[t]hey can't all be in it" (254), which various characters involved in the investigation stress repeatedly.

In his summary of the evidence preceding the big revelation, Poirot yet again stresses the different nationalities of the passengers, but this time, in a rhetorical backflip, he uses this enumeration as a rhetorical device to support his theory that ties the passengers together as a group: "[i]n America there might be a household composed of just such varied nationalities—an Italian chauffeur, an English governess, a Swedish nurse, a French lady's maid and so on" (262). Marc Alexander performs a rhetorical analysis of this passage and concludes that the enumeration of passengers and their nationalities is used as a concrete example for Poirot's otherwise rather lofty claims that only an American household could assemble people of such varied nationalities, and he argues that these examples form "the rhetorical thrust of the argument" Poirot is building (2009, 21). Listing and parallelism in this passage function as a rhetorical support structure for Poirot's argument. The "and so on" at the end of the list turns the enumeration into what Alexander calls "a series example," which implies that countless other points could be added to the list to further support the argument (2009, 21).

As the example from *Orient Express* shows, categorization lends itself to the manipulation of the reader's attention and assumptions. A very basic approach to using categorization to such purpose is to veil the importance of a clue by subsuming it into a higher-level category. This is, for example, used in *Ackroyd* (see 31) and *Crooked House* (1949) (see 175), both of which include an important item in their enumeration that is subsumed under its hypernym rather than made visible as the basic level term right away.[19] In *Crooked House*, the object, a chair, is mentioned only two pages later, but in *Ackroyd*, several chapters go by before the object—the dagger that will be used as a murder weapon—shows up again, divorced from the context it was originally enumerated in. This constitutes "a twist on the more usual detective fiction device of nesting a significant object—a clue—in amongst insignificant ones" (Stewart 2019, 185) and makes it harder to connect the list item to the clue the original context provides.

Variations on the technique of nesting a significant object among insignificant ones can also be observed in *Clouds* and in *Hickory*. *Clouds* uses the sheer mass of objects enumerated over four entire pages under the heading of passengers' belongings to conceal the two objects that can prove the murderer's guilt (see 83–86). Detective Poirot's comment (following this list) that the list "seems to point very plainly to one person as having committed the crime" (87) remains the only hint to the reader that a suspicious object *can* be identified among the passengers' belongings. Readers are provided with no guidance as to what kind of clue or which category of object they are supposed to look for and thus lack the analytical tools to successfully process the mass of information they are confronted with. The passage plays with the issue of visibility discussed above and illustrates the kind of interpretative glitch that can result from what Mainberger designates as a reader's "insufficient familiarity with the functional context"[20] of the list, that is, a lack of knowledge about the principle(s) that induced the creation of the list (2003, 19).

Hickory takes yet a different approach to concealing clues among list items. The plot of the entire novel is based around the circumstance that objects which initially appear together in a single list are, in fact, to be attributed to two different lists, which record the involvement of three different people. The disentanglement of what belongs on which of these lists is the central problem to be solved in this novel:

Evening shoe (one of a new pair)
Bracelet (costume jewellery)
Diamond ring (found in plate of soup)
Powder compact
Lipstick
Stethoscope
Ear-rings
Cigarette lighter
Old flannel trousers

Electric light bulbs
Box of chocolates
Silk scarf (found cut to pieces)
Rucksack (ditto)
Boracic powder
Bath salts
Cookery book.
(*Hickory*, 9)

This list is initially presented to Poirot in the above order, labeled as an enumeration of stolen goods. When confronted with this list, the characters discuss the "totally unrelated nature of the objects" (10) and try in vain to come up with a principle that connects them all—with what Madeleine Frédéric calls a "synthetic formula" (1986, 106)[21] to comprise the enumerated items. Frédéric argues that enumerations tend to be governed by a semantic principle that unifies the constituent items and renders them recognizable as part of a semantic field that functions like a caption or heading for the enumeration (see ibid.). If such a synthetic formula is not (or not satisfactorily) provided, readers will try to come up with one themselves to make sense of the list. This is exactly what Poirot attempts when he is first confronted with this "haphazard collection" (11). He points out that "[w]hat is so intriguing is all the different categories represented here" (13) and immediately engages in coming up with a classification system that sorts the items into more coherent groups. His ordering system hinges on the semantic principle of value. He divides the items into "small trifles" (13) of little value that are connected to vanity, things that can be sold for a profit (such as the stethoscope), and "things that it would seem were not worth stealing," such as the light bulbs. He also remarks that the cut-up silk scarf fits neither of his categories and seems to be the result of a "deliberately vindictive" action (15).

Interestingly, the principle that eventually enables Poirot to reorder the list and separate the items relevant to the investigation from the ones merely stolen by a girl to draw her love interest's attention (marked in italics below) is temporal succession.[22] Again, the theme of (in)visibility plays a crucial role in determining the proper ordering principle that unlocks the clues contained in the list. Chronology is not a structuring principle that is made visible in the text: the physical and very visible nature of the objects themselves distracts from the invisible principles of temporal succession that readers are aware of but do not consider. As a possible theme, chronology is not discussed in the text until Poirot asks to have the initial list rearranged.

The restructured version of the list is reprinted in full on pages 166–167 of the novel. The space in which this rearrangement is allowed on the page promotes the importance of this discovery and suggests that the reordering of items is not to be seen as a mere repetition of previously known information but rather as a new and important clue. Indeed, the reordered chronological list already hints that three rather than two parties must be involved in the events:

> Rucksack (Len Bateson's)
> Electric light bulbs
> *Bracelet* (Genevieve's)
> *Diamond ring* (<u>Patricia's</u>)
> *Powder compact* (Genevieve's)
> *Evening shoe* (Sally's)
> *Lipstick* (Elizabeth Johnston's)
> *Ear-rings* (Valerie's)
> Stethoscope (Len Bateson's)
> Bath salts (?)
> *Scarf* <u>cut in pieces</u> (Valerie's)
> *Trousers* (Colin's)
> *Cookery book* (?)
> Boracic (Chandra Lal's)
> Costume Brooch (Sally's)
> Ink spilled on Elizabeth's notes.
> (*Hickory*, 166–167, highlights mine)

In the above quoted list, the three constitutive elements are marked as follows: italics indicate the items related to the love interest, plain writing items are related to a drug smuggling business and efforts to conceal the smuggler's identity, and the underlined items hint at the involvement of a third party drawing the strings in the background.

The chronologically reordered final list Poirot receives omits two of the previous items that are related to the love interest but also contains the additional item "Ink spilled on Elizabeth's notes" (167) that calls into question the synthetic formula chosen earlier as a header since it fits none of the object-related categories. The additional item contributes to changing Poirot's view on the case, since it necessitates a rethinking of the synthetic formula that ties the items together. Sabine Mainberger has pointed out that most categorization systems are fluid and that adding additional items to the list will often draw attention to the arbitrariness of the previous classification because the new item can easily be integrated into the list once a different connecting principle is chosen (see 2003, 53). Once the stolen goods (*italics*) are edited out of the above quoted list, what remains can be subsumed under evidence for the involvement of the character Nigel Chapman, and the list now functions as a written proof thereof. With the new order, the list thus also gains the new purpose of identification.

Despite the flexibility of the form, lists invite us to think in categories. Detective fiction places great emphasis on the shared features or properties of objects in the formation of these categories. Such an approach to categorization advocates a "rationalistic dictate" (ibid., 53)[23] which the entire genre buys into. This kind of pattern of thinking is predestined to avail itself of the form of the list to demonstrate its practicability and inevitability. With its tight focus on ordering structures and obsession with "proper order" of things (148) and with its numerous discussions and deliberations about categorization strategies, *Hickory* could be read as a meta-commentary on the hidden mechanisms that govern detective fiction. Restoring the chaos that the seemingly unrelated list items represent to this proper order rests on detective Hercule Poirot. That such a miraculous restoration of order is possible is taken for granted as one of the core assumptions of the detective fiction genre. Even before it is clear that the list will become the basis for a murder investigation, Poirot shows interest in the puzzle it poses because it is his function in the story to solve such puzzles. Chapter 2 states that "Poirot knew quite well that somehow and somewhere there must be a pattern [in this list]" (16) and thus demonstrates the genre's strong ties to what Mainberger designates as a rationalistic dictate.

Christie expertly makes use of (and sometimes deliberately breaks) these genre rules and relies on the reader's unthinking acceptance of them to set up manipulative plot structures and achieve her surprise effects. Be it the assumptions that classifications are fixed that she plays with in *Hickory*, or the assumption that lists present relevant information and only have to be put in the right order to reveal their secret that she plays with in the encrypted notebook in *Clouds*, Christie is keenly aware of her reader's ideas about genre rules and ordering mechanisms, which so frequently show themselves in the genre's lists. "[E]numerative structures" in particular, Eva von Contzen argues, "require the reader's input in order to be rendered meaningful" (2021, 49), and according to Wolfgang Iser, readers "cannot help but try and supply the missing links that will bring the schemata together in an integrated gestalt" (1978, 186). List structures are thus a particularly effective means of manipulating readers' expectations.

The Fair Play Rule

When Marc Alexander discusses Christie's *Orient Express*, he remarks that detective fiction could be considered a "core genre of manipulative writing" (2009, 13); yet, the rule catalogs from and general agreements on the so-called Golden Age[24] of detective fiction state fair play with the reader as their most important principle. This section shall discuss how such contrary impulses can be reconciled.

The expression *fair play* serves as an umbrella term for all the detailed rules that the rule catalogs of the Golden Age (discussed in Chap. 2) put on record. If, however, one takes a closer look at Ronald Knox's "Detective Story Decalogue" or the points that feature in the "Detection Club Oath," rules such as "No hitherto undiscovered poisons may be used" or "No accident must ever help the detective" (Knox 1976, 195) seem more geared toward preventing deus ex machina solutions and sloppy plotting than fairness in the OED sense of "Honesty; impartiality, equitableness, justness; fair dealing" with regard to the reader (*OED*, s.v. no 6).

The reader, in fact, only features in three of Knox's ten rules, and only rule VIII has something to say about clues, the list-based element of the story that is the most frequent target of reader manipulation: "VIII. The detective must not light on any clues which are not instantly produced for the inspection of the reader" (1976, 196). Knox's wording suggests that clues should not be omitted from the text only to be produced out of thin air to support an explanation. The rule, however, carefully avoids statements that imply clues need to be contextualized or explained—the two operations reader manipulation is most often based on. A more sloppily worded variation of Knox's commandment appears in the "Detection Club Oath." It asks prospective members of the Detection Club: "[d]o you solemnly swear never to conceal a vital clue from the reader?" (Haycraft 1976, 198) and through the use of the word "conceal" invites interpretations that configure fairness as an absence of deception or ambiguity. If these rules are to have any authority over the realities of the genre, fair play has to be understood in a much broader sense: as a summons to avoid implausible explanations but allow for ambiguities.

In fact, many of the detective novels that apparently violate one or several of Knox's rules—such as Christie's *Ackroyd*—are ranked among the most popular specimens of their genre. This would suggest that readers do not mind or possibly even expect and enjoy being manipulated, as long as the solution they are presented with at least in hindsight proves to be plausible and motivated by the plot and clues the reader has followed.

In both their focus on problem solving and their often enumerative structure, in which suspect after suspect is questioned with regard to the resolution of a mystery, detective novels of the Golden Age, and especially those of Agatha Christie, bear resemblance to the text genre of the riddle. Riddles frequently describe their object in a series of brief characteristics, each of which contains a hint, and thus can be argued to possess "enumerative character" (Mainberger 2003, 98).[25] Detective fiction functions according to the same principle, as Mainberger also points out briefly. The characteristics enumerated in a riddle frequently seem to contradict one another (ibid., 99), as is also the case with clues provided to the reader in detective fiction. Both detective fiction and riddles afford heightened reader engagement through the inclusion of a number of such (contradictory or non-contradictory) characteristics. According to Mainberger, it is the explicit purpose of a riddle to provide clues that "suggest a certain solution and then create surprise by flouting the expectations they set up" (ibid.).[26] The same could be said about the Golden Age detective novel.

The close ties between these two text genres are founded in their affinity to the list form and its affordances. The enumerative structure in which riddle characteristics or witness testimonies are frequently presented confronts readers with an abundance of information and invites them to fill in the blanks left between individual items, characteristics, or bits of information. As elaborated above, the order and wording of such bullet-point-like information is often deliberately misleading and used to create surprise by revealing causal connections different from those the information initially seems to point to.

This reshaping of (causal) connections between items inscribes an undeniably playful element into both riddles and detective fiction that, paradoxically, raises the expectation that one's expectations about the outcome will be defied. Since detective fiction is an essentially plot-driven genre, it heavily relies on suspense for its effect, which the constant play with expectations helps to create. Suspense results from ambiguity and the reader's inability to get to the solution before the fictional detective does and therefore could be considered a more or less direct result of manipulating the reader through misleading their expectations.[27]

But if being confronted with misleading information, surprise twists, and false clues is inscribed into the genre expectations for detective fiction, a closer look at what is meant by fair play under these circumstances is necessary. Fairness to the reader, in this case, is not to be understood as an absence of ambiguity but rather concerns the production of a solution that incorporates elements previously mentioned in the text and therefore aims at plausibility and story world logic.

A crucial distinction between the detective novels of the Golden Age and those detective stories that were published toward the end of the nineteenth century lies in the conceptions of knowledge that the logic of these texts is built around. Even though detective fiction is such a closely knit and easily recognizable genre, conceptions and representations of knowledge differ widely across different timelines and subgenres. In Golden Age fiction, knowledge (as a means of solving the puzzle and piecing clues together) tends to be text-inherent, that is, information necessary for arriving at the right solution has to be mentioned or at least hinted at in the printed text (suzhet). Furthermore, the analysis of evidence in Golden Age novels is based around circumstances which would be considered common knowledge by a majority of the readers. Stephen Knight, for instance, points out that most of the central clues in Christie's fiction revolve around the realm of domestic activity (such as the proper time of year to light a chimney fire) rather than venture into complex laws from the realms of science (see Knight 1980, 109). Knox implicitly includes this conception of knowledge in his fourth commandment when he writes "[n]o hitherto undiscovered poisons may be used, nor any appliance which will need a long scientific explanation at the end" (1976, 195). Elaborate scientific explanations and procedures (which, e.g., play a central role in Austin Freeman's Dr. Thorndyke stories) are considered undesirable because they are likely to fall outside the realm of common knowledge the majority of readers will have access to.[28]

Christie's novels also play fair with their readers in the sense that they make clear what kind of knowledge they expect the readers to resort to and what kind of investigative work is to be performed. *The Notting Hill Mystery* discussed in the previous chapter, for example, requires the reader to compare and cross-reference information given at various points of the story and to reassemble the information given at various points into a chronological timeline that will reveal patterns and discrepancies. Christie's novels, by contrast, provide an overview over the information mentioned at various points in the story in maps, tables, or summaries and thus take this kind of work out of the reader's hands.

Clouds, for instance, contains a map depicting which passenger occupied which seat on the plane (the crime scene) that immediately follows the table of contents and thus signposts even before the story begins that diligence is not what this text asks of its reader. Similarly, *Orient Express* features a map of the train coach in which the crime was committed that indicates which passenger occupied which berth (see 76). Starting from the Golden Age, maps of the house or crime scene became a standard feature of the clue puzzle mystery (see Knight 1980, 109–110). This development testifies to the fact that Golden Age novels expect their readers to draw connections between pieces of information rather than task them with creating an overview of which information is available at which point in the story.

LISTS AS THE DETECTIVE'S TOOL: CREATING ORDER

Lucie Doležalová has argued that "[i]n a literary context, lists seem to embody a lack of story; one often skips lists in novels because they do not seem to move the events forward" (2009, 1). In the Golden Age detective novel, it seems to be the other way around. Lists are used to summarize important plot points for the reader; they frequently contain or hide clues, and in the case of Agatha Christie, her fictional detectives use them as a means to order their thoughts. Since these lists promise the reader access to the detective's thoughts and (through the medium of writing) function to give the detective's reasoning process a physical shape, they draw rather than deflect the reader's attention.

Representing Thoughts

When used as a tool by Christie's detectives, lists are often the means of representing the progression of the investigator's thoughts. Toward the end of *Orient Express*, Hercule Poirot writes down ten questions that give the chapter in which they occur its title and that he considers crucial for the solution of the case:

Things needing explanation.
1. The handkerchief marked with the initial H. Whose is it?

2. The pipe-cleaner. Was it dropped by Colonel Arbuthnot? Or by somebody else?
3. Who wore the scarlet kimono?
4. Who was the man or woman masquerading in Wagon Lit uniform?
5. Why do the hands of the watch point to 1.15?
6. Was the murder committed at that time?
7. Was it earlier?
8. Was it later? (210)

The order and grouping in which Poirot poses these questions grants the reader insight into his thought processes. Questions five through eight build upon one another and thus show a clear progression of thoughts. Question five suggests that the watch is an important clue, and Poirot's successive questions first spell out the obvious implication of that clue and branch out from there to demonstrate that he finds the obvious interpretation suggested by question six misleading or unconvincing.

Furthermore, the disjointed syntax that leaves the relation between successive list items undetermined allows Poirot to explore alternative interpretations (see questions 2; 5–8) without having to deliver a coherent theory—a feat that is usually expected of detective characters. The list form, together with the phrasing as questions rather than statements, allows the reader a rare glimpse into Poirot's thought processes without giving away his conclusions. Urs Stäheli considers it a unique affordance of the list form to offer an "ordering system that brings together heterogenous content without having to provide a foundational unity" (Stäheli 2011, 86).[29] In Poirot's case, the numbered ordering system creates the impression that the detective has a clear overview over and is in control of the investigation without him having to give away details about specific conclusions that can be drawn from the list of questions. Poirot's list both emphasizes the considerable number of missing links (and thus the difficulty of the task Poirot is confronted with) and highlights his capability to succeed at this task.

Briefly contrasting Poirot's list with the considerations of his colleague and assistant M. Bouc shall further illustrate my point. In the chapter following the one that poses Poirot's ten questions, the reader is granted insight into M. Bouc's thoughts about the case. Bouc's thoughts are presented in paratactical sentences of continuous text, frequently separated by "…" to mark pauses in thought and, at first glance, do not appear too different from Poirot's list of questions:

Assuredly I must think. But as far as that goes I have already thought …
Poirot obviously thinks this English girl is mixed up in the matter. I cannot
help feeling that this is most unlikely … The English are extremely cold.
Probably it is because they have no figures … But that is not the point. It
seems that the Italian could not have done it—a pity. (216)

Although Bouc's thoughts also revolve around the suspects and pose
questions, the effect on the reader is one of confusion, disorder, and a lack
of structure.

Through the numerous uses of the pronoun "I" as an indicator of
Bouc's opinion, the passage evokes the impression of speculation and
stands in stark contrast to Poirot's seemingly impersonal questions. The
formal structure in which the passage is presented further reinforces this
effect. With the "…" the text includes a typographical sign for an omission, a disconnection, or a missing link that draws attention to itself and
evokes the impression that Bouc is unable to follow through with any
particular train of thought. The invisible gaps in Poirot's list, on the other
hand—if they are noticed at all—rather convey the idea of highly condensed information. The graphical representation of Poirot's questions in
numbered list form as opposed to the continuous text used for Bouc's
thoughts makes Poirot's list appear even more concise and to the point.
The list form casts Poirot's questions as "synecdochic," meaning that the
brevity of the items seems to conceal a nexus of wider implications, whereas
Bouc's thoughts appear rather "periphrastic" in their failure to arrive at
the core of the problem (see Barney 1982, 191).[30] Poirot's list, therefore,
not only represents the content but also the ordered and structured quality of his thoughts.

Poirot's list of ten questions is not only presented to the reader on the
printed paper of the page; the novel also explicitly mentions that Poirot
writes down on a sheet of paper both the list of questions and the list with
the passengers' profiles discussed above (see 205; 210). By making his
thoughts visible through a written medium, the detective awards his reasoning process physical shape. A statement made in writing is generally
considered more permanent than oral statements that can be more easily
modified or disavowed.

Giving physical shape to his thoughts and preserving them in the form
of a written artifact enables Poirot to allow his colleagues (and the reader)
easier access to them. Poirot hands his written list of passenger profiles to
Bouc to help his colleague "refresh [his] memory" (205) of the facts of

the case. Additionally, he hands his list of ten questions to Bouc to provide him with a basic grid to anchor his considerations in. This way, Poirot offers his colleague an opportunity to reenact his reasoning process. In the context of detective fiction, where seeing as the detective's primary means of perceiving and interacting with the empirical(ly perceptible) world is inscribed with such crucial ideological importance, this material aspect moreover contributes to making Poirot's considerations appear more convincing.

In Christie's detective novels, such a contemplation of facts, often in written down form, frequently replaces the need for taking actions. Stephen Knight even argues that "[h]ard work, activity, professionalism and the positivistic mysteries of contemporary forensic science," which are so important to the stories of Dr. Thorndyke discussed in the following chapter, "are all thrown out together" in Christie's crime stories and are replaced by "peaceful reflection," which can reestablish order just as well (1980, 110).[31]

The list of passengers' belongings in *Clouds* (see 83–86) serves as a means for such reflection and is a case in point. The list is written down on a piece of paper that takes on an importance that transcends that of the material objects it represents. The full documentation of the passengers' belongings and the matching of each object with its owner are of central importance to Poirot's detective work in the novel; yet, Poirot never handles or even sees the objects the list represents. The written documentation of signifiers replaces the need for engagement with the actual signified, even for those objects that in the end turn out to have been instrumental to the crime.[32]

Poirot's list of ten questions, as well as the list of belongings in *Clouds*, exist as objects within the story world and are therefore situated on the level of the diegesis. Lists outside the diegesis that are directly addressed to the reader, such as the score sheet in Wheatley's *Herewith the Clues* discussed in Chap. 3, are rare in Christie's novels, and it is even rarer that they contain clues.[33] With the exception of the table of contents, all lists discussed in this chapter that are used by detective figures exist as objects on the diegetic level. These lists are usually composed by Poirot and serve either as a memory aid to himself or as a visual representation of his observations used to summarize or point out case details for his colleagues or assistants. The typographical emphasis of the empty space around those lists among otherwise continuous text grants them and, moreover, turns these lists into signposts for the reader.

The reader is confronted with the exact same information in the exact same phrasing as Poirot's assistants in the story world; therefore, or so the text seems to suggest, the reader also has the same (fair) chance of solving the puzzle as the detective's assistants do. The seeming absence of the mediating instance of the narrator in these lists functions to involve the reader more deeply into the story. It suggests that the reader and the characters who are presented with Poirot's lists in these instances share the position of narratee within the text's communicative structure. This shared position creates the impression that readers can get involved in the investigation in the same way as the assisting characters and ties in with the idea posed above that investigative work requires no physical action but rather consists of the compilation and interpretation of text-based media. This may be one of the reasons for the extraordinary popularity of Christie's clue puzzle novels. Lastly, the reader is likely to equate the list form's apparent lack of mediation with a lack of deception and accept the list's content at face value.

Concealing Thoughts

The illusion that lists lack a mediating instance can not only be used to create facticity; it also works to obscure logical connections from the reader. This is used to build suspense in *A Murder Is Announced* (1950), where Christie's spinster detective Miss Marple disappears suddenly and leaves behind only a list of clues without explanations. The list strongly suggests she has resolved the mystery yet leaves the readers and the characters who find it in the dark about the kinds of connections to be drawn between the items: "Lamp. Violets. Where is bottle of aspirin? Delicious Death. Making enquiries. Severe affliction bravely borne. Iodine. Pearls. Letty. Berne. Old Age pension" (256). Marple's list has both the reader and the characters who find it at a loss. "Does it mean anything? Anything at all? I can't see any connection" (256), one of the characters comments.

Lists "convert [...] continuous material (e.g. narratives, arguments, descriptions) into discontinuous, isolated items" (Stäheli 2016, 14) and therefore can work as summaries for the list-maker while at the same time they defy interpretation by someone else. Stäheli's argument revolves around how the standardization process that comes with indexing items can be a powerful tool for producing knowledge and exerting control for those who create the index, and he also draws attention to the political implications of such invisible power structures (see 2016, 16). Although the political implications of listing and indexing are commonly disregarded in detective fiction, Christie's lists regularly showcase the power that a list-maker (usually the detective) wields and the powerlessness that those unfamiliar with the list's logic are confronted with.

Marple's list suggests that the items she listed can be fitted into a coherent narrative that points to the guilt of a certain suspect. For her, the discontinuous bullet points on the list serve as shorthand for this narrative, but for an onlooker without insight into her thoughts, it is almost impossible to reconstruct her reasoning steps. Even though the list gives the impression of boxes being checked off a mental cross-reference list, syntactic connections that could draw attention to cause-effect logic or chronology remain absent. Moreover, the lack of a synthetic formula (see Frédéric 1986, 106) (such as a suspect's name), which could provide an external reference point to serve as a guideline on how to connect the clues, prevents readers from recreating the logic that unifies the list from the perspective of the list-maker.

Eva von Contzen remarks that enumerative forms "exponentiate possible decoding mechanisms because they maximize gaps" (von Contzen 2017, 235).[34] Paradoxically, even though the lack of a guiding mediating instance allows more direct access to Miss Marple's thoughts—the rapid succession of items simulates how quickly she fits the clues together—it, at the same time, leaves open a multitude of possible interpretative strategies without any leads on how to prioritize them. The immediacy of the list that seems to provide the reader with direct access to Marple's thoughts at the same time serves to obscure the detective's conclusions.

A lack of mediation and the absence of a synthetic formula are not the only ways in which lists can conceal the logic according to which they were compiled. Christie's *The ABC Murders* (1936) presents a list of victims that flaunts an ordering logic that seems obvious in order to conceal the hidden logic according to which the murders are committed. As the title already suggests, the killer in *The ABC Murders* seems to follow the letters of the alphabet in picking out his victims: Alice Asher is killed in Andover, followed by Betty Barnard killed in Bexhill, followed by Sir Carmichael Clarke, who meets his end in Churston. At each of the crime scenes, an ABC railway guide is found,[35] which implies that the killer follows the railway guide's alphabetical order in picking out his next victim and location. This initially prompts the conclusion that a serial killer is at work, whose killings meticulously follow an alphabetical order and are thus to be situated outside more conventional patterns of and motives for crimes, such as a personal relation between killer and victim. Detective Poirot, however, eventually points out that the ABC pattern does not only deviate from conventional motives for murder but is also internally inconsistent[36]:

> There was something haphazard about the procedure of A B C [the killer] that seemed to [Poirot] to be at war with the alphabetical selection [...] To be consistent, the murderer should have chosen his towns in some definite sequence. If Andover is the 155th name under A, then the B crime should be the 155th also—or it should be the 156th and the C the 157th. (247–248)

The fact that the murderer's choices within the strict alphabetical order of his killings seem random allows Poirot to see that the ABC order is used as a front to conceal a personal motive. Poirot picks apart the ordering structure of the crimes, and his close examination of the logic behind the list of victims enables him to unmask the killer and expose the ABC killing list as an imperfect construct to deflect attention from the one victim whose death afforded the killer personal gain.[37] At the same time, Poirot's analysis emphasizes the criminal's imperfect command of such ordering structures and contrasts it with Poirot's mastery.

Breaking Down the Problem: Managing Boundaries

"[T]o list is to attempt to comprehend," writes Stephen Barney (1982, 223) in his discussion of lists in Chaucer's *Canterbury Tales*. This is certainly true in the context of detective fiction, where lists not only work to manipulate the reader's attention or to display the detectives' thoughts, but also function as reasoning tools and structuring aids to facilitate detective work. The structuring properties of the list make it a fitting tool to draw clear boundaries around a subject matter within the space of a page and select and highlight what is relevant. At the same time, lists can be used to break larger problems down into smaller, tick-off-able topics and therefore make them appear more manageable.

It is a detective's task to narrow down possible fields of inquiry and to compartmentalize information. A choice of focus that is too broad is detrimental to drawing accurate and sensible conclusions (see Gitelman 2014, 7) and will distract from the more relevant points of inquiry. The form of the list is an ideal tool for such compartmentalization because it operates on processes of selection that force the list-maker to make judgments of value and relevance in order to pick out from the mass of information the items which will yield concise results. Compartmentalizing information makes it appear more manageable, and drawing clear boundaries round a subject matter functions to establish clarity and order or at least the semblance thereof.

Poirot is not the only detective character who resorts to this investigative strategy. At the beginning of the murder investigation in *Clouds*, inspector Japp attempts to create an overview over the case that allows him to rank the suspects according to their possible involvement. For this, he picks two distinct categories on which he bases his deliberations: possibility—dependent on the situational factors of timing and proximity—and probability—recognizable motive and access to the means—that any particular suspect could have committed the crime:

> This is where we stand. Jane Grey. Probability—poor. Possibility—practically nil. Gale. Probability—poor. Possibility—again practically nil. Miss Kerr. Very improbable. Possibility—doubtful. Lady Horbury. Probability—good. Possibility—practically nil. (79–80)

The list continues in ascending order, ending with the most likely suspects. The clarity and plausibility of the categories chosen veils the fact that the reasons for Japp's assessment of a suspect as more or less likely to have committed the crime are not discussed and have to be inferred. It is the form rather than the content of Japp's deliberations that lends it rhetorical force. Even though Japp's assessment of the suspects turns out to be entirely inaccurate, the list's "random sequence makes it apt for a display of formal order" (Barney 1982, 194) and thus serves to temporarily accomplish clarity despite its ultimate inaccuracy.

Japp's act of listing goes beyond a mere description of the current state of the case. Even though his list shares with descriptions the property of creating an overview and painting a clear picture for his audience, it takes on an additional prescriptive function in suggesting actions to be taken in the further investigation (i.e., to first consider the more likely suspects). Even though lists and descriptions can overlap, "only the former are immediately recognizable and enactive as a skill and practice" (von Contzen 2018, 323) and thus stand out against mere description. Inspector Japp's list transforms the information it is based upon through the act of writing. Spelling his deliberations out on paper awards them a durable quality that contributes to eliciting an affective response: his act of ordering affords a sense of mastery and security (see ibid., 324). Such mastery is a common skill ascribed to detective figures, and it is frequently tied to the ability to use lists for the purposes of order and categorization. Through the processes of selection and ordering, the list form suggest an intellectual pervasion of the material that is lacking in a mere description.[38]

The act of listing takes on a quasi-performative quality in its capacity to create meaning: even if the classifications performed turn out to be incorrect later, they at least temporarily create order and satisfy both the characters' and the readers' need for clarity. The act of labeling options, facts, observations, or alternative actions, for example, by assigning them numbers or letters of the alphabet, imbues them with a significance that is uncoupled from interpretation and its results. As is the case with the list, the purpose of such labeling lies in creating a specific appearance rather than specific content. The form of the list constitutes "the ideal medium for the creation of new ordering principles" (Stäheli 2017, 367) because its minimal syntax makes it amenable to the inscription of ever new meanings. Numbering or alphabetical category labels (as, e.g., those used in *Crooked House* (see 127)) serve to compartmentalize information and stand in for and cover up the unnamed assumptions on which they are based. By referring to commonly accepted and widely used alphabetical or numerical ordering systems, such labels claim and repurpose the regulatory authority of those systems for their list's specific context.

Strategies of compartmentalization similar to those the list affords can be realized in the continuous text through the use of punctuation. When detective Poirot delivers explanations about the circumstances of a crime (most frequently toward the end of a novel), he tends to do this in an enumerative style that is characterized by a fast-paced succession of facts and ideas that are separated by dashes with conspicuous frequency. These dashes signal pauses in Poirot's explanations, which in turn prompt readers to fill in the blanks left by Poirot and supplement missing connections. Moreover, the dashes create the appearance of breathlessness and fast-flowing thoughts. They serve as visual markers to break up the text and give even continuous text paragraphs a list-like aspect (see e.g. *Clouds*, 207).[39] The discontinuous visual appearance the dashes create allows Poirot's explanations to draw on the affordances of the list form, and the visual compartmentalization of information thus achieved supports the impression that Poirot's explanations create order and coherence despite the gaps they leave.

Besides using lists for the compartmentalization of complex problems, Christie's detectives also employ them for concretization—another strategy to reduce complexity. Concretization is a process which aims at giving abstract facts and circumstances a more tangible shape. It makes problems measurable and awards a degree of comparability that makes issues (appear) more accessible and thus more manageable. Lists are a frequently employed tool to perform such concretizations, because they "assemble disparate items into ordered classes of things, making problems amenable to targeted, cross-boundary intervention" (de Goede et al. 2016, 3). In their capability to create comparability or measurability, lists can thus work as a problem-solving strategy because they assemble a variety of items under a common denominator.

An example of this can be found in *Clouds*, when Poirot attempts to find out which of his suspects could have benefited from the victim's death. To assess the effect the murder had on each suspect's life, Poirot creates a list:

> Miss Grey. Result—temporary improvement. Increased salary.
> Mr Gale. Result—bad. Loss of practice.
> Lady Horbury. Result good, if she's CL 52. [i.e. if she corresponds to the encrypted notebook entry titled CL 52]
> Miss Kerr. Result—bad. (207)

This list frames the effect of the murder in terms of financial gain, which makes it possible to assess the result the crime has on each person's life in terms of a concrete, binary plus/minus logic. Picking the gain or loss of money as the criterion that best demonstrates the effects of the murder makes this effect countable and comparable in terms of numbers that seem to provide an objective measuring standard. Framed like this, Poirot's list functions to not only compile information, but to create new semantics "in producing contingent referentialities that come to appear as obvious" (de Goede et al. 2016, 5). Poirot's list constitutes a concretization of the problem that allows him to divide his suspects into three subcategories (financial gain/loss/no effect) and thus opens up a new path for the investigation—to focus on the suspects who had something to gain.

Even though the concretized evaluation system thus created appears plausible at first sight, its logic does not hold up to closer scrutiny. Besides disregarding the emotional effects that can play into or result from involvement in a crime, Poirot's list entirely disregards the proportionality of risk and results in committing a felony. The idea that someone might risk the severe sentence that a murder charge can result in for the sole reason of a temporarily increased salary seems absurd or even ridiculous. The comic effect that the detective fiction genre's obsession with facts and figures can have will be discussed in the following section.

LISTS AND HUMOR: A META-COMMENTARY ON DETECTIVE FICTION

Lists in Agatha Christie's novels do not always serve the purposes of the investigation or of manipulating the reader's expectations. Christie seems well aware of the abundance of lists she uses in her novels and of how closely the way her detectives use those lists tie them to categorization strategies and the realm of sober, objective investigative work and structured logical thought. Christie's novels, however, do not only use the form of the list as part of the detectives' methodological toolkit or as a device for reader manipulation. The form of the list also works to poke fun at detective fiction's reliance on these very categorization strategies. This becomes evident in two distinct ways: first, the self-referential hints to categorization strategies in connection with detective work and the impulses to order and structure entangled with them, and second, the humorous use of the list for (stereotypical) characterization, which relies on the list's tendency to restrict itself to essential and relevant details.

Toward the end of *Clouds*, shortly before Poirot reveals the identity of the murderer, he remarks to his audience that deaths can be divided "into two classes—deaths which are my affair and deaths which are not my affair" (248). Being used to Poirot's elaborate explanations and categorizations, at this point in the story, readers expect to be given information that will illustrate circumstances of the crime or give hints to the identity of the murderer; quite possibly readers would expect a list of further subclassifications or at least a detailed explanation. But the categories Poirot proposes in this situation are tied only to his personal experience and thus directly opposed to the aspirations for objective categories one would expect to precede the methodical uncovering of a murderer's identity. Such a statement seems to presuppose that detective Poirot is to be considered the central reference point for objective judgment, and it self-consciously ridicules the self-importance it displays. Poirot's statement serves as a sort of tongue-in-cheek comment on his apparent omniscience and unbelievable investigative skills. It stands as a benevolent and self-referential nod to the fact that Poirot's assessments always turn out to be correct and thus serves as comic relief while at the same time cementing Poirot's extraordinary position and abilities.

The importance of categorization strategies and ordered thought is similarly satirized at the beginning of *Hickory*, where Poirot's secretary Miss Lemon is introduced as a very efficient person. The reader learns that "the whole of Miss Lemon's heart and mind was given, when she was not on duty, to the perfection of a new filing system which was to be patented and bear her name" (2). Miss Lemon's unusual hobby foreshadows the concern with order and the importance of correctly putting together information around which the central plot of *Hickory* revolves. At the same time, by the novel's publication date in 1955, most readers can be assumed to be familiar with the important role that ordering and correctly allocating information generally play in Christie's detective novels. Miss Lemon's concern with a system that will bring order out of chaos to the degree of "perfection" (2) can be read as a comment on both detective fiction's obsession with bringing order to a chaotic world and the genre's common disregard of character development or topics outside the immediate vicinity of the crime.[40]

In a similar manner, *Clouds* humorously comments on the overly inflated importance of categorization and matching pieces of information in detective novels when the two characters Jane and Norman discover a list of things they have in common and on the basis of that list decide they are made for one another:

> They liked dogs and disliked cats. They both hated oysters and loved smoked salmon. They liked Greta Garbo and disliked Katharine Hepburn. They didn't like fat women and admired really jet-black hair. They disliked very red nails. They disliked loud voices, noisy restaurants, and negroes. They preferred buses to tubes. (141)

It is not only the random accumulation of unrelated details that have little to nothing to do with personality that is responsible for the humorous effect of this list. The matching of random interests seems to take on an almost mathematical precision in this excerpt. Quality, this list suggests, is achieved through an accumulation of quantity (that levels qualitative differences). Thus, this list makes the creation of a love match appear to function in the same way as the yes/no logic of matching clues to suspects that readers are familiar with from this genre. The list thus pokes fun at the overly analytical approach to the world that is so typical of detective fiction.

The second way in which lists and their properties are used humorously in the novels of Agatha Christie is as a characterization device. When Poirot interviews the writer Daniel Clancy in *Clouds*—at this point in the investigation one of his suspects—the reader first gets a description of Clancy's rather chaotic room that serves to characterize the writer's scatterbrained personality. A cursory glance at his room reveals "papers strewn about, cardboard files, bananas, bottles of beer, open books, sofa cushions, a trombone, miscellaneous china, etchings, and a bewildering assortment of fountain-pens" (159). The putting together of food items, instruments, professional equipment, leisure items, furniture, and tableware displays no apparent order other than that the items are Clancy's property and thus has a satirical effect.

Satire, Stephen Barney remarks, "magnifies and deals in 'disorderly profusion,' [and thus] naturally uses lists" (1982, 217), which enable the putting together of many disparate items in a small space. The combination of disorder and the sheer number of items is responsible for the comic effect in the example above because the chaotic enumeration acts contrary to the reader's expectation that a professionally successful adult must have a means of organizing their life and duties that continues to ensure their professional success. Furthermore, the variety of things listed implies a lack of focus that is also considered impedimental to a successful career. Lastly, the passage draws on the cliché that absentmindedness and the lack of social skills implied by the lack of order are typical traits of a writer's personality.[41]

This humorous nod at the writing profession is self-referential in a similar manner to the ways in which Poirot's and Norman and Jane's use of categorization and mathematical precision quoted above are. Those examples have characters applying the processes of categorization and comparison so typical for detective fiction to a context displaced from the investigation in order to make a meta-commentary on the importance but also inflated use of categorization and combination systems in detective fiction. The Clancy example takes this up on an even more abstract level: the list not only characterizes Clancy as a typical representative of the writing profession but also makes a comment on the writing medium (and its creators) in written form. Choosing the form of the list—which has long been known to be employed to stake claims to authority and truth for its objective depiction of facts (see Mainberger 2003, 102; 108)—for this seems to give the grossly stereotypical and exaggerated comment a serious undertone that contributes to the humorous effect.

NOTES

1. Despite Christie's innovative use of form, her works have drawn surprisingly little attention. A cursory MLA search yields only about 200 search results for "Agatha Christie" since 2000, compared to about 1500 for "Arthur Conan Doyle" for the same period.
2. If not indicated otherwise, all translations in this chapter are my own. The original phrasing will be provided in the footnotes. Here: "Die einfache Form ist paradoxerweise in der Dekodierung höchst komplex."
3. For a discussion of these terms, see Sklovskij (1991, 170).
4. A list of abbreviations can be found at the beginning of this book.
5. For a discussion of Knox's "Decalogue," see chapter two (38–40).
6. "diégétisation du récit."
7. Gutkowski discusses the possibility that one of the chapter titles could serve as a hint to the reader that Sheppard is deliberately misrepresenting factual connections (see 2011, 55).

   Some German translations, such as the 1997 edition published by Goldmann (München), trans. Friedrich Pütsch, do not include the table of contents in the novel and furthermore leave out the chapter titles and replace them with ascending numbers. This takes away from the reader a potential clue and a means of characterizing Sheppard.
8. Sheppard does tell lies but only in direct speech. Thus, he cannot be considered an unreliable narrator. In his role as narrator, he correctly (if sometimes incompletely) represents events and dialogue as they occurred. According to Gutkowski, Sheppard "tells the truth, but can make the receiver catch an oxymoric 'false reality'" (2011, 52), which represents a rather creative violation of pragmatics. Even Sheppard's direct lies often exploit the affordances of form to enhance their credibility; he, for example, uses the list form's ties to facticity to make a number of hypotheses he voices (that include statements he knows to be false) appear as objective observations (see 159–160).
9. "denn zwischen In- und Exklusion eines Elements gibt es keinen Kompromiß."
10. "Die Liste fungiert [...] als eine Kulturtechnik zur Herstellung von Übersichtlichkeit."
11. The reading strategies of cross-referencing and comparison are discussed in more detail in chapter three: The Dossier Novel.

12. "[Ein] Untergehen der Gegensätzlichkeit und Unverträglichkeit des Aufgezählten wird forciert durch das Wiederholen von Elementen oder auch nur Strukturen—durch strengen Parallelismus."
13. In *Hickory*, Nigel Chapman does turn out to be guilty, but the rhetorical firework described here successfully veils that he must have had an accomplice.
14. Stäheli makes his argument for travel guides, but it can be applied equally well to detective fiction.
15. Unless indicated otherwise, all emphases have been removed from quotations for better readability.
16. "Bausteine einer kohärenten und sinnhaften Erzählung."
17. "Alles scheint gesagt—und das Wichtigste bleibt offen."
18. Ina Hark makes a similar argument and argues that Christie's strategy of concealing the identity of the guilty party in *Orient Express* depends on three points: (1) on "the reader's familiarity with detective story conventions that dictate that some suspects must be innocent"; (2) on the fact that Christie "delays sketching in a complete picture of the Armstrong household" (the Armstrong case itself is only mentioned about a quarter into the book); and (3) on Christie "play[ing] up the international diversity of the passengers," which makes it unlikely that they might be linked (see 1987, 40).
19. For basic level categories, see Rosch (1976).
20. "unzureichender Kenntnis des Funktionszusammenhangs."
21. "la formule synthétique."
22. When Poirot asks the original list-maker (Mrs. Hubbard) to chronologically reorder the items, the reader is also informed about the schema responsible for the items on the original list being presented in their initial order: Mrs. Hubbard first listed items that seemed peculiar to her and thus stuck out in her memory, and classified the rest as (in her opinion) either important or unimportant things (see *Hickory*, 138).
23. "Wer Klassenbildung auf die Frage nach gemeinsamen Merkmalen an den Elementen reduziert, unterstellt sich einem rationalistischen Diktat."
24. For a definition and brief discussion of the term, see chapter two (30–32).
25. "[der] aufzählende Charakter vieler Rätseltexte."
26. "durch zusammenpassende Hinweise eine Lösung nahezulegen und der so aufgebauten Erwartung am Ende überraschend zu widersprechen."
27. It has been argued that many of Christie's novels violate the principle of fair play. This claim, however, is based on a misinterpretation of the idea of fair play as an absence of deception, as discussed above.
28. Knox's fourth commandment, in fact, seems to be geared directly at Austin Freeman, who is singled out in the commandment's explanatory text as a negative example.

29. "nur die Liste bietet ein Ordnungsmodell an, das Heterogenes zusammen-
führt, ohne eine fundierende Einheit annehmen zu müssen."

30. Stephen Barney uses these terms to define how lists convey information.
According to Barney, lists "tend to be rather synecdochic than periphrastic" (1982, 191).

31. Knight also argues that the suggestion that private contemplation can solve
a problem just as well as professional action provides an "illusion of effective self-help and self-sufficiency" that the clue puzzles of the interwar
period frequently catered to (1980, 110). The idea that the reader can act
as a detective in these clue puzzles and can be "clever enough—in play at
least—to construct defences against a murderer" (Knight 2004, 88) further feeds into this idea.

32. In a similar manner, the novel as a written medium that invites readers to
become active as detectives may evoke the impression that detection can be
performed through contemplation alone and does not require the detective to get their hands dirty.

33. It could be argued that the extradiegetic table of contents in *Orient Express*
provides a clue to the guilt of all suspects through its tripartite division, in
which it groups together a chapter named after each passenger, one named
after the conductor (who also turns out to be involved in the crime) and
one each named after the murder weapon and the passengers' luggage.
Under the Heading of "Part 2 The Evidence" the grouping suggests a
relation among the items grouped together that can be established through
their direct involvement in or relevance for the crime.

34. "Im Enumerativen sind die Mechanismen der Dekodierung potenziert, da
die Leerstellen maximal sind."

35. The ABC railway guide lists railway stations in alphabetical order.

36. Compare, for example, the killing list in *And Then There Were None* (1939),
where the victims are apparently killed in order of the magnitude of their
guilt (245), an internal ranking logic which makes intuitive sense because
it matches two linear developments.

37. This novel is another instance of an investigation conducted almost entirely
through the examination of textual media rather than physical action or
forensic analysis.

38. The security that Japp's list elicits, however, is short-lived. Toward the end
of his list, Japp includes detective Hercule Poirot as a highly likely suspect
and thus problematizes the logic his list is based on. Japp's list is an attempt
at imitating the skill Poirot has at his command when making lists and
categorizing evidence, and it ultimately demonstrates that he lacks Poirot's
mastery.

39. Janine Barchas makes a similar point in her essay about the use of the dash
as a stylistic element in the work of Sarah Fielding. She argues that the
dashes function to "convey […] information through graphic rather than
verbal means" (1996, 633) and can provide additional information about

the conversation by, for example, indicating a character's emotional state (See 1996, 633–641).

40. The simplicity that comes with such a narrow focus in turn reinforces the idea of a manageable and order-able world that detective fiction promotes.

41. The characterization of a typical American in chapter eleven of *Clouds* similarly employs stereotyping in connection with typical properties of the list to achieve its comic effect (see 126).

CHAPTER 5

Excursus: The *Thorndyke* Novels and the Language of Science

My hypothesis was perfectly sound, perfectly consistent in all its parts,
and perfectly congruous with all the known facts.
—Witness *(288)*

Richard Austin Freeman has been called "the dean of scientific detective story writers" (Donaldson 1971, IX), and his character Dr. Thorndyke is known as the detective who "sowed the seeds of the modern forensic crime novel" (Curran 2010, 30). This assessment likely derives from the headspinning display of expert knowledge from fields as diverse as chemistry, photography, medicine, jurisprudence, and graphology[1] that usually feature in the resolution of Thorndyke's cases. Unremitting references to proper scientific procedures and explanations on the use of scientific equipment further strengthen this image. This aura of scientific expertise portrays Dr. Thorndyke (and through him, science) as both infallible and, at least theoretically, imitable. In order to vouch for the validity of the examinations and experiments described in the novels, Freeman claimed to have performed many of them himself; he thus draws on his own status as a medical expert to support that of his character. In fact, many of the prefaces to be found in Freeman's novels emphasize that all the forensic procedures and scientific facts the novels are based around have their origin in the real world. Some of the early Thorndyke short stories even included images of pieces of evidence examined under the microscope,

© The Author(s) 2023
S. J. Link, *A Narratological Approach to Lists in Detective Fiction*,
Crime Files, https://doi.org/10.1007/978-3-031-33227-2_5

such as a nerve ganglion or different types of human hair (see Donaldson 1971, 91) that effectively conveyed a sense of realism to Freeman's readers.

It is the idea of knowledge, or more precisely, expert knowledge, on which the reputation, reception, and marketing of these novels hinge. But what exactly counts as knowledge? Freeman's novels aim to make readers believe that Thorndyke's methods are scientifically sound and rely on hard, reproducible facts; yet, actual displays of expert knowledge (usually) only occur at the very end of the novels and function to support rather than establish theories. The idea that Thorndyke's decisions and actions are guided by well-established expert knowledge, however, pervades almost every page. In this brief excursus, I will unravel the role of expert knowledge in Freeman's *Thorndyke* novels and show how the idea of Thorndyke's competence and expertise is created more through the language and forms associated with scientificity than the display of scientific proficiency itself. I will further discuss how Thorndyke's method of investigation depends neither on his much emphasized expert knowledge nor, or only rarely, on empirical observations made at crime scenes. To an astounding degree, Thorndyke's success as a detective hinges on creative imagination rather than established scientific procedures.

CREATING SCIENTIFICITY

Most of the *Thorndyke* novels are told from the first-person perspective of Thorndyke's assistant Christopher Jervis. Thorndyke's relationship to Jervis seems loosely based on that of Sherlock Holmes and John Watson: Jervis is a medical practitioner, and his relation to Thorndyke is situated somewhere between friend, apprentice, and fan. Jervis's perspective awards the reader access to observations and some medical background knowledge but allows Thorndyke to keep his knowledge to himself until the case needs to be resolved at the end. Jervis's outside perspective on Thorndyke's accomplishments crucially contributes to creating an image of Thorndyke as a brilliant thinker.

Framing: Language and Form

Contrary to what many of the prefaces announce, Thorndyke's status as an expert in the novels is primarily established through the language he uses and through taking advantage of forms associated with scientificity rather than displays of scientific prowess itself.[2] Thorndyke frequently supports his image as an expert by name-dropping and alluding to real-world experts and their works. Those references, however, usually do not play a significant role when it comes to the resolution of the mystery; instead, they create the impression that Thorndyke's vast knowledge is important to his investigations, while, in fact, their sole function is to make him appear credible. Similarly, much of Thorndyke's dialogue that concerns the interpretation of evidence is rendered in list form, and it is this form, I argue, more than the content of his observations that makes his statements appear judicious and unbiased.

A particularly striking example of this strategy occurs in Freeman's first *Thorndyke* novel, *The Red Thumb Mark* (1907), in which Thorndyke presents his evidence in the manner of a mathematical equation, in which "X" stands in for the identity of the culprit:

[L]et us just recapitulate the facts which our friend X has placed at our disposal.
First: X is a person concerning whom I possess certain exclusive information.
Second: He has some knowledge of my personal habits.
Third: He is a man of some means and social position.
Fourth: He is a man of considerable knowledge, ingenuity and mechanical skill.
Fifth: He has probably purchased, quite recently, a second-hand 'Blick' fitted with a literary typewheel.
Sixth: That machine, whether his own or some other person's property, can be identified by a characteristic mark on the small 'e.'
If you will note down those six points and add that X is probably an expert cyclist and a fairly good shot with a rifle, you may possibly be able, presently, to complete the equation, X=? (*Thumb*, 112–113)[3]

This passage is noteworthy in at least three respects. Firstly, none of the six "facts" Thorndyke enumerates even remotely depend on his medico-legal or forensic (or any other) expert knowledge. It is the form of representation and the language of mathematics and logics used to convey them that helps to depict these observations as hard facts. The bold print of the enumerative headers, moreover, contributes to the impression of ordered thought conveyed here. Sabine Mainberger has argued that the use of consecutive numbering alone suggests that the speaker behind an enumerative statement wields a certain amount of control over the items recorded (see Mainberger 2003, 167), and Thorndyke's collection of what he labels as facts aims to do exactly that.

The second point worth noting is the extent to which this list repre-sents detective work. Thorndyke's language creates a framework in which detection is depicted as the equivalent of a math problem, where a prede-termined equation inevitably renders a single solution if the equation is correctly solved for the variable X.[4] Thorndyke ultimately breaks down the complex network of interactions that an investigation depends on to the simple three-character equation "X=?" Simplifications in the manner of X equals A or B let Thorndyke make use of what Mainberger calls the "declarative power" and the "postulate quality" inherent in lists and defi-nitions (Mainberger 2003, 92, my translation).[5] Thorndyke thus validates the content he wishes to convey through the authoritative force of the form he employs.

Lastly, the six items of Thorndyke's enumeration are logically orga-nized in a funnel structure that proceeds from general to particular. The first two points refer to environmental factors, more precisely, the sus-pect's relation to Thorndyke. The third and fourth items refer to the crim-inal himself and point out identificatory qualities, and the last two points Thorndyke mentions refer to a particular object in the criminal's posses-sion. The logical structure behind the items Thorndyke enumerates becomes more specific as it progresses and thus is endowed with an almost performative quality. The funnel structure creates the impression that the exclusionary work the list seems to call for as a method of investigation is already being performed with the mentioning of each consecutive item. The first list item, therefore, seems to define a fixed group of possible sus-pects (i.e., anybody on whom Thorndyke possesses nontrivial informa-tion), and each consecutive point appears as a next logical step to narrow down the list thus created. Such fantasies of the controllability of environ-mental factors and a finite number of possible variables are key functions conveyed through the language and list structures that are so particular to the *Thorndyke* novels.

When investigating his cases, Thorndyke usually formulates a number of speculative statements which he calls "hypotheses" to express ideas that cannot yet be supported by evidence.[6] Frequently, these hypotheses are stated in list form. In *The Red Thumb Mark*, for example:

> there are four conceivable hypotheses: (1) that the robbery was committed by Reuben Hornby; (2) that it was committed by Walter Hornby; (3) that it was committed by John Hornby, or (4) that it was committed by some other person or persons. The last hypothesis I propose to disregard for the present and confine myself to the examination of the other three. (*Thumb*, 24)

By labeling his cogitations as "hypotheses" (rather than, say, speculations or ideas), Thorndyke conjures up the context of a scientific laboratory and thus veils his own, possibly biased, position as the creator of the list.[7] At the same time, the word field of scientific procedures and customs employed here suggests that there are conclusive means of testing his hypotheses already at his disposal. The display of numbers before each hypothesis helps to create the impression that a variety of possibilities on the topic under investigation have been considered and that these possibilities are comprehensive, that is, the number of options to consider is finite. In the example above, the enumerative form suggests that the scope of the investigation will be limited to the examination of only four hypotheses,[8] one of which will lead to a solution.

The fourth hypothesis, however, hides an infinite number of other possibilities from drawing immediate attention. Eric Griffiths has suggested that in an arrangement of items, "[t]he order of items of information is itself an item of information" (2018, 13), and this is also the case for Thorndyke's hypotheses in the example above. The hypotheses seem sorted in order of likelihood or importance. Hypothesis number four casually acknowledges that there may be other approaches worth considering, but the infinite possibilities that remain besides Thorndyke's first three hypotheses are summarized into a single etcetera[9] that is immediately disregarded from further consideration. Even though Thorndyke claims to take an unbiased view of his cases and to consider them "apart from [his] opinions on the subject" (*New Inn*, 26), his hypotheses are hardly unbiased. It is the form in which they are represented that conceals this fact.

Thorndyke's repeated use of lists and the connotations they evoke enable him to present basically any statement he makes as scientifically sound. Thorndyke uses lists to convey what he considers to be facts and thus turns the list into a form that creates facts. Liam Cole Young makes a similar argument about popular music lists, in which, he argues, the choice to list individual music titles into a ranking "inscribes the list itself as a viable or legitimate form through which to organize and communicate information" (2013, 508). The mere form of the list lets Thorndyke's experimental or speculative statements appear like scientific procedures. In *The Mystery at Number 31, New Inn* (1912), for example, Thorndyke proposes an experimental triangulation method based on listing directions and road properties with the help of a compass in order to identify an unknown location his assistant Jervis is repeatedly escorted to. He suggests that Jervis take notes in the manner of:

9:40 S.E. Start from home.
9:41 S.W. Granite stones.
9:43 S.W. Wood pavement. Hoofs-104.
9:47 W. By S. Granite crossing. Asphalt. (31)

The list form, which neatly divides the entries into columns that indicate the time, direction, and properties of the surroundings, conveys the impression that the data thus collected is precise enough to render an exact result. Listing elements in this manner, however, conceals a number of factors capable of causing considerable variations and thus distorting the result obtained. First and foremost, the list hides that time is only a reliable indicator for distance under the condition that speed remains consistent. Nevertheless, Jervis follows Thorndyke's instructions, and with the help of his notes, cross-referenced with a street map of the town, the two investigators succeed in drawing up a map that leads them to the desired location (Fig. 5.1). The visual representation of the map thus produced is included in the text and is meant to serve as a piece of physical evidence for the validity and exactitude of the method it was created with,[10] not unlike the microscope photographs that were included with some of Freeman's early short stories.[11]

As Jervis and the reader follow Thorndyke creating this map, Thorndyke initially speaks of the "roughness of the method" (*New Inn*, 115), as if to acknowledge the experimental nature of his approach, but his next sentence already re-frames his previous statement and suggests all it takes is "a few more proportional measurements for the satisfaction of proving the case by scientific methods" (ibid.). The mentioning of "measurements" being taken appears to be enough to qualify Thorndyke's approach as sufficiently scientific. Similarly, in the short story "A Wastrel's Romance," Thorndyke quotes probabilities to support his argument: "the chances are a thousand to one that the door that the key will open is in some part of Dockhead" (309). The numbers he quotes, however, seem randomly chosen, and no source or reference is given to explain those odds. It is the concept of probabilities and not the actual calculations that matter, just as it is the concept of scientificity much more than the descriptions of scientific proceedings that forms the backbone of Thorndyke's reputation.

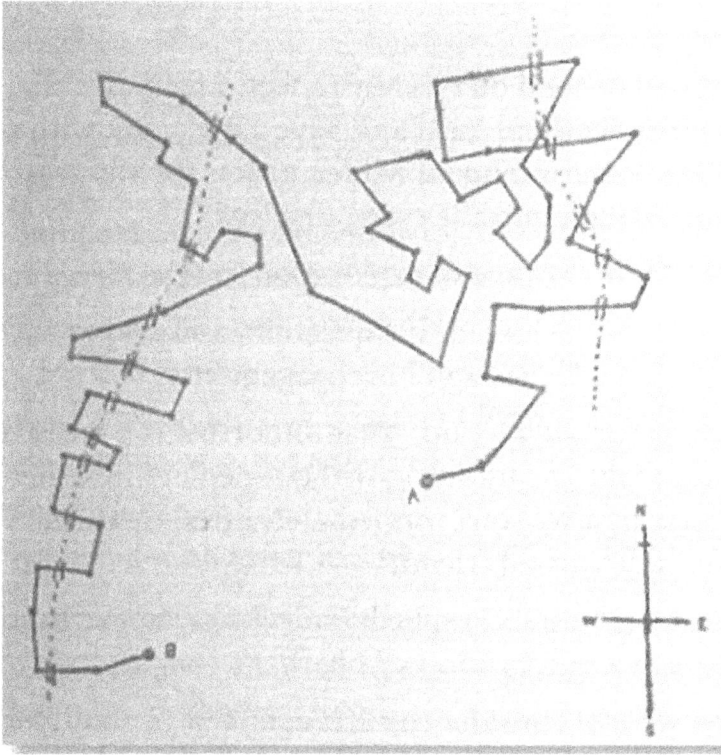

Fig. 5.1 Thorndyke's map

Expert Knowledge

Freeman's *Thorndyke* novels contain numerous references to real-world expert literature and abundant descriptions of police or forensic proceedings. The characters regularly consult specialist books such as Alfred Pearce Gould's *Elements of Surgical Diagnosis* (1884) (see *Witness*, 139) and frequently perform chemical analyses (such as the Marsh test for detecting arsenic), which the texts describe in minute detail in order to let the reader follow along the testing procedure (see "Brodski", 229). The emphasis put on the importance of following procedures and scientific practices at times verges on the didactic.[12] Thorndyke, for example, draws attention to the importance of accuracy when performing scientific operations when he explains that "[w]e must label this [piece of evidence] at once or we may confuse it with the other specimens" (ibid.). The didactic element becomes even more prominent in the references to the merits or in the critique of renowned contemporary scientists such as Gregor Johann Mendel (see *Witness*, 24) and Sir Francis Galton (see *Thumb*, 31; 68).[13] Such references give both Thorndyke's story world audience and Freeman's readers a glimpse at the kind of knowledge that Thorndyke would consider general education for practitioners in his field. At the same time, these references establish Thorndyke's identity as an expert in a variety of scientific disciplines.

The purpose of these manifold references goes hand in hand with the effect produced by the frequent use of the form of the list: both techniques create a backdrop of scientificity for Thorndyke's investigations. The foregrounding of expert knowledge supports an ideology that is characterized by a "belief in the attainability of incontrovertible, objectively verifiable truths, and a naively optimistic belief in the capacity of a 'scientific' approach grounded in 'pure reason' to uncover those truths" (van der Linde/Wouters 2003, 81) that is typical of the *Thorndyke* novels.[14] Much of the appeal of the clearly structured working processes and scientific practices Thorndyke advertises lies in the implicit promise that following such protocols will yield reproducible results, and characterizing Thorndyke as a brilliant thinker who relies on these practices awards this strategy additional weight.

The scientific and medical references are sometimes themselves displayed in the form of the list and therefore suggest that the subject matter dealt with in an investigation can easily be classified into clearly separable categories. The novel *A Silent Witness* (1914), for example, contains a list of deformities of the human hand that are presented as useful information for identifying a person: "[l]ost fingers, stiff fingers, webbed fingers, supernumary fingers, contracted palm, deformed nails, brachydactyly and numerous other abnormal conditions" (285). The enumeration of these deformities in the manner of categories suggests that the identification (and, by implication, the apprehension) of a suspect or perpetrator is a matter of working through routine lists of criteria that require simple yes/ no decisions. In a similar fashion to Thorndyke's list of hypotheses discussed above, this classificatory list, too, contains in its final item a kind of etcetera that at the same time includes a potentially infinite possibility of further options.[15] Paradoxically, those options appear easily manageable because of the limited space their abstraction into a single list item takes up on the page.

Freeman's novels employ the verifiable validity and reliability of the scientific methods they describe to corroborate the idea that Thorndyke's (very different) method of investigation is just as reliable, reproducible, and scientifically sound as the sources he quotes and the (chemical) tests he performs. Similar to the language of scientificity used in *Thumb*, the novel *A Silent Witness* has Thorndyke explain his process of reasoning in terms of a chemical reaction:

> I would draw your attention to the interesting way in which, when a long train of hypothetical reasoning has at length elicited an actual, demonstrable truth, that truth instantly reacts on the hypothesis [...]. I may compare the effect to that of a crystal, dropped into a super-saturated solution of salt, such as sodium sulphate. So long as it rests, the solution remains a clear liquid; but drop into it the minutest crystal of its own salt, and, in a few moments the entire liquid has solidified into a mass of crystals. (291)

This description implies that the way in which Thorndyke reasons and creates hypotheses is comparable to a chemical reaction that, once initiated, will inevitably progress to a resolution. Furthermore, the comparison suggests that such a chemical reaction of hypothesis and evidence can be as consciously provoked as the dropping of a crystal into a sodium sulfate solution.[16] Moreover, the crystal and the solution share properties on the molecular level ("its own salt"), which, transported to the context of Thorndyke's hypotheses, implies that there is an inevitable, natural connection between the (possibly random) creation of hypotheses and the successful resolution of a case. Lastly, the solid aggregation state of the end product of the chemical reaction awards the appearance of tangibility to Thorndyke's method. While the detective (as the agent who drops the crystal into the solution) plays a crucial role as the instigator of this (chemical or investigative) process, the criminal and the crime itself have no place in Thorndyke's analogy, except, maybe, as the receptacle in which the reaction takes place and which does not play a role for the reaction itself. The sole purpose of the crime (or receptacle) is that it contains facts (or, in the analogy, a chemical solution) that can react on the detective's actions. The analogy thus denies the criminal any possibility to outsmart the detective. Similar to the language of mathematical equations used in *Thumb*, it is the language of chemistry rather than an application of the scientific discipline itself that validates Thorndyke's conclusions in this example.

The purpose of such metaphors is to fuse the palpability and reliability of scientifically tested and approved procedures with the modus operandi of detective work, and with Thorndyke's approach to investigations in particular. Such a fusion, however, veils and aims to veil that a detective's ability to responsibly handle a piece of evidence (such as correctly taking a fingerprint)[17] is clearly distinct from their ability to analyze and process observations and decide what may serve as evidence (such as making sense of a variety of fingerprints found at a potential crime scene). One is a mechanical process, and the other is a creative one.

The importance of science as a signifier of reliability and stability extends even to the paratexts of these novels. The prefaces and publisher's notes included in several of the novels and short story collections draw on the author's status as a medical expert, and they emphasize the accuracy of Freeman's fictional representation of actual methods and procedures. In the author's preface to the volume *John Thorndyke's Cases*, Freeman informs his readers that he "[has] been scrupulous in confining [him]self to authentic facts and practicable methods" and that "the methods and solutions described in [the stories] are similar to those employed in actual practice by medical jurists" (1). The Publisher's Note preceding *New Inn* similarly vouches for the author's "broad base of knowledge" in various disciplines and his status as a "capable medical doctor" himself (n.p.).[18] The Preface to *Thumb* not only goes as far as to reassure the reader of the novel's accurate portrayal of scientific procedures but also takes it upon itself to "draw[…] attention to certain popular misapprehensions on the subject of finger-prints and their evidential value" (7) and to announce that the novel will set right such beliefs.

The attitude the *Thorndyke* novels take toward their readers, as well as the lists used in the novels, diverge significantly from those that appear in the novels of Agatha Christie discussed in Chap. 4. While in Christie's novels, the reader is encouraged to interact with the lists and try to make sense of them in the context of the investigation, the lists and scientific references in Freeman's novels serve to corroborate Thorndyke's status as expert, whose knowledge and methodical competence are to be admired rather than emulated. At times, the lists and scientific explanations in Freeman's novels take on an almost didactic quality. Readers are not supposed to solve the case but rather marvel at Thorndyke doing so.[19] For this reason, it does not matter if the solution Thorndyke proposes for a case brings to light details or clues formerly unknown to the reader (see, e.g., *Witness* 283; 288), while in a Christie novel, such a feat would be considered a grave breach of the fair play rule. The *Thorndyke* novels dangle before the reader Thorndyke's method of investigation as an approach hypothetically available to anyone, yet, at the same time, Thorndyke's unceasing insistence on the importance of expert knowledge makes clear that, in practice, only very few people exist who meet the requirements to be able to apply this method.

SCIENCE MEETS CREATIVITY: HYPOTHESIZING ABOUT THORNDYKE'S METHOD

Thorndyke's method gives the appearance of being solely based on scientifically sound and reproducible reasoning. As the above sections have shown, the mere labeling of Thorndyke's thoughts as hypotheses awards them authority and claims to scientificity. The individual investigative steps Thorndyke takes, however, are often situated closer to the realms of creativity than science. Thorndyke uses scientific methods and procedures to confirm rather than to create results. The lists, scientific language, and expert knowledge that are so abundant in the novels thus create an aura of scientificity around what is essentially a creative process. Such an approach clashes strongly with the ideal of mechanical objectivity as "blind sight, seeing without inference, interpretation, or intelligence" (Daston and Galison 2007, 17) that came to dominate conceptions of science around the mid-nineteenth century and continued to be influential in the early twentieth century.

The inseparability of science and creativity in Thorndyke's approach to investigation becomes evident in Thorndyke's repeated explanations of his method:

> Shuffle your data about. Invent hypotheses. Never mind if they seem rather wild. Don't put them aside on that account. Take the first hypothesis that you can invent and test it thoroughly with your facts. [...] Then try with a fresh one. (*New Inn*, 158)

Thorndyke's explanation reads like a step-by-step instruction manual. The short, paratactic statements are easy to follow. The simple grammatical structure invites the idea that the implementation of those instructions can also be easily accomplished. The list-like structure further suggests that the process of coming up with a solution is linear and a matter of trial and error, and that errors will be easy to identify. Variations of this explanation occur throughout the Thorndyke stories (see, e.g., *Witness*, 229; *New Inn*, 91), and although not all of them are presented in list form, the idea of a set of easy-to-follow instructions remains the same.

That Thorndyke's instructions are not as straightforward or easy to follow as they seem becomes clear when other characters talk about his abilities. Thorndyke's assistant Jervis at one point describes the detective in terms of a "magician offer[ing] you his hat to inspect" (*Witness*, 211) to then conjure up something material out of thin air, and Thorndyke's employee Polton describes his abilities in terms of artistic genius:

> Ordinary men have to reason from visible facts. He doesn't. He reasons from facts which his imagination tells him exists [sic], but which nobody else can see. He's like a portrait painter who can do you a likeness of your face by looking at the back of your head. I suppose it's what he calls constructive imagination, such as Darwin and Harvey and Pasteur and other great discoverers had, which enabled them to see beyond the facts that were known to the common herd of humanity. (ibid., 258)

Both descriptions have in common the creation of something from nothing, that is, the creation of something that is not based on graspable or observable facts. Both Jervis and Polton have a scientific or medical background that, so Thorndyke repeatedly implies, should grant them access to Thorndyke's allegedly scientific way of thinking and methods. Yet, both of them are incapable of describing what they observe Thorndyke do in terms that render it accessible to others.

Polton's statement makes evident the tension between creative imagination and scientific method that the *Thorndyke* novels are characterized by. Polton's words make apparent this paradox, but at the same time he attempts to brush over it: he emphasizes Thorndyke's reputation and renown as a scientific thinker by putting him in a line with scientists "such as Darwin and Harvey and Pasteur and other great discoverers" (ibid.) presumably known to the reader.[20]

The vocabulary around concepts such as "data," "tests," and "verification" (ibid., 210–211) that Thorndyke describes his method with stems from the semantic field of laboratory environments, whereas other characters describe what he does in terms of magic, art, and creative imagination. In "The Art of the Detective Story," Freeman himself emphasizes that a good detective story involves both "ratiocination" and "imagination" (Freeman 1976, 9). Freeman's novels are known for being centered around "the positivistic mysteries of contemporary forensic science" (Knight 1980, 110), and for Thorndyke's meticulous application of expert knowledge to solve his cases, but a closer look reveals that this knowledge only serves to give a scientific shine to what is essentially a creative process.

Science, of course, always involves a degree of creative thinking, and "knowledge is the mostly provisional result of artful, often messy, laborious, multifarious, ineffective and time-consuming work," and is thus closely connected to creative acts (Erchinger 2018, 3).[21] The *Thorndyke* novels conflate the practical and reproducible processes of experimentation that are associated with the paradigm of science which Daston and Galison have termed *mechanical objectivity* with the creative aspects of science that are, for example, involved in coming up with hypotheses. The novels strive to portray the creative aspects of science as similarly reproducible as the mechanical following of established procedures. By portraying Thorndyke's investigative methods through formal structures and vocabulary associated with scientific and laboratory contexts, Freeman's novels create the impression of scientificity and reproducibility. Ultimately, they paint a picture of the creative aspects of Thorndyke's method *as* scientific in the sense of being unbiased, reproducible, and mostly automated proposed by Daston and Galison (see 2007, 321).

Thorndyke's compilation and use of reference works is a particularly striking example of this conflation of creative imagination and mechanical objectivity. The use of reference works has a long tradition in detective fiction. Henderson, the detective in Adams's *The Notting Hill Mystery*, both brings up real-world reference works and organizes his own case file with a number of referencing tools, and Conan Doyle's Sherlock Holmes frequently consults encyclopedias and self-compiled reference works.[22] The *Thorndyke* novels take up this tradition but modify it to accommodate Thorndyke's method.

Just like Sherlock Holmes, Thorndyke often uses his self-compiled case index to back up the hypotheses he creates. Thorndyke's index, however, is not based on actual cases but on imaginary ones. In *Thumb*, the first *Thorndyke* novel, the detective explains how at an early stage in his career he plotted a number of imaginary murders and ways in which they could be detected, and he lists criteria that went into his considerations. Thorndyke furthermore "added, as an appendix to each case, an analysis with a complete scheme for the detection of the crime" in order to turn his cases into "fully indexed" volumes of "really valuable works of reference" (114).

The belief in and appeal of thinking in detectable and repeatable patterns is clearly evident in Thorndyke's explanation and unites the appeal of working with prototype models with the idea that scientific thinking is constituted by attention to minute details and a detached attitude that has its origins in the mid-nineteenth century (see Daston and Galison 2007, 27). Thorndyke uses the cases in his imaginary case collection as "elaborate prototypes" (*Thumb*, 115) for the actual cases he investigates, even though these prototypes are the sole result of his imagination rather than the abstraction of a pattern observed from actual cases.[23] Thorndyke relies upon these prototypical case models to confirm his hypotheses and thus handles them in a similar fashion to material pieces of evidence found at crime scenes. An initially creative process is thus referred to as an established scientific method.[24]

Thorndyke claims to have "acquired as much experience from those imaginary cases as […] from real ones," and to have learned the hypothesis-based method he currently employs to solve cases from them (*New Inn*, 159; see also *Witness*, 253). Thorndyke's method is thus based on a model of knowledge in which the investigator is already in possession of a set of prototypical solutions to any possible case and, in near-omniscient fashion, only needs to classify new observations and allocate them to a finite number of predetermined categories. Those categories already exist in the investigator's "mental catalogue," which, van der Linde and Wouters argue, is a common feature to detectives who base their conclusions on knowledge acquired before the investigation begins (2003, 76).

The investigator's mental index, in similar fashion to Thorndyke's written case indices, thus "produces an imaginary of control" and "suggests the idea that complex narratives can be dissected into discrete units" (Stäheli 2016, 23).[25] Thorndyke thus champions the idea that everything that concerns an investigation is knowable and can be explained with rational thought, so that solving a case comes down to narrowing down a finite number of options. This becomes evident when Thorndyke explains:

> each time that you fail to establish a given case, you exclude a particular explanation of the facts and narrow down the field of inquiry. By repeating the process, you are bound to arrive at an imaginary case which fits all the facts. Then your imaginary case is the real case, and the problem is solved. (*New Inn*, 159)

Such statements are based on the idea that the investigator has or can gain access to all and any of the details that are relevant to a case, and they preclude the possibility that anything can be genuinely new (and thus fall outside established patterns of categorization).

Thorndyke's position as an expert and the list's formal vicinity to scientific disciplines such as statistics mutually reinforce one another to portray the investigative steps the detective takes and the conclusions he draws as inevitable scientific causality. Those features also imply that a number of facts can only be arranged into one feasible hypothesis. Freeman's novels combine the idea that the world and its contents are knowable to science with the comprehensive capacity of creative imagination, and they portray the latter quality in terms of the former. This strategy effectively veils the limits of meticulously following established forensic procedures that depends on hard facts and idealizes scientific reasoning as a means of creating stability and warding off chaos or harm. The following chapter will elaborate on the role that knowledge and its concrete representation plays in Arthur Conan Doyle's *Sherlock Holmes* stories.

NOTES

1. As will be shown in this chapter, the differentiation between science and pseudo-science is not clear-cut and does not matter for the effect achieved in the novels.
2. Dr. Thorndyke's medical degree is already part of this strategy. By awarding his detective such a degree, Freeman emphasizes his role as an expert and inspires trust in his opinions and abilities.
3. Unless indicated otherwise, all emphases have been removed from quotations for better readability.
4. This is not the only novel in which the investigation is compared to a math problem. See also, for example, *New Inn*, where Thorndyke's aide Jervis compares a case to a math problem: "the Blackmore case is like an endless algebraic problem propounded by an insane mathematician" (188).
5. "Sätze wie x ist a,b,c machen sich "das deklarative Moment und den Postulatcharakter von Definitionen zunutze, und das heißt den autoritativen Gestus der definierenden Aussage."
6. For similar settings, see, e.g., "Brodski" (213); *Osiris* (108); *New Inn* (26).
7. See Mainberger (2003, 107), who argues that the form of enumeration conjures up an impression of objectivity because a list eliminates all hint to its creator and makes it seem like the items themselves establish connections.

8. Thorndyke frequently employs the power of concrete numbers to support his position as an expert and award credibility to his statements. See, for example, *Witness*, where Thorndyke categorizes: "I considered the possibilities; and at once they fell into two categories [...]" (282).
9. For a similar use of the etcetera, see "Brodski" (213).
10. Paul K. Saint-Amour draws attention to "knowledge's inseparability from representation" (2015, 186) and points out the impossibility to capture knowledge divorced from subjectivity. For a more detailed discussion of maps and visual representations, see Chap. 5, which discusses the affordances of these phenomena in conjunction with Bruno Latour's essay "Drawing Things Together" (1990).
11. When the Thorndyke stories first appeared in *Pearson's Magazine*, they were "accompanied by enlarged photographs of microscope slides prepared by Freeman, which purported to be those Thorndyke produced in court" (Binyon 1989, 16–17). The inclusion of real photographs supposedly made by a fictional character deliberately blurs the boundaries between real world and story world. The photographs serve as material evidence for Thorndyke's expertise and credibility, and they are meant to put him on a level with real-world expert witnesses whose statements are reputable enough to be accepted as evidence in court.
12. *Thumb* even makes these didactic aspirations explicit in its preface, which declares that "the book may serve a useful purpose in drawing attention to certain popular misapprehensions on the subject of finger-prints" (7) and thus help to rid its audience of such misapprehensions.
13. Gregor Johann Mendel (1822–1884) is famous for his pea plant experiments that allowed him to explain rules of heredity, and Francis Galton (1822–1911) is known for his work in statistics, eugenics, and for his pioneering work in dactyloscopy.
14. Van der Linde and Wouters talk about the ideology of Doyle's *Sherlock Holmes* stories, but the statement is equally, maybe even more, true for the *Thorndyke* novels.
15. On the potential infinity of lists, see Eco (2009, 363–369); on finite vs. infinite lists, see also Mainberger (2003, 10).
16. The passage plays with the double meaning of the word "solution" as both the mixing proportion of chemical substances and the (re-)solution of a logical problem. The double meaning of the word exists in a number of different languages, for example, in German, Italian, Spanish, and French.
17. This process is described in great detail in *Thumb*, where the procedure reads almost like an instruction manual (see 20).
18. Assurances by the author such as "I may add that the experiments described have in all cases been performed by me, and that the micro-photographs are, of course, from the actual specimens" (*Cases*, 1) further support

Freeman's status as a trustworthy expert on the subject matter he represents.

19. Interestingly, Freeman is considered the inventor of the inverted detective story, where the reader supposedly has all the clues, and the interest lies in how the crime is detected rather than in who committed it. The preface to the short story collection *The Singing Bone*, which contained the first inverted detective stories, for example, announces that "the ingenious reader is interested more in the intermediate action than in the ultimate result" (196). But even in Freeman's inverted detective stories, readers generally do not have access to the expert knowledge or means to processing clues that are necessary to solve the case the stories present. Cynthia Bily remarks that "[t]hough all necessary clues are laid out before the reader, it would be a rare reader, indeed, who was sufficiently versed in Egyptology, chemistry, anatomy, or archaeology to make sense of all the evidence" (2008, 676).

20. Polton is presumably referring to the physician William Harvey (1578–1657), biologist Charles Darwin (1809–1882), and chemist and biologist Louis Pasteur (1822–1895) here.

21. The strict distinction between arts and sciences itself is mostly a product of the nineteenth century (see Erchinger 2018, 20–21).

22. The use of reference works in the *Sherlock Holmes* stories is discussed in more detail in Chap. 6.

23. The appeal of such prototype models is also evident in the work of Thorndyke's real-world contemporaries. Francis Galton, for example, tried to create prototypical images of criminal personalities by overlaying photographs of individual perpetrators (see, e.g., Worthington 2011, 128). Galton, however, worked inductively by combining and comparing many individual cases, while Thorndyke creates the prototype first and then uses it to classify individual cases. For the application of this method to generate medical knowledge, see Hess and Mendelsohn (2010, 296).

24. In *A Silent Witness*, Thorndyke labels this approach to solving cases as "synthetic method" (253).

25. For a more detailed discussion of indices in the *Sherlock Holmes* stories, see Chap. 6.

CHAPTER 6

Lists and Knowledge

SHERLOCK HOLMES AND THE (VICTORIAN) DREAM OF TOTAL KNOWLEDGE

[W]hen you have eliminated the impossible, whatever remains, however improbable, must be the truth. (*Sign*, 51)[1]

This statement voices the belief that an explanation must be true because other explanations are considered impossible. The conclusion, however, is logically invalid because finding and correctly disproving all possible alternative explanations would require omniscience.[2] I have argued before that the fascination of the *Holmes* stories does not so much rest on the (sometimes non-existent) crimes committed in them but rather on how the mysteries they present are explained away with observations that at least seem rational. The character of Sherlock Holmes embodies what Stephen Knight calls the "Victorian romance of knowledge" (1980, 79), the idea that total knowledge is attainable through rational thought. Sherlock Holmes's exceptional success at what he labels as the science of deduction is inextricably linked with the vast body of knowledge he commands. This knowledge enables him to identify patterns in his cases which, by implication, are also valid across society as a whole.

In "The Adventure of the Blanched Soldier," Holmes states that "[i]t is my business to know things. That is my trade" (59) and thus suggests that the trade of detection relies on exhaustive background knowledge.

© The Author(s) 2023
S. J. Link, *A Narratological Approach to Lists in Detective Fiction*,
Crime Files, https://doi.org/10.1007/978-3-031-33227-2_6

When Knight speaks of the "Victorian romance of knowledge," he refers to the idea that advances in science and technology can open up wells of knowledge that will enable an individual to gain total understanding of their surroundings. The character Sherlock Holmes is a projection surface for the idea that Truth—"not just the truth behind this or that mystery, but Truth as a conceptual abstraction, an intellectual and ethical ideal" (Smajić 2010, 71)—is attainable through acute observation and the sorting of perceptions into previously established categories of knowledge.

When Holmes claims that his "simple art, [...] is but systematized common sense" ("Soldier", 64), he suggests that the capacity to meaningfully structure knowledge is not the preserve of the Romantic genius but accessible to anyone who knows the correct method of systematization. Perhaps surprisingly, the systematizations Holmes performs heavily rely on paper technologies. These are made prominent throughout the stories in the frequent appearance of a case index Holmes has compiled, as well as in his habitual consultation (and creation) of reference works and print-based sources of knowledge. Such reference works visualize knowledge in both detail and scope, and depend on lists and listing techniques for their visual presentation. The unifying impulse that comes with the presentation of systematized lists is not restricted to the level of textual representation. Eva von Contzen has argued that "lists are instances of cultural coherence and cultural identity; they are indicative of a particular view on the world" (2021, 35); in this case, they are indicative of a tendency in Victorian culture to imagine knowledge as comprehensive and controllable.

In addition to providing a structure for the assembled knowledge on the layout level, lists also afford a degree of abstraction that makes pattern recognition easier. This chapter aims to show how lists, through structuring the reference works that are so important to Sherlock Holmes's investigative method, are at the very basis of the impressive feats of knowledge and detection he performs. The mere reference to listing techniques in absentia suffices to flesh out the body of knowledge that Holmes commands in the reader's mind, even if that body of knowledge has no counterpart outside the story world. Holmes's knowledge and feats of detection appear so impressive to readers not only because they are proof of his striking intelligence but also because of the underlying structuring system they imply. Doyle's *Sherlock Holmes* stories contain numerous references to written works and paper technologies that have proven successful strategies of information management outside the story world. These references award the ungraspable and vague body of expert knowledge to which Sherlock Holmes lays claim to unquestioned validity.

Too Much to Know: Knowledge and Paper Technologies

Before I turn my attention to the representation of knowledge in the *Sherlock Holmes* stories themselves, I would like to briefly discuss the interconnection between knowledge and the paper technologies that are essential to its transmission (in both real-world contexts and the Sherlock Holmes stories). As the title of a recent monograph by Ann Blair indicates, there is simply *Too Much to Know* (2010) for any individual to achieve a comprehensive overview of all there is to know. Reference books such as encyclopedias, Blair explains, have functioned to store, sort, select, and summarize information for their readers for centuries (see 2010, 3) and "typically offered a larger collection of excerpts than most individuals could amass in a lifetime" (ibid., 63). Information provided in encyclopedias has been preselected and efficiently summarized by editors, whose editorial decisions are no longer visible in the texts that readers consult. However multifaceted the information presented in an encyclopedia entry may be, encyclopedic texts always contain value and relevance judgments made by the work's editors. The in- or exclusion of any particular entry alone constitutes an evaluation of its relevance. The task of considering various sources to make those judgments is thus taken out of the reader's hands and saves them significant amounts of time. At the same time, the invisibility of the editors' decisions creates an aura of objectivity and authority that is further supported by the label *encyclopedia*. The term originates in the Greek phrase *enkuklios paideia*, which translates as "common knowledge" or "general education" (see ibid., 12), and thus promises universality in its scope of representation.[3]

Such promises of comprehensiveness and authority made indices, the paper technology which made all this knowledge accessible and served as a finding aid, a highly valued asset of encyclopedias. A continuation of the selection and summarizing processes at work in an encyclopedia, indices could save readers even more time, and they were appreciated to a degree where (early modern) "printers boasted of them on title pages or apologized when they were missing" (ibid., 143). Indices make the knowledge stored in reference works searchable and visually highlight relevant key terms,[4] just like they render invisible those terms that compilers consider less relevant. An index sorts and presents its work's knowledge in neatly separate units and signals to its readers the immediate availability of this knowledge. This way, indices produce "an imaginary of control" (Stäheli

2016, 23) that suggests to readers that encyclopedias put at their command any piece of relevant knowledge at any time.

Such "totalizing proclivities" are typical of the Victorian and Edwardian worldview, and they are clearly reflected in the reference works of the period (Saint-Amour 2015, 202). Paul K. Saint-Amour draws attention to the "epistemological arrogance" (ibid.) of the Victorian and Edwardian worldview that he sees reflected in the eleventh edition of the *Encyclopædia Britannica* (1910–1911). This arrogance is founded in an aspiration for comprehensiveness—and hence, control—that encyclopedias lead their readers to believe they have to offer.

According to Urs Stäheli, encyclopedias and similar reference works reflect the "dream of a Universal Index" (2016, 23) that stems from a human desire for wholeness and unity. The idea behind dreaming of such a comprehensive text is based around "the reduction of complexity of the world in order to produce a new controllable complexity" (ibid.).[5] This entanglement of unity and control, which will prove highly important to the *Sherlock Holmes* stories and their Victorian context, can already be observed much earlier in Denis Diderot's 1755 *Encyclopédie*. Diderot's entry for "encyclopedia" reads:

> ENCYCLOPEDIA, noun, feminine gender. (*Philosophy.*) This word signifies *unity of knowledge* [...] In truth, the aim of an *encyclopedia* is to collect all the knowledge that now lies scattered over the face of the earth, to make known its general structure to the men among whom we live, and to transmit it to those who will come after us. (Diderot 1964, 277, emphasis in original)

The ideas of unity and complexity that can be rendered controllable through specific techniques and technologies are at the center of the myth that has developed around the figure of Sherlock Holmes. The four basic ordering techniques of "storing, sorting, selecting and summarizing," which Blair describes as crucial to the function of reference works (2010, 3),[6] play a major role in the context of Doyle's *Sherlock Holmes* stories. They expound how Sherlock Holmes manages information and determine how knowledge is represented.

This unifying impulse is closely connected to a second major affordance of paper technologies that features centrally in the *Holmes* stories: the power to extrapolate general laws from an assortment of particular examples. With regard to the production of medical knowledge, Volker Hess and J. Andrew Mendelsohn have demonstrated that paper technologies adapted from scholarly work, such as "keeping registers, tabular formatting, and […] extracting," made it possible to view formerly isolated case material in conjunction and to extrapolate general laws from individual patient histories (2010, 296). These are the very techniques that Doyle's detective claims to have mastered and that are repeatedly referred to in order to justify Holmes's vast knowledge.[7] Hess and Mendelsohn focus their attention on the production of medical knowledge from the seventeenth to nineteenth centuries and name "[c]ollecting, formatting, selecting, reducing, comparing [and] sorting" as key techniques "of mastering on and by paper" (ibid., 287). They thus stress the importance of the very same ordering techniques that Ann Blair discusses in the context of reference works. This is only one way in which this ordering and classifying impulse interlocks with a "wider history of ordering the world on and through paper" (ibid., 287).

In their exploration of the history of *Objectivity* (2007), Lorraine Daston and Peter Galison point out how the written collection of knowledge in reference works serves as calibrating and learning tool for scholars new to a subject area (see 2007, 26). Reference works (such as the ones Blair, Hess, and Mendelsohn, and Daston and Galison discuss) centrally rely on a unified form of representation to convey expertise to their readers and to make apparent the kind of order that lies at their heart. Daston and Galison, for example, examine the images printed in scientific atlases to reveal changing conceptions of knowledge and objectivity over time. The brevity that the depiction of information in reference works necessitates both makes information easily visible and condenses it. Abstraction and condensation award reference works additional legitimacy because they make it possible to assemble a broad range of (potentially contradictory) topics under the unified material shape and layout of a printed volume. The mediality of printed objects thus endows them with an "aura of epistemic unity" (Starre 2017, 250, my translation)[8]—with the impression that information assembled in the same material shape shares a common source. The materiality of a reference work fuses disparate items and thus feeds into the claims to authority that are always an undercurrent in those works. The following sections will elaborate on how the interconnection of knowledge and paper technologies discussed above serves as a backdrop for the representation of knowledge in Doyle's detective fiction.

Listing Knowledge and the Encyclopedic Impulse

The paper technology of listing as a tool of understanding features at the very beginning of *A Study in Scarlet* (1887), in which Sherlock Holmes makes his first appearance. This opening foreshadows the importance of listing as a categorizing instrument for the novel and the stories that are to follow. Already in chapter two of the novel, John Watson pens down a list of Sherlock Holmes's various areas of knowledge and expertise in order to come to an understanding of Holmes's character (for both himself and the reader):

> Sherlock Holmes—his limits
> 1 Knowledge of Literature: Nil.
> 2 Knowledge of Philosophy: Nil.
> 3 Knowledge of Astronomy: Nil.
> 4 Knowledge of Politics: Feeble.
> 5 Knowledge of Botany: Variable. Well up in belladonna, opium, and poisons generally. Knows Nothing of practical gardening.
> 6 Knowledge of Geology: Practical, but limited. Tells at a glance different soils from each other. After walks has shown me splashes upon his trousers, and told me by their colour and consistence in what part of London he had received them.
> 7 Knowledge of Chemistry: Profound.
> 8 Knowledge of Anatomy: Accurate, but unsystematic.
> 9 Knowledge of Sensational Literature: Immense. He appears to know every detail of every horror perpetrated in the century.
> 10 Plays the violin well.
> 11 Is as expert singlestick player, boxer, and swordsman.
> 12 Has a good practical knowledge of British law. (15–16)

This list illustrates a number of categorization and sense-making strategies that are at work throughout the entire *Sherlock Holmes* canon. First and foremost, it features knowledge as a central category around which Holmes's skill as a detective is based. Holmes's expertise in subjects as different as chemistry and sensation fiction, as well as his ignorance in areas that Watson considers common knowledge—the first items in his enumeration—makes up a considerable part of the fascination the character elicits. Especially Holmes's lack of knowledge in areas Watson considers to be part of general education seems at odds with his reputation as a successful detective.[9] Even though Holmes's physical prowess is an important part of his heroic appeal, Watson's qualification of some of Holmes's skills as "practical" has a derogatory ring to it that implies practical skills are less desirable or at least easier to achieve than intellectual understanding. The neat numbering that structures Watson's list furthermore implies comprehensiveness by presenting a countable and hence manageable set of knowledge categories that seem worth considering. The ninefold repetition of the word "knowledge" itself partly accounts for this effect and moreover leaves the reader with the impression that they have received information about Holmes's areas of expertise even though most of Watson's categories point out Sherlock Holmes's lack of knowledge in them. Through his list, Watson defines a scope of possible knowledge categories that is portrayed as a fixed and "finite set" with stable relations that "always produce the same effect" (Moretti 1988, 145).[10] At the same time, the objective appearance of the list conceals its ideological biases. In a similarly prescriptive way, many of the *Holmes* stories propagate the idea that any set of observations or clues can only have one correct meaning that can be apprehended and comprehended by the expert (see ibid.). The appeal of the character Sherlock Holmes is firmly anchored in the idea of control that stands behind such assumptions of a world that follows a clear, sortable structure.

Watson's list sets out to systematically enumerate and rank the subject areas in his list from "nil" to "immense" knowledge. This act of categorization will also prove typical to the way in which Sherlock Holmes perceives and classifies his surroundings. Enumerative structures feature centrally in classifications that work with defining features (see Mainberger 2003, 73). In the *Holmes* stories, they can be found, for example, when Sherlock Holmes analyzes the appearance of potential clients or describes the content of rooms. Both actions usually result in a remarkably clear and coherent picture of the respective person or surroundings. That picture is drawn together from details that initially appear isolated and, by themselves, unremarkable. This act of definition is exactly what Watson's list-making tries to achieve with Sherlock Holmes: Watson attempts to draw a clear picture of who Holmes is by enumerating a set of defining features.

Watson's list, however, does not keep up its initially clear systematization. The last three items on the list appear like afterthoughts and no longer fit into the ascending order of proficiency. A closer look, furthermore, reveals that the categories Watson chooses to describe Holmes's areas of expertise appear themselves rather random and follow no established cataloging or referencing system.[11] Even this arbitrariness emerges over and over again in Doyle's stories running through the Holmes canon and its aspirations to order like a Sinfieldian faultline.[12] Missing explanations tend to materialize out of thin air, and references that are necessary to fill plot holes tend to have no referent in the contemporary scientific methods that Holmes seemingly values so highly.[13] Frequently, paper technologies are used to strengthen the reliability of made-up and often implausible referents.

The Adventure of the Reference Works
The reference works Sherlock Holmes both consults and compiles are as much a trademark of *Sherlock Holmes* as Holmes's violin, his pipe, and John Watson. Watson himself remarks at the beginning of "Creeping Man" that "[a]s an institution I was like the violin, the shag tobacco, the old black pipe, the index books" (191). The index books, or rather the listing and categorizing strategies that they stand for, are used as a tool for understanding as much as the method of close observation of details Holmes so frequently and prominently propagates, yet they do not feature in Holmes's description of his methods.

In *The Sign of Four* (1890), Sherlock Holmes names three criteria that, in his eyes, make a good detective. He remarks about a colleague that "[h]e possesses two out of the three qualities necessary for the ideal detective. He has the power of observation and that of deduction. He is only wanting in knowledge, and that may come in time" (4). Deductions[14] can be made on the basis of close observation that allows one to detect patterns and anomalies in them. In order to correctly classify the information thus obtained and place it within the relevant context, however, knowledge is required, and knowledge is inseparable from reference works in Doyle's detective stories. In his study *Ghost-Seers, Detectives, and Spiritualists*, Srdjan Smajić points out the connection between seeing and knowing in detective fiction. According to Smajić, a detective's powers of observation are not only related to seeing but also to reading, "or rather seeing as reading. The visible world is a text, the detective its astute observer and expert reader" (2010, 71). Smajić argues that Holmes's ability to read clues, and thus his seemingly superior vision, is based on the encyclopedic stock of knowledge he can draw on. This knowledge is what enables him to instantly collate and categorize the observations and deductions he makes: "[i]f seeing for Holmes means instantaneous knowing, this is because he makes sure (and Doyle makes sure to remind his readers) that in the work of detection, knowing comes before seeing" (ibid., 123). The superior vision ascribed to detectives would thus depend upon the power of relating what is seen to knowledge previously gained,[15] and seeing, on which the power of observation hinges, becomes a matter of knowing what to look for.[16] Smajić thus ascribes to the detective the powers of selecting and sorting that Ann Blair considers as affordances of reference works.

Stephen Knight calls Holmes an "expert in the use of reference works" (2004, 56) and argues that this quality complements the character's aura of scientificity. Though true, Knight's statement lacks precision. The way in which reference works are used in *Sherlock Holmes* not only complements but in fact crucially contributes to creating this aura of science and precision. The classificatory, encyclopedic impulse that dominated scientific thinking in the nineteenth century is reflected in the way Doyle's stories represent knowledge through reference works and the classifications contained therein. Textual forms such as lists, tables, and precise definitions can transport scientific connotations and authority to new contexts, including detective fiction, because they are frequently used in scientific environments.[17] The frequent occurrence of reference works in *Sherlock Holmes*, consequently, fulfills a legitimizing function: the knowledge Holmes commands is the foundation of and backdrop to his success, and is solidified in the material shape of the printed books he has authored. "Detection is, or ought to be, an exact science" (*Sign*, 3), Holmes claims, and few things, apparently, can be more exact than a set of definitions made visible in print.

Several *Holmes* stories feature enumerations of alphabetical entries from reference works. In "A Scandal in Bohemia," for instance, Holmes consults the "Continental Gazetteer," that is, a geographical dictionary, and reads out the entries that precede the one he is looking for: "Eglow, Eglonitz—here we are, Egria. It is a German-speaking country—in Bohemia, not far from Carlsbad" (5). Such insertions of alphabetical enumerations help to define what counts as knowledge and implicitly guarantee that knowledge is stable—upon opening the volume, readers will always find the same information in the same order. More importantly, whenever Holmes consults a reference work, the entries seem to tell him everything he needs to know about any conceivable subject.[18] The entries are presented as exhaustive in their depth, and the variety of subjects that can be included in an alphabetical enumeration expands this exhaustiveness to breadth as well as depth.[19]

Even more volatile sources of intelligence, such as the oral information Holmes receives from his contact Langdale Pyke, are described in terms of printed and more durable sources to award them additional reliability. Pyke is referred to as Holmes's "human book of reference upon all matters of social scandal" ("Gables", 101). Knowledge, in Doyle's detective stories, seems to be defined by what can be found in reference books, often in those supposedly written by Holmes himself.[20]

The idea that knowledge is stable, traceable, and manageable frames how Holmes investigates any particular case or set of circumstances he is confronted with. Holmes's way of conducting investigations presupposes that he knows quasi everything there is to know about his field of expertise. Claims that "[t]here is a strong family resemblance about misdeeds, and if you have all the details of a thousand at your finger ends, it is odd if you can't unravel the thousand and first" (*Scarlet*, 19)[21] estify to an encyclopedic approach to knowledge that is list-like to the core: seemingly unknown or inexplicable occurrences are correlated with lists of existing phenomena and can thus be broken down to their constituent parts and fully explained through their resemblance to items that have already been listed. For Holmes, thus, "[t]here is nothing new under the sun" (ibid., 29); he only encounters variations on previously known circumstances.

The close connection between knowledge and memory implies that the structure through which knowledge is portrayed in the *Holmes* stories is also applicable to Holmes's memory, which he consults in a similar manner as one would an encyclopedia. Holmes's knowledge appears to come sorted into distinct categories that remain accessible independently from one another and can be searched if the correct keyword is available.[22] Gerhard van der Linde and Els Wouters, in their paper on various bodies of knowledge in detective fiction, also make explicit the connection between knowledge, memory, and the way reference works are consulted:

> Confronted with a set of events for which he has to find a rational explanation, the detective could use this body of knowledge [of facts previously known] as basis for a kind of encyclopedia, in which phenomena are grouped, annotated, and contextualized, and for a "dictionary" which enables him to interpret certain gestures and other observable phenomena. (2003, 76)

A view of knowledge and experience, in which everything can be fitted into an already existing referencing system, Paul K. Saint-Amour remarks, tends to subject everything it encounters to a "descriptive rationalism"

and runs risk of "bullying the world into compliance with its organizational grids and drives, of typifying Enlightenment arrogance in its claim
to encompass the known" (2015, 186). Such "Enlightenment arrogance"
assumes that there is a fixed set of relevant items to know, which can be
meaningfully assembled and made accessible to the expert. This is defining
for the worldview propagated in the *Holmes* stories.

Holmes, however, goes even further and claims that:

> [t]he ideal reasoner, [...] would, when he had once been shown a single fact
> in all its bearings, deduce from it not only all the chain of events which led
> up to it but also all the results which would follow from it. [...] [T]he
> observer who has thoroughly understood one link in a series of incidents
> should be able to accurately state all the other ones, both before and after.
> ("Pips", 109)

Similar to the way in which knowledge is portrayed in terms of the clear
definitions provided in reference works, this idea promises that not only
the present but also the past and the future can be compartmentalized into
neatly separable categories that maintain a linear relation to one another.[23]
The fantasy of control and mastery that Holmes's idea of the ideal rea-
soner projects is rooted in Enlightenment philosophies about science;
thus, Neil Sargent argues, "the analytical detective story adopts a teleo-
logical view of history," in which past and present stand in a fixed and
stable relation to one another, which allows the detective to follow back a
clear trail of evidence that leads from present results to past events and
enables them to "explain the hidden causal principles behind the mystery"
(2010, 288). In conjunction, Holmes's knowledge and keen observational skills allow him to detect "a natural and transcendent order whose
determinism is so all-embracing that even the smallest details signify the
whole" (Jann 1990, 690). According to Holmes's logic, access to any one
piece of evidence, however small, should thus enable him to unravel the
entire case.

Holmes's near omniscience, of course, poses practical problems of
implementation for Doyle, who has to convincingly represent Holmes's
limitless expertise and ingenuity in his stories. For this reason, Holmes
seems to have at his disposal a quasi-infinite assortment of reference works,
few of which have equivalents outside the story world. This allows Holmes
(and Doyle) to rely on the mere mechanics of referencing rather than on
concrete references themselves to legitimize claims he makes. Without

having to provide actual proof, Holmes can thus refer to his self-authored monograph on different types of tobacco ash to support his claims about a piece of evidence, and readers will (have to) accept this reference as a credible validation of his statement without being able to consult its source (see, e.g., *Sign*, 4; "Identity", 66). Replacing actual references with the more abstract mechanics of referencing thus makes it possible to fill in plot holes and logical blanks that could otherwise threaten to undermine the neat, orderly worldview the stories try to convey. The following section will examine how the referencing techniques Holmes uses to display the encyclopedic scope of his knowledge award legitimacy and an aura of scientific precision to absent or entirely imaginary referents.

The Case of the Case Index: On Absent Referents
Holmes makes frequent use of reference works, but rarely mentions concrete titles save those of his self-authored works. The reference works he uses usually remain vague, as in the passages "[h]e picked a red-covered volume from a line of books of reference on the mantelpiece" ("Bachelor", 217) or "[m]ake a long arm, Watson, and see what V has to say" whereupon Watson reaches for "the great index volume to which he referred" ("Vampire", 114). Thus, it is the mechanics of referencing rather than any concrete source of references that fulfills a function in the stories.

In a number of short stories and novels, Holmes refers to an indexed list of cases and general knowledge he has compiled. This index frequently serves to explain where Holmes has obtained a piece of information that seems to appear almost miraculously, and it symbolizes the tremendous scope of experience and knowledge he can draw on. Just by awarding his compilation of case notes the label *index*, Holmes claims for himself not only possession of but also mastery over a vast body of knowledge. Urs Stäheli has pointed out how "[t]he index is—through its very existence—a witness for mastery," how it "creates the impression of total understanding" (2016, 23) and conjures up "dreams of total knowledge" (ibid., 19).[24] Holmes's index thus allows him to claim for himself absolute control over the knowledge assembled in his index without him ever having to reveal the criteria for creating an ordering system that enables such mastery. Holmes's index is thus more than a simple finding aid; the act of indexing becomes "a tool for understanding and acting in the world. Indexing [is] [...] demonstrating and discovering something" (Hess and Mendelsohn 2010, 289). The mere use of the term index thus suggests that Holmes has not only collected a lot of information but that he also has total command over the contents of his index and understands all the implications that the information contained therein bears.

The reliability of statements that Holmes makes on the basis of the fictive information in his index is substantiated by the mentioning of real-world place names and concrete temporal references. Statements such as "[y]ou will find parallel cases, if you consult my index, in Andover in '77" ("Identity", 61–62), or "[t]here was a parallel instance in Aberdeen some years back, and something on very much the same lines at Munich the year after the Franco-Prussian War" ("Bachelor", 227–228), let Holmes spontaneously create facts that fit the current case. The references to places such as Andover or Munich that readers would be familiar with from real-world contexts serve to corroborate and legitimate the information that comes attached to them.

The system behind what kind of information is entered in Holmes's index is only hinted at in the vaguest of terms, but never clearly explained or displayed. Watson informs the reader that "[f]or many years [Holmes] had adopted a system of docketing all paragraphs concerning men and things, so that it was difficult to name a subject or a person on which he could not at once furnish information" ("Bohemia", 8). He thus points out both the scope and instant retrievability of the indexed information. The rather vague reference to "men and things" as subjects of Holmes's interest metonymically stands in for *everything* and only superficially evokes the impression of delineating clear areas of interest. Moreover, when Holmes reads out the index entry he made on Irene Adler, frequent interjections and exclamations such as "hum!", "ha!", "yes!", and "quite so!" ("Bohemia", 9), that signify satisfaction, even complacency, with the information he has collected, highlight his information management skills. Every bit of information Holmes reads seems to prove relevant to his current case, and the impression is evoked that his brilliant note-taking system at times even surprises Sherlock Holmes himself. Although the stories mention Holmes working on his index, for example, "cross-indexing his records of crime" ("Pips", 98)—which, again, hints at a sophisticated ordering system behind the index—concrete statements about the underlying principle of organization remain absent.

In the same way, actual content of the index is, with few exceptions, only referred to rather than represented in its concrete wording. This strategy of representation opens up an infinite referencing potential that makes it possible to insert new addenda whenever and wherever they are needed. Listing strategies as they occur in an index "make it possible not only to link but perhaps more importantly to de-link the spaces they generate from other spaces" (de Goede et al. 2016, 8) and thus invoke an infinity of possibilities without raising questions about how new additions fit into the established system. Holmes can make countless additions to the information supposedly contained in his index without running risk of disturbing the causal or sequential relations between individual index items. The mere existence of an index, catalog, or other directory, Sabine Mainberger argues, sets up expectations of a well thought-out structure and convincing categorization (see 2003, 3). Holmes's index leans on that assumption, and the authority the term alone carries functions like a self-fulfilling prophecy.

The *Holmes* stories, however, feature not only the often mentioned case index to provide an invisible background structure and inexhaustible source of information, but also flaunt a number of monographs and scientific articles, written by Holmes himself, that are frequently quoted and drawn upon to back up his claims. This might be attributable to:

> one of the characteristic features of the analytical detective story, namely, the assumption that material circumstances are presumed to be more disinterested, and thus more reliable, witnesses to the truth of a factual assertion than witnesses who provide direct testimony. (Sargent 2010, 293)

A statement that is written down and can be accessed in printed form may thus appear to have greater argumentative force than the very same statement made orally. This holds true for oral and written statements made within the fictional world, even though both kinds of statements are represented to readers on the same level, that is, through printed words. The mere reference to something that exists in the material form of a printed volume awards its contents authority. In *Sign*, Holmes states:

> I have been guilty of several monographs. They are all upon technical subjects. Here, for example, is one "Upon the Distinction between the Ashes of the Various Tobaccos". In it I enumerate a hundred and forty forms of cigar, cigarette, and pipe tobacco, with coloured plates illustrating the difference in the ash. (4)[25]

The reference to "technical subjects" suffices as a marker for scientific validity and makes it unnecessary to mention methodological approaches or specific areas of expertise; the fact that these works exist in print is enough to vouch for their legitimacy. The enumeration of three different classes of tobacco—cigar, cigarette, pipe—promises a classificatory system in which the sorting and selecting operations Ann Blair considers central functions of paper technologies (see 2010, 3) have already been performed. These operations implicitly guarantee the reliability of the information presented. Additionally, the word "enumerate" and the concrete number of specific entries mentioned signify both specificity and comprehensiveness. This conjures up contexts of objectivity and scientific methodology that are further supported by the reference to "coloured plates" which function as material evidence for Holmes's claims.

When Holmes makes classifications such as:

> [t]he fish you have tattooed immediately above your right wrist could only have been done in China. I have made a small study of tattoo marks and have even contributed to the literature of the subject. That trick of staining the fishes' scales of a delicate pink is quite peculiar to China. ("League", 29)

it is not the statement itself that convinces readers of his ingenuity, but rather the method that seems to stand behind it. In this particular case, Holmes's statement conveys the idea that there is a homogeneous category that could be labeled Chinese tattoo art and that a thorough study thereof might enable one to easily identify all its constituent members. Furthermore, the level of detail given is so striking that it renders the statement immediately convincing. Ben Parker has cleverly argued that "the methodological material and references in the *Sherlock Holmes* stories produce only a 'method effect,' akin to Roland Barthes's effet de réel," and that this "method effect 'produces' a scientific or logical procedure that is nowhere carried out in the narrative form" (Parker 2016, 449).[26] The central element of the *Holmes* stories is thus "not the presence [...] but the aura of decodable clues" (ibid., 450). Parker, however, does not elaborate on the fact that such a "method effect" would not be possible without the frequent reference to ordering and referencing systems that award Holmes's explications credibility through their formal properties alone.

The enjoyment that readers gain from reading stories about Sherlock Holmes, Parker suggests, "is not in being shown the answer to a brain teaser" but rather relies on the pleasure of witnessing "an impressive and nonduplicable feat" (2016, 453). The explanation that is provided for any mysterious set of circumstances is much less important to such a reading experience than the idea of a structured and knowable world that under-lies even the most absurd of Holmes's deductions. The framework of indexing and referencing through which Holmes legitimates his claims to knowledge turns potentially random statements into hard facts that are made visible (and thus also replicable) through their material existence as printed product.[27] The tight interlacement of knowledge and visibility is not only kept up but expanded on in modern adaptions of the *Sherlock Holmes* material, as will be discussed in the remainder of this chapter.

Knowledge and Visibility: The BBC's Sherlock

In his article "Drawing Things Together," Bruno Latour states that "we can hardly think of what it is to know something without indexes, bibliog-raphies, dictionaries, papers with references, tables, columns, photographs, peaks, spots, bands" (1990, 36). All these practices of conveying knowl-edge bear close resemblance to the phenomena that this book has described as list-like. Another shared feature of these practices is that they all, in varying degrees, constitute instruments of visualizing a certain (predeter-mined) kind of order. The following sections are dedicated to an examina-tion of this entanglement between knowledge and visibility.

In order to illustrate this connection, I examine the two closely related forms of lists and maps with respect to their capability to convey, compart-mentalize, and visually represent knowledge. Lists and maps share a num-ber of affordances. They are frequently mentioned together, but the nature of their relation is rarely commented upon. Latour, for example, even though he makes abundant use of the form of the list in his argu-ment, does not reflect upon the properties of the form he employs. Eva von Contzen, in her analysis of "Experience, Affect and Literary Lists," refers to both listing and mapping as practices that are non-narrative but frequently appear in narrative texts (see 2018, 325), but does not investi-gate how these two practices interrelate. Even in the specific context of detective fiction, the conjunct appearance of lists and maps has been remarked but not reflected upon. In his account of the history of crime fiction, Julian Symons names maps of crime scenes and the appearance of listed information (e.g., in the form of printed timetables) as two phenom-ena that both became popular in crime fiction during the Golden Age (see 1985, 103–104). This contemporaneity implies a close proximity between the two phenomena that Symons, however, does not elaborate upon.

Drawing on Latour's observations on the importance of imaging and visualization techniques for scientific change, this section of the chapter will first take a close look at the nature of the relations between lists and maps and the affordances those forms share and then demonstrate by the example of the BBC show *Sherlock* (2010–2017) how the detective fiction genre conjunctly uses lists and maps as tools to visualize, spatialize, and compartmentalize thought processes. The specialized knowledge that marks a detective's particular power and appeal rests on a combination of those aspects, which prove central to the show's rendering of the detective's comprehensive gaze as universally accessible.

Making Meaning Visible: Shared Affordances of Lists and Maps

In 1986, Bruno Latour first published his article "Drawing Things Together," in which he describes visualization techniques as a key element to scientific development. Rather than seeing changing economic circumstances or the emergence of some sort of new mindset as the cause for scientific change, Latour emphasizes the interconnection of visualization and cognition and examines writing and imaging techniques as possible elementary causes for scientific innovation. Latour poses the order that such practices of inscribing can afford as the focal point around and through which change can originate.

This kind of order, Latour emphasizes, is not created invisibly in the brain of some genius but is constituted in how we put down observations in writing. According to Latour, writing and visualization techniques are a necessary (but not sufficient) element of scientific revolution: the final result of any scientific practice is always rendered in writing or visually on paper (see 1990, 22).[28] Gaining support for a new theory, thus, is the direct consequence of a clearly organized, visualized presentation of ideas and results. Diagrams, maps, columns, and so on are all concise and clearly recognizable visualization strategies that afford the kind of order, structure, and visual clarity that Latour deems necessary for the efficient transmission of information.

In order to foster scientific change and render results convincing, Latour argues, visualization techniques need to exhibit a number of affordances that condition their cogency and universal applicability: they must be "superimposable" (ibid., 22), and as textual objects, they need to "have the properties of being mobile but also immutable, presentable, readable and combinable with one another" (ibid., 26). Relations between writing and cognition often express themselves through such "immutable mobiles" (ibid.), which can be transported into new contexts without losing their essential qualities. These "immutable mobiles" thus provide a "two-way connection [...] that allow[s] translation without corruption" between an object of investigation and an audience (ibid., 28).

Maps (as well as lists) are prime examples of textual objects that feature the affordances Latour mentions. They both condense and simplify information and thus "mobilize larger and larger numbers of events in one spot" (ibid., 41); half a page of a map or diagram can replace pages and pages of description.[29] In addition to providing such succinct overviews over information, maps remain instantly recognizable as forms (in the sense of Caroline Levine) that can perform the same kind of operation across an infinite variety of contexts. They are, thus, both immutable and mobile.[30] Since maps show only the abstracted bare bones of what they represent, they lend themselves to superimposing different sets of data: a map of a certain area can show altitude differences, population density, climate diagrams, or roads, or it can superimpose a combination of these sets of information over one another and, for instance, combine information on roads and altitudes. Their high degree of abstraction renders maps an ideal tool to present an abundance of data in a relatively small and accessible space. As meeting places between word and image, maps (and other visualization tools) are capable of both mobilization and immutability and, thus, according to Latour, possess the two key aspects of generating scientific impact (see ibid., 31). Additionally, the recognizability of the form itself, independent of the content it conveys, carries connotations from the context of its use, such as associations with objectivity and facticity, that are difficult to disentangle from the message it transmits.

Most of the affordances that Latour ascribes to maps and other tools of inscription also apply to the form of the list. In fact, Latour himself makes copious use of lists to support his arguments.[31] Lists and maps are intimately related in the way they shape processes of meaning-making and share a number of affordances that play key roles in the transmission (and representation) of knowledge:

1. Visibility: Lists and maps both appear as distinct and recognizable (immutable) forms that remain instantly visible amid masses of other data or text, and through this visibility and recognizability, they draw immediate attention. Their visual nature awards both lists and maps spatial qualities. Media scholar Liam Cole Young points this out when he writes that "[a] paper list is a series of marks that materializes a technique of spatial data organization" (2017, 37). Similarly, in his investigation of lists, Jack Goody implicitly acknowledges the connection between thought processes, visibility, and spatialization when he chooses the curiously spatial example of the itinerary to illustrate one of his three list categories (see 1978, 80).[32]

2. Simplicity: A key aspect that helps to render lists and maps instantly visible is their tendency to compress large quantities of information into relatively small spaces. Maintaining clarity when rendering data in such abstracted and condensed form demands a certain simplicity of representation. Latour points out how the "flat" quality of inscriptions, which is responsible for their clarity and the impression that nothing remains hidden in them, "enables mastery" through the very simplicity it projects (1990, 44). He even uses the form of the list as one possible example of such a "flat surface that enables mastery" (ibid.).

3. Facticity: The reduction of complexity that lists and maps share often leaves implicit the connections and relations between the items represented. At the same time, these forms suggest that the combinations they present make inherent sense. In leaving connections implicit and stripping items of their descriptive contexts, lists and maps create gaps which can hide the personal or ideological bias of the list- or map-maker, and create the illusion that they depict objective facts rather than representations. This aspect has particular relevance for lists and maps in detective fiction. In *Crime Fiction*, John Scaggs discusses the significance of realist spatial settings, which can be seen in "[t]he use of maps, along with the use of titles that fix a particular event in spatial terms" in Golden Age crime fiction (2005, 51). He even implicitly connects this phenomenon to the abundant appearance of lists in these novels. Scaggs argues that the "objectified sense of place" that is created through the inclusion of crime scene maps in Golden Age novels is usually accompanied by an equally "objectified sense of time in the proliferation of times, clocks, timetables, and alibis" (ibid.), which is often used to conjure up an air of facticity in detective novels and tends to be represented in the form of the list.

4. Comprehensiveness: The impression of facticity is supported by the degree of compression these forms afford. Compressed accounts usually consist of the essentials of an argument or depiction that are representative of larger contexts; thus, such accounts appear comprehensive by implication. Maps and lists appear as what Latour calls the "final stage of a whole process of mobilization" that constitutes the result of an entire "cascade of ever simplified inscriptions that allow harder facts to be produced at greater cost" (1990, 40), and that render complex issues in simple forms. The simpler the inscription, Latour suggests, the harder the fact appears, not least because information condensed and coded into an image is considerably harder to disprove than a statement (before one could do this, the process of condensation would have to be reversed to lay bare the information that resulted in the image). This brevity and conciseness makes lists, maps, and other inscriptions appear as both objective and comprehensive: whatever details remain visible in a compressed depiction of data are automatically considered as important and representative of what has been left out. In detective fiction, this list-based comprehensiveness frequently serves to epitomize the detective's all-encompassing gaze.

5. Flexibility: The property of being mobile (as Latour terms it) or, in Caroline Levine's words, of being able to travel across a wide variety of contexts (see 2015, 7) renders the forms of the list and the map infinitely adaptable to new contexts without changing their basic functionality: a decorative map functions according to the same principles as a strategic one.

Both lists and maps constitute powerful tools through which knowledge can be created, transmitted, negotiated, and reorganized. The remainder of this chapter will use the BBC series *Sherlock* as an example to demonstrate how lists and maps can be used to direct the audience's perception and conception of knowledge.

Knowledge, Lists, and Maps in the BBC's Sherlock

In 2010, the BBC aired the first episode of *Sherlock* (2010–2017), a show that adapts the material of Arthur Conan Doyle's *Sherlock Holmes* stories to a contemporary setting.[33] Over the four seasons of the show, its protagonist Sherlock is presented as "a millennial thinker" whose "youthful technological expertise" enables him to handle digital information with exceptional speed and efficiency (Stein and Busse 2012b, 10). Just like with Doyle's nineteenth-century model of the famous detective, knowledge and observation are portrayed as the foundation of Sherlock's exceptional skills. Contrary to Doyle's original stories, however, *Sherlock* tries to give its audience direct access to the detective's thoughts as he is having them rather than explain his conclusions after the fact. In this manner, *Sherlock* tries to portray the, at first glance, almost magical skill set of its protagonist as potentially accessible to anyone. Sherlock's expertise and skills, so the show suggests, are not the result of innate genius but rather a matter of finding the right access points to information and navigating an overwhelming supply of data efficiently. To promote this idea of universal accessibility, *Sherlock* takes a strongly visualized approach to representing knowledge that allows viewers access to Sherlock's thought processes.[34] The show uses lists, maps, and other visualization tools in order to portray knowledge as spatialized field, the successful maneuvering of which requires navigational rather than interpretative skills.

Spatialization and Accessibility

Whenever the BBC's version of Sherlock Holmes analyzes a situation, the show chooses to display typed words as a screen overlay floating next to clues that draw Sherlock's attention. These overlays often appear as lists of keywords, mapped out around suspects or clues, that visualize Sherlock's cognitive activity and give the audience direct access to his perception. *Sherlock*'s first episode, "A Study in Pink" (S1, E1),[35] introduces the audience to many of the devices the show employs to provide access to Sherlock's mind and therefore offers itself particularly well as a case study. In this episode, the screen overlays are meant to help the audience comprehend Sherlock's thought processes as he deduces information from the dead body of a woman found at a crime scene. The audience is first presented with a close-up shot of a detail that draws Sherlock's attention, such as the dead woman's hands and fingernails. Subsequently, Sherlock's thoughts or conclusions (in this case, that the woman is "left handed") appear next to the details.

The fact that the audience is invited to watch Sherlock think becomes clear at the latest when he observes a detail and the screen overlay writing changes as Sherlock considers different options. The audience can see that the woman has scratched the letters "RACHE" into the floorboards with her fingernails. The screen overlay first displays a German dictionary entry that tells the audience "Rache" is the German word for "revenge." This screen overlay, however, is followed by a reverse shot back to Sherlock's face, in front of which the dictionary entry is still displayed in mirror writing within Sherlock's direct line of sight [24:40].

This suggests that the words the audience can read on screen are what Sherlock sees when he looks at a clue: if we look back at him, the words are mirrored because from the character's point of view, they are still there and displayed in regular writing. Furthermore, when Sherlock moves the victim's hand, the words that float next to it also move along the screen.

This shows that the words are part of Sherlock's perspective and perception, and it also serves to emphasize the visual approach that *Sherlock* takes to knowledge: the protagonist's conclusions are literally spelled out before his face, displayed in written letters next to his object(s) of observation.[36] The audience is not only presented with the result of Sherlock's conclusions but becomes witness to his actual thought processes. This becomes clear when the dictionary entry in mirror writing shatters underneath his gaze and the camera cuts back to a close-up of the clue. The image of the scratched letters is now overlayed with the letters "RACHE" and permutations of letters that could be added to form a different word.

Allowing the audience this kind of access to Sherlock's cognitive processes serves a twofold purpose. First, it demystifies the miraculous conclusions the audience might be used to from Doyle's *Holmes* stories and thus presents Sherlock's deductions and the knowledge he draws on as an accessible and objective tool that can potentially help anyone to map out a path from an observation to its one and only correct interpretation.[37] Secondly, as Louisa Stein and Kristina Busse remark, the thought processes visualized in the show "serve doubly to tie the viewer to Sherlock's unique subjectivity" (2012b, 12)[38] and render the character more accessible to the audience despite his impressive and seemingly unreachable skill set. The show's deliberate shift from the character's last to first name even further contributes to rendering him more accessible (see ibid., 12).

Sherlock uses both visual and sound effects to support its portrayal of Sherlock's cognitive activity, but the key to providing this kind of accessibility is the visualization of his knowledge and thoughts. The words that appear as lists of observations on screen are dynamic, like Sherlock's thoughts, and visually represent how one thought inevitably triggers another. In the scene from "A Study in Pink," for example, a close-up of the woman's right hand and the ring she is wearing is overlayed with the word "married," and then the word "unhappily" is added above the original thought. This is followed by a set of rotating numbers that represent how Sherlock calculates the period of time for which the woman has been married. As the numbers settle on "10+," the word "years" fades in and is added to the list of bullet point thoughts [25:18]. This shows how each of Sherlock's deductions serves as the basis for the logical next step on an inevitable path to the correct solution and thus suggests that there is a linear path from making an observation to arriving at the correct conclusion.

In "Drawing Things Together," Latour emphasizes the importance of both visualization and spatialization to achieve such an effect:

> What is so important in the images and in the inscriptions scientists and engineers are busy obtaining, drawing, inspecting, calculating, and discussing? It is, first of all, the unique advantage they give in the rhetorical or polemical situation. 'You doubt what I say? I'll show you'. (1990, 35–36)

The visualization of Sherlock's cognitive processes serves as demonstration and affirmation of his methods at the same time. Through visualizing Sherlock's thought processes, the show not only awards them credibility but also makes them appear falsifiable and thus scientific. In Doyle's original *Sherlock Holmes* stories, the reader is only presented with Holmes's fantastical conclusions and some explanations in hindsight, which corroborate Holmes's status as genius and are aimed at inspiring awe. *Sherlock*'s protagonist, on the other hand, presents the audience not only with the result but also with the cognitive process that maps out the way by which Sherlock arrives at his conclusions. Sherlock's observations are shown on screen rather than just summarized. The audience shares his perspective and can see for themselves how he forms conclusions from his observations.

The show anchors Sherlock's thoughts in space by having the words float next to or, in some cases, even through[39] the physical object an observation is made about. This is central to the show's rhetoric and its portrayal of knowledge. Latour has pointed out that the greatest advantage of inscriptions in a scientific context is that "[t]he two-dimensional character of inscriptions allow [sic] them to merge with geometry" and thus to make paper (or, in the case of *Sherlock*, screen-) space congruent with real space, that is, three-dimensional, observable reality (ibid., 46). Through its visualization techniques, *Sherlock* renders its protagonist's thoughts as both mobile and immutable in the sense of Bruno Latour. The spatialized inscriptions make his thoughts appear mobile—and thus valid because they remain reproducible in a variety of contexts—and immutable because of their anchoring in physical space and the mapped-out path to a definite and correct solution they portray.

This representation of knowledge as spatialized pathways is not unique to the show's protagonist but is also adopted by the other characters in the show. In "A Study in Pink" the perpetrator explains how he manipulated his victims, remarking "I know what people think. I know what people think I think. I can see it all like a map inside my head" [1:13:30]. Statements like this support the show's spatialized way of portraying knowledge. In order to get where you want to go, *Sherlock* suggests, all you have to do is to read the map of possibilities right and take the correct route. Detection, and, by implication, knowledge, the audience is told, requires navigational rather than interpretative skills.

Navigating and Interpreting Knowledge
In their introduction to the volume Sherlock and Transmedia Fandom, Louisa Stein and Kristina Busse discuss how Sherlock's digital know-how is based around the two basic operations of searching and filtering (see 2012b, 11). The show makes these two processes visible through screen overlays whenever Sherlock contemplates a problem or analyzes a clue, and allows the audience to follow along his path of thought through words and images that float over the screen. From these screen overlays it becomes clear that Sherlock uses his phone (as a metonymical extension of the Internet) and his memory almost interchangeably. In "A Study in Pink," for example, Sherlock examines a victim's wet coat and then uses his smartphone to check the weather conditions in the vicinity of London. The screen overlay shows the keywords displayed on Sherlock's phone and highlights the search path he selects through the menu (see [25:56]), which inevitably leads him to a single possible location where the victim could have come from. Visually, Sherlock's (external) search with his smartphone is represented in the same way as his internal thought processes: arriving at the correct solution is displayed as a matter of choosing the correct path through a number of options, some of which must be filtered out. The parallel the show draws between cognitive processes and an Internet browser's search function implies that finding the correct solution to any given problem is a matter of selecting the appropriate route from a readily available menu.

> The processes of searching and filtering impact the way we as a culture understand our relationship to both information and visibility. Search and filter convey the rendering of insight through the sorting of information and the making visible of preferred or more relevant findings. Sherlock's dependence on the protocols of search and filter in his deductive processes highlights the way in which, according to Lev Manovich (2001), digital logics become cultural logics become personal logics. (Stein and Busse 2012b, 11)[40]

Similarly, information that does not appear to be worth consideration according to these digital logics can be easily edited out. As becomes evident from the rotating, shattering, and disappearing screen overlays discussed in the previous section, Sherlock discards thoughts with the swipe of a hand or the blink of an eye, as if they could simply be deleted once he has rated them as irrelevant to the current endeavor.

Visibility, or the mastery thereof, is closely related to power in the context of detective fiction.[41] Seeing, as the above quote hints, is portrayed as insight. Two fundamentally different processes, one related to perception and the other to cognition, are equated here (as they are, too, in Doyle's original *Sherlock Holmes* stories) to foreground clarity over complexity and render the cognitive operations Sherlock performs as "flat" in Latour's sense (see 1990, 44). This flatness not only awards Sherlock the power to make visible what information he needs, whenever he needs it, but also enables the show to present his thought processes as linear and easily traceable. The flat inscription surface of the map lends itself to this very operation and is frequently used in *Sherlock* to provide clarity and accessibility when displaying how Sherlock thinks.

In "A Study in Pink," for example, Sherlock, on foot, pursues a suspect in a taxi through Soho. He compensates for the taxi's superior speed with his detailed knowledge of the city, and "[m]uch like a computer calculates a route from point A to B, Sherlock visualizes the fastest way to catch up with the taxi" (Kustritz and Kohnen 2012, 95). Following a shot in which Sherlock puts his hands to his head as a signal that he is thinking, the audience is shown a map of London, zooming in on Soho. On the map of Soho, a red line appears across the streets, making visible the most likely route for the taxi to take (see [53:23]). The scene is presented in crosscuts between this map and images of street signs, traffic lights, and construction sites supposedly flashing through Sherlock's mind and serving as explanations why he can predict where the taxi will turn. This not only demonstrates Sherlock's enormous and incredibly detailed knowledge of London but, as Kustritz and Kohnen remark, portrays the city of London itself as a "map of visual information that can be reproduced, organized, and accessed" by Sherlock (ibid.). In Sherlock's mind, the complex events that occur in a city are simplified into a flat representation that becomes predictable and controllable. To succeed in his pursuit, all Sherlock needs is the skill to navigate his mental map of London more efficiently than the taxi navigates the streets of London.

Once Sherlock has calculated the best route to take, the audience sees shots of him and John Watson sprinting along narrow alleys and up stairwells, intercut with the map of Soho, on which a second, green line now makes visible the route Sherlock has chosen for his pursuit. The green line does not keep to the official streets marked on the map but cuts through building blocks and unmapped back alleys, and thus demonstrates that Sherlock's knowledge of London surpasses even the computational power of a navigational algorithm such as Google Maps (see ibid.). This scene epitomizes the show's portrayal of knowledge as visualizable and spatialized, accessible, listable, and easily navigable.

One striking instance which illustrates the navigational logic of Sherlock's knowledge occurs toward the end of the episode "A Study in Pink," when Sherlock uses the GPS signal of the victim's (missing) phone to track its location through a website (see [1:00:56]). Once the phone is located, a flashing dot on a map and a bleeping sound indicate the completion of the search. When Sherlock looks at the screen that displays the phone's location, he starts reassembling clues in his head to identify who the killer might be, and the audience can follow the process through questions he voices in his mind and corresponding images of clues and key situations displayed on screen. While Sherlock reviews his memories of facts of the case, the bleeping sound, by which the website indicates the phone has been located, continues and becomes integrated into Sherlock's thoughtscape displayed on screen. The continuation of this sound shows that Sherlock is busy locating who and where the killer might be, and—since the bleeping signals the completion of the GPS localization of the phone—that the solution is already hovering at the edge of his perception. This draws yet another parallel between Sherlock's cognitive processes and digital navigation and calculation of data points, and implies Sherlock's mind works like a computer. Moreover, it expands on the spatialized representation and visual approach to knowledge the show engages in. What makes the BBC's Sherlock exceptional is his instinctive command over navigational processes, which renders him able to control (digital) information through the operations of searching, filtering, and visualization.

Memory as Objective Data

Already in Arthur Conan Doyle's *Sherlock Holmes* stories, the process of organizing knowledge is portrayed as stunningly spatial. Even when leaving aside the inherently spatial organization of the books and encyclopedias Doyle's Sherlock Holmes resorts to so often, the prevalence given to space in the organization and description of memories is striking in both Doyle's original and the BBC adaption.

In *A Study in Scarlet* (1887), Doyle's Sherlock Holmes introduces the image of the "brain attic" to describe how he processes and remembers information:

> I consider that a man's brain originally is like a little empty attic, and you have to stock it with such furniture as you choose. A fool takes in all the lumber of every sort that he comes across, so that the knowledge which might be useful to him gets crowded out, or at best is jumbled up with a lot of other things, so that he has a difficulty in laying his hands upon it. Now the skillful workman is very careful indeed as to what he takes into his brain-attic. He will have nothing but the tools which may help him in doing his work, but of these he has a large assortment, and all in the most perfect order. (14)

In this quote, knowledge and memory are described in terms of physical space and material items. The location of the attic at the top of a house equals the position of a person's head (and hence brain) on top of the body and functions to anchor the analogy in physical space. The degree of detail to which Holmes's elaborations are taken is striking: as storage space, the attic of a house allows its owner perfect control not only over what is to be stored there but also over how and according to which ordering system the "furniture" is to be arranged. A successful arrangement allows the attic's owner to "lay[...] [their] hands upon" and thus retrieve the items they seek at any time. At a closer inspection, the degree of control over one's memory that Holmes's analogy suggests, of course, turns out to be illusory, but in the context of Doyle's *Sherlock Holmes* stories, it functions to portray human memory as an array of objective data that can be stored or deleted at will and that can be retrieved in the exact same condition in which it was stored.

In the episode "The Great Game" (S1, E3), the BBC's *Sherlock* echoes Holmes's statement about his brain attic when Sherlock tells John Watson: "[l]isten. This is my hard drive and it only makes sense to put things in there that are useful. Really useful. Ordinary people fill their heads with all kinds of rubbish. And that makes it hard to get at the stuff that matters. Do you see?" [4:50]. This metaphor takes up Doyle's idea that memories can be stored, arranged, and deleted at will, and additionally emphasizes the machine-like efficiency of organizing data this way by having Sherlock compare his brain to a part of a computer. Sherlock's proficiency with and constant use of technology also feeds into this idea.

The notion of "technology as an extension of [our] physical body" has already been proposed by Marshall McLuhan (1994, 47), and the so-called extended mind thesis suggests that "cognition is often […] continuous with processes in the environment" (Clark and Chalmers 1998, 10), that is, that our cognitive processes can become coupled with external resources that are at our regular disposal (see ibid., 11). Clark and Chalmers take the calculator as their example to explain what they term "active externalism" (ibid., 9), in which external features come to play an "ineliminable role" in our cognitive processes (ibid.). New technologies foster such active externalism to an unprecedented degree.[42] Sherlock's phone as metonymical extension of the Internet functions as seamless extension of his "mental database" (Kustritz and Kohnen 2012, 97), which suggests that Sherlock's memory has an equally objective quality and machine-like efficiency.

In "The Hounds of Baskerville" (S2 E2), Holmes's brain attic idea is taken up again and expanded according to the characteristics discussed above. Holmes's brain attic in this episode becomes Sherlock's "mind palace."[43] The change of terminology reflects the increase of proportions that comes with the inclusion of the Internet into the well of knowledge Sherlock can draw on. Additionally, the inflated size functions to flaunt Sherlock's habitual arrogance: by labeling his own mind a palace, he points out its extraordinary size and contrasts it with an ordinary person's mind, which might perhaps be compared to a house rather than a palace.[44]

The episode "The Hounds of Baskerville" has Sherlock investigate a secret research facility, from which, allegedly, a giant genetically engineered hound has escaped. When trying to draw a connection between seemingly disparate clues, Sherlock retreats to the aforementioned mind palace. The show's trademark floating words then allow the audience to follow Sherlock into his mind palace. The scene starts with a blurry image of the word "hound," displayed within a circle of orange light. The image triples and fades as Sherlock proceeds to the next thought. The way the word is displayed is reminiscent of the image of a research object as it appears when looking through a microscope that is out of focus. This implies that Sherlock's mind works like a scientific instrument that, if properly used, will yield a clear image of his object of research.

This microscope reference can be seen as an updated version of the traditional Holmesian magnifying glass, which already symbolizes the detective's insight and attention to detail in Doyle's stories. Furthermore, the visual metaphor of Sherlock's mind as a microscope suggests that reaching the correct solution is a process of mechanical adjustment that is both repeatable and calculable, and thus that the kind of analysis Sherlock is performing can be reproduced by anyone who has been instructed in how to do so. By analogy, this manner of representation also suggests that the object of Sherlock's investigation—his memories, in this particular scene—can be handled like any material object examined under a microscope: it can be viewed from different angles, but will essentially remain unchanged. The memories that Sherlock reviews in this scene, thus, are portrayed as objective data, which remains accessible and unchanged indefinitely.

As the scene proceeds, this impression is further strengthened by the way Sherlock navigates his thoughts. As the words and clues he is trying to connect appear in print before his closed eyes, Sherlock makes swiping motions with his hands to navigate his associations, which is reminiscent of the way information can be reviewed on electronic devices with a touchscreen.

Sherlock, for example, pins the word "liberty" to the side of his mental screen and moves it around as he goes through different associations, and he swipes through information he retrieves from his memories in a way that is reminiscent of scrolling through a website. He uses his hands to sort through memories and swipe aside associations he rejects as being unimportant to his current objective. Furthermore, the mise-en-scène has words appear between Sherlock's outstretched hands and at times suggests that he is holding them as one would hold a material object (see [1:10:51]). The way Sherlock uses his hands further reinforces the impression that his thoughts and memories are as graspable as material objects, retrievable with the touch of a hand, and as unchangeable and thus objective as data stored on a digital device. *Sherlock* thus portrays "[m]ind, body, and data [as] part of an overtly integrated information system" (Taylor 2012, 139) and highlights the physical level involved in cognition that is also a prominent focus of the extended mind thesis. *Sherlock* brings into prominence not only the huge amount of data that Sherlock constantly has at the tip of his fingers, but also his ability to access any piece of information that is part of this network as easily as one would retrieve a physical object from its storage space.

The mind palace metaphor, through which this scene is framed, illustrates how Sherlock is able to "mobilize larger and larger numbers of events in one spot" through the very techniques that Latour describes as central to scientific innovation (1990, 41). By mapping Sherlock's cognitive activity onto the imaginary yet concrete mental space of his mind palace, the show portrays Sherlock's abstract mental map as reproducible and objective. Sherlock's knowledge seems firmly anchored in physical and digital space, which creates the impression of order and accessibility. In the mind palace scene, John Watson explicitly draws attention to this spatial aspects of Sherlock's thought process when he explains to a scientist that Sherlock's mind palace is "a memory technique. A sort of mental map. You plot a map with a location, doesn't have to be a real place, and then you deposit memories there" [1:10:16]. Watson's portrayal of knowledge as mappable and of memories as something that can be deposited like a physical object reinforces the idea that knowledge requires navigational rather than interpretative skill. Both maps and lists, in the show, become tools to visualize cognitive processes and turn personal observations and memories into scientifically graspable data.

Compartmentalization
The strong spatial aspect of how *Sherlock* represents knowledge foregrounds issues of compartmentalization and classification that connects the show back to its origins in Doyle's stories. The brain attic metaphor, which compares pieces of knowledge to furniture that can be arranged and retrieved at will (see *Scarlet*, 14), suggests that different aspects of knowledge are as clearly distinguishable as individual pieces of furniture and that they remain independent from one another. The view of "physicality as information" (Taylor 2012, 134), that is, the idea that material objects carry traces of their history that can be observed and unambiguously correlated with an interpretation, is closely linked to a view of knowledge as compartmentalized that can be found in both Doyle's *Sherlock Holmes* and the BBC's *Sherlock*.

The idea of easily distinguishable and neatly separable units is central to the portrayal of knowledge and order in both texts. The list Watson makes to categorize Sherlock Holmes in *A Study in Scarlet* presents a range of categories that appear to be separate and clearly discriminable because they are rendered in a consecutively numbered column in a layout that visually disconnects the list items from one another. Such a presentation glosses over discontinuities and unintuitive classificatory choices Watson makes, such as listing literature (item 1) and sensational literature (item 9) as separate categories (see *Scarlet*, 15). Watson's list presents the story world as based on a clearly identifiable (and hence, reproducible) order. The word lists of Sherlock's observations that *Sherlock* uses to display its protagonist's deductions and make them accessible to the audience fulfill a similar function. Each word or prompt appears attached to a concrete physical object or aspect of a person and thus has a fixed place in the story world. The words are anchored in observable space in a similar way to how Watson's list in *A Study in Scarlet* relies on its concrete layout to achieve its effect. Both strategies of representation order the world they comment upon and use physical space to evoke the impression that the conceptual space and cognitive processes they stand in for can be as easily separated from one another as can the physical locations of the concrete list items.

Another parallel compartmentalizing and classifying strategy can be found in Sherlock Holmes's use of (frequently fictional) reference works and the way in which the BBC's Sherlock uses the Internet as a source of information. The way in which Sherlock harnesses the Internet to come up with pieces of information that miraculously propel his investigation forward is equally stunning to the audience as the way in which Doyle's Sherlock Holmes retrieves pieces of information that perfectly match the current case when he consults reference works. Both versions of the famous detective remain credible when they perform such feats because they can lay claims to specialized knowledge the other characters (and the audience or the readers) lack. Sherlock's digital proficiency is portrayed as exceptional and as far surpassing that of an average human being and is "key to presenting his rationalist intelligence in the BBC series" (Bochman 2012, 148). Similarly, Doyle's Sherlock Holmes lays claims to knowledge acquired during past investigations as well as to the ability to know which pieces of information may be relevant to his profession. Holmes points out that his brain attic only comprises "the tools which may help him in doing his work" (*Scarlet*, 14) and thus presents his ability to efficiently compartmentalize information as the key to his success as a detective.

Yet, neither Holmes's reference works nor the websites Sherlock consults are sources that Doyle's readers and the audience of the BBC show can verify. Many of Holmes's reference works are simply fictional, and though the audience of the BBC's *Sherlock* will likely have access to the Internet, the Internet itself is such a vast and entangled mesh of content that the origin of any particular piece of information is as untraceable as the source of Sherlock Holmes's information in Doyle's stories. The premise upon which such unlimited and yet untraceable knowledge can appear believable is that this knowledge derives from an identifiable source of information that presupposes some kind of classificatory system the detective knows how to apply and that this source of information is potentially, but not actually, accessible by others than the detective himself. Both Holmes's reference works and Sherlock's use of the Internet fulfill those conditions and consequently grant these detectives near omniscience without the taint of supernatural powers. Holmes relies on the mechanics of referencing that Doyle's readers would be familiar with, and *Sherlock* emphasizes how its protagonist's proficiency is a matter of navigational skill.

Even though the two detectives are more than a century apart, both are based around the idea that knowledge and reason are central tools in ordering an otherwise chaotic world. Both characters in particular and both story worlds in general employ lists and list-based referencing systems and categorization strategies to create an appearance of order that ultimately remains inaccessible to Doyle's readers and *Sherlock*'s audience. Lists and reference works in both story worlds appear as a way of portraying the detective's reasoning as based on a replicable step-by-step method, yet at the same time their fragmentary nature guarantees that only the detective can perform those steps and thus appears as an exceptional rational genius.

Toward the end of "Drawing Things Together," Latour concludes that "[i]f you want to understand what draws *things* together, then look at what *draws* things *together*" (1990, 60, emphasis in original). This chapter has been an attempt to do exactly that and show how aspects of visibility and representation influence what kind of information we conceive of as knowledge and how we depict and evaluate it in any given context. Both Doyle's *Sherlock Holmes* and the BBC show *Sherlock* choose a take on knowledge that focuses on its representation over delineating the exact kind of knowledge content that enables a detective to conduct a successful investigation. Both texts use listing and referencing tools to create a plausible (and visible) backdrop for their detective's expertise and thus make it possible for a mere reference to a thing to stand in for the thing itself. The figuration of knowledge that stands behind that strategy is decidedly different from the interconnections of knowledge and listing techniques that have been discussed in the previous chapters. My conclusion is going to situate these different approaches to representing knowledge in the larger context of detective fiction and tie them to the different kinds of implied readers that the texts I have discussed imagine as their audience.

NOTES

1. References to individual stories will be abbreviated if the title is not mentioned in the text. Unless indicated otherwise, all emphases have been removed from quotations for better readability.
2. Due to the popularity of the *Sherlock Holmes* stories, this kind of fallacy has become known as Holmesian fallacy (see rationalwiki.org/wiki/Holmesian_fallacy).
3. For a detailed discussion of the etymological origins of the word "encyclopedia," see Blair (2010, 12).
4. This chapter uses the terms "encyclopedia" and "reference work" interchangeably.
5. Detective fiction as a genre pursues a very similar endeavor and often transforms the complexity of the real world it draws on into structured text that can be more easily disentangled or controlled.
6. Many characteristics of printed reference works, from reader-friendly layouts to indexing and alphabetical order, go back to practices adapted from medieval manuscripts (see Blair 2010, 5).
7. Compare, for example, "[t]here is a strong family resemblance about misdeeds, and if you have all the details of a thousand at your finger ends, it is odd if you can't unravel the thousand and first" (*Scarlet*, 19).
8. "Die Medialität des gedruckten Buches verleiht dem Katalog darüber hinaus [eine] Aura von epistemischer Einheit." Starre makes his argument about the unifying capacity of short forms and uses the catalog of the American Library Association—a bibliography of a tremendous number of books—as his example.
9. The list almost ironically illustrates the clash of Watson's expectations and Holmes's actual skills—and thus Watson's lack of understanding for how Sherlock Holmes works.
10. Moretti makes his argument about the unvarying cause-effect relations in Holmesian deductions. Watson's list depicts knowledge categories as similarly stable.
11. Watson, for example, does not list "history," one of the nine main categories in the Dewey Decimal Classification (first published 1876) that is still widely used in libraries today. Furthermore, he lists "Literature" and "Sensational Literature" as two separate categories, and "Botany," "Geology," and "Chemistry" could probably be subsumed under *Natural Sciences*. For a discussion of the Dewey Decimal Classification, see Starre (2017, 240).
12. According to Alan Sinfield, a faultline is a rupture in any given ideology that questions the conditions of its plausibility. Texts inevitably produce faultlines. See Sinfield (1992).

13. Holmes, for instance, is often described as performing chemical analyses at the beginning of a story (see, e.g., *Scarlet*, 7–9), but he does not employ such analyses to process evidence in a case.

14. Deriving conclusions from observation, as Holmes often claims to do, would actually be inductive reasoning, as Stephen Knight pointedly remarks (see 1980, 86). Holmes, however, relies on deductive reasoning when he draws conclusions on the basis of background knowledge about other cases, so either term seems appropriate.

15. This contributes to presenting the power Holmes commands as an acquired ability rather than innate genius.

16. Smajić also relates his observations to Foucault's study of the archive: Smajić discusses Foucault's study of the rapidly growing interest in the archive during the nineteenth century, and he then argues that the *Holmes* stories represent a "fantasy about exhaustive encyclopedic knowledge and boundless archival resources which vouch that no clue will be overlooked or misinterpreted" (2010, 124).

17. Stephen Barney points out something quite similar in the context of Chaucer's medieval list-making. He argues that because medieval science was mostly represented in lists, Chaucer repeats this form (which is associated with scientific content) in his own works (see 1982, 214).

18. In "Bohemia," for example, consulting the "Continental Gazetteer" enables Holmes to identify the origin of an embossed piece of paper. The reference work is used to assign a definite meaning to the appearance of the letters "Eg" on the paper (5). Holmes further uses expressions such as "of course" (ibid.) to support the impression that the meaning he allocates to the letters is the correct one.

19. The short story "The Red Headed League," for instance, lists "Abbots and Archery and Armour and Architecture and Attica" (36) as entries of the *Encyplopædia Britannica* that can be found in close proximity to one another.

20. Evidence, for Holmes, is almost always material. Psychological observations nearly never play a role for how Holmes investigates. A notable exception is the short story "A Scandal in Bohemia."

21. Compare also: "League" where Holmes states: "[a]s a rule, when I have heard some slight indication of the course of events, I am able to guide myself by the thousands of other similar cases which occur to my memory" (27). Thus, Holmes basically argues knowledge is finite, and he has acquired all knowledge useful to his profession.

22. See, for example, how he describes his brain attic (for an analysis of the passage, see pp. 181–182 in this chapter). The idea of "laying [one's] hands upon" (*Scarlet*, 14) any given piece of knowledge suggests that Sherlock Holmes envisions his brain as a kind of mental library and that

knowledge items can be cataloged like books. In his short story "The Library of Babel," Jorge Luis Borges envisions a library that contains books in which "all possible combinations of the twenty-two orthographic symbols [...] that is, all that is able to be expressed" are recorded (1998, 115). Hence, Borges's narrator reasons, the library's books contain all possible knowledge in the universe. Borges's short story ridicules this idea, but Doyle's Sherlock Holmes advocates a very similar conception of knowledge as the foundation for his investigative method.

23. Franco Moretti argues that the detective fiction genre itself "does not permit alternative readings" (1988, 144) and thus reflects this kind of thinking in presenting certain chains of events as inevitably linear in their logic.

24. Stäheli argues that indices are a potentially dangerous tool because they appear as objective information but veil the process of how and by whom they have been created. This sense of danger is entirely absent from the *Sherlock Holmes* stories. Detective fiction casts the authority of the detective—and, by implication, the authority of the sources and references they choose to employ—as trustworthy by default. With Holmes's indices, Doyle even goes one step further than that: Holmes's near omniscience and status as the creator of those indices affirm him as an authoritative source of information, and in a feat of circular reasoning, the existence of Holmes's indices as material, printed sources of information that Holmes, with his authority as a detective, considers worth consulting makes them appear as trustworthy sources of information that Holmes can safely base his conclusions on.

25. Similarly, in "Identity," Holmes talks about unique features of a typewriter and once again refers to one (at this time even yet unwritten) of his monographs. He mentions there are fourteen characteristics that support his claim, but the actual characteristics remain unnamed (66).

26. Roland Barthes's reality effect describes how literary descriptions of space can evoke verisimilitude without a concrete extratextual signified (see 1968).

27. This is already shown in the etymology of the word "index," which is related to seeing and vision: the Greek word for display, epideixis, is related to the Latin word index, which signifies list. Both words have the same root. Lists, thus, could be said to "show the visibles" (Barney 1982, 203).

28. Latour argues that writing alone cannot explain changes in scientific practice. Where there are competing systems or hypotheses, it is always the one with the most faithful followers that will win. Visualization, however, is fundamental to gaining new allies for a field or theory (see 1990, 23–24).

29. Maps tend to represent physical space and render concrete objects abstract, whereas diagrams usually represent conceptual space and give abstract subjects a more concrete representation. Both rely on the same operations of

simplification and condensation to facilitate easy visual access to their object of representation. Other forms of visual representation such as drawings or equations are situated along the same sliding scale, and the distinctions between individual forms of visual representation are not always clear-cut.

30. Caroline Levine's traveling forms (i.e., forms that stay recognizable across time and space (see 2015, 7)) bear clear resemblances to Latour's immutable mobiles.

31. See, for example, the many lists Latour includes on pages 35–37 of "Drawing Things Together." Urs Stäheli is one of the few critics who problematize Latour's copious use of lists in his Actor Network Theory (see 2011). Ian Bogost has even created a tool that generates Latour litanies from randomized Wikipedia page APIs, the "Latour Litanizer" (See Bogost 2009, n.p.).

32. Goody differentiates between three general categories of lists: inventories (which are retrospective), shopping lists (that are prospective), and lexical lists. He cites the itinerary as an example for the shopping list category (see 1978, 80).

33. To avoid confusion, I will refer to Doyle's original character as (Sherlock) Holmes and use only the first name Sherlock to refer to the protagonist of the BBC series.

34. While *Sherlock* makes its protagonist's thought processes accessible to the audience in a way that lets them follow Sherlock's thoughts, this technique does not necessarily render Sherlock's way of thinking reproducible.

35. The episode's title is a reference to Doyle's *A Study in Scarlet* and features many intertextual allusions to Doyle's novel.

36. An interesting variation on this occurs in the first episode of the second season, "A Scandal in Belgravia," when Sherlock encounters Irene Adler and is unable to draw any conclusions from her appearance. Instead of the bits of personal information the audience is usually presented with when Sherlock scrutinizes somebody, the screen overlay only displays a number of question marks (see [25: 16]).

37. Funnily enough, the one and only correct solution is different for Doyle's original text and the *Sherlock* episode.

38. This is similar to Doyle's Sherlock Holmes: on the one hand, uniqueness and individualism are emphasized through Sherlock Holmes's seemingly unreachable genius, and on the other hand, the stories (falsely) present his deductive methods as universally accessible and based on common sense.

39. In "A Study in Scarlet," Sherlock holds up the victim's wedding ring, and the word "dirty" appears near the outside, while the word "clean" is displayed on the inside of the ring, half hidden by the front of the ring (see [25:25]). The floating words, and hence Sherlock's thought processes,

thus behave like material objects that can be in front of or behind other objects, which makes them appear graspable.

40. Stein and Busse base their argument on Lev Manovich's monograph *The Language of New Media* (2001).

41. On theories of vision in connection to detective fiction, see Smajić (2010). See also the work of sociologist Urs Stäheli (2016), who discusses how indices can be powerful tools because they render *in*visible the process of how they are generated.

42. It could be argued that lists, too, count among the technologies that constitute an extension of our cognitive processes into the physical world as described by Clark and Chalmers because they are a common tool that facilitates thought processes through visualization.

43. In *Sherlock*, Sherlock is not the only person to use such mnemonic techniques to his advantage. In the episode "His Last Vow" (S3, E3), Sherlock's antagonist Charles Augustus Magnussen uses information stored in his own mind palace for blackmail.

44. The use of spatial and architectural metaphors for mnemonic techniques has a long tradition and goes back to the method of loci that, according to myth, was invented by the ancient Greek poet Simonides of Ceos (see Zielinski 2014, n.p.).

CHAPTER 7

Conclusion: Models of Knowledge in Detective Fiction

In *Postmodernist Fiction*, Brian McHale calls detective fiction "the episte-mological genre par excellence" (2001, 9). The genre's concern with the transmission, reliability, and the objects of knowledge, McHale argues, is defining for what he calls the *epistemological dominant* detective fiction shares with most modernist texts (ibid.). Each chapter of this book has explored aspects of generating, delimiting, manipulating, verifying, and organizing knowledge as it is transmitted between text and reader and/or utilized by detective figures. I have shown how inextricably these episte-mological concerns are linked to the forms—in particular, the form of the list—that transport them.

Even within the confines of the genre of detective fiction, however, *knowledge* is by no means a unified category; between story worlds, and across changing historical and ideological backgrounds, conceptions of knowledge shift and adapt to both the role of the reader and the function of the detective in the respective texts. In some texts, such as the fiction of Agatha Christie, detection relies on knowledge that entirely depends on clues situated in the story world, whereas Austin Freeman's *Thorndyke* novels, for example, frequently reference areas of expert knowledge that exist as professional fields outside the text to validate the detective's con-clusions. In yet another way, Doyle's *Sherlock Holmes* stories draw on bod-ies of knowledge that are entirely imaginary and are neither anchored in the real world nor displayed as an element of the story world accessible to

© The Author(s) 2023
S. J. Link, *A Narratological Approach to Lists in Detective Fiction*,
Crime Files, https://doi.org/10.1007/978-3-031-33227-2_7

readers. The final section of this book aims to highlight how the various conceptions of knowledge discussed in the previous chapters are inseparable from the roles these novels assign to their readers and from the lists and list-like devices that are crucial to defining those roles.

Perhaps the most intuitive and probably the most widely spread expectation of the kind of knowledge relations readers will encounter in a work of detective fiction arose during the Golden Age in the first half of the twentieth century: the idea that all clues necessary to solve the mystery must be featured in the text, and that, therefore, solving the puzzle the text presents is a matter of sharp observation and logical combination. Golden Age fiction requires no specialized knowledge of either its detectives or readers, and the combinations necessary to solve a case are generally based on common sense. Moreover, the texts present readers (and detectives) with puzzles that can be solved by contemplation and communication and do not require detectives to display any physical prowess. In this setup, readers have the chance to match the detective. The facts that most frequently further the investigations of a Hercule Poirot or a Miss Marple are from the domestic realm and thus accessible to a wide range of readers (see Knight 1980, 109).[1] In *A Murder Is Announced*, for example, it becomes important that a door's hinges have recently been oiled, and *The Murder of Roger Ackroyd* features a piece of furniture that has been moved as an important clue.

Basing the knowledge an investigator needs to succeed on common experience and clues featured in the text is an ideal condition upon which the roles of reader and detective can become merged with one another. It is the detective's task to *read* clues rather than conduct forensic experiments or draw on experience gained in past investigations, and the Golden Age's promise of fair play—of a plausible story that is based on clues accessible to the general reader—invites readers to take on the role of detectives themselves and try their hand at reading the patterns provided by the text to identify the solution of the mystery.

Both the novels of Agatha Christie discussed in chapter four and the *Murder Dossiers* of Dennis Wheatley and J.G. Links discussed in chapter three invite their readers to become active as investigators and promise them a fair chance of success. Christie's novels do so implicitly through their authors' membership in the Detection Club (founded in 1928): all members of the club had to swear to observe the rules of fair play in the "Detection Club Oath," which served as a signpost for the club's high professional standards (see Haycraft 1976, 197). In contrast, Wheatley and Links directly promise their readers in the author's note preceding *Murder off Miami* that the material readers find in the dossier is presented "without any extraneous or misleading matter," and they even point out the passage in the dossier where readers will have "all the available evidence […] to hand" (n.p.) that is necessary to solve the case.

While both Wheatley and Christie engage their readers in the act of detection, they do so in rather different ways. *Murder off Miami* is designed to bear the greatest possible resemblance to a real-world police file and promises a realistic detection experience to the reader. The *Murder Dossiers* even go as far as insinuating that the reader will actually be responsible for the outcome of the investigation and for apprehending the suspect. The author's note to *Murder off Miami*, for instance, directly asks the reader to decide "who *you* will arrest" for the murder (n.p., emphasis in original). Subsequent dossiers cut back on the verisimilitude aspect and instead rely on their game-like nature to keep readers engaged. For this degree of involvement, basing the knowledge required to solve the mysteries in the material itself is of course vital. The lists that organize the various pieces of evidence are essential to facilitate the reader's easy access to the information needed for their investigation because they either summarize information or serve as a navigational tool that allows the reader to easily locate pieces of information in different parts of the dossier.

Christie's novels, on the other hand, rely on their readers' expectations to find the clues they need concealed in the text, and the anticipation of these clues becomes the basis for misdirecting the reader's attention in order to manipulate the conclusions readers draw. Rather than framing her stories in terms of verisimilitude and a realistic experience, Christie structures her novels in a way that exploits (potential) ambiguities to create suspense. Misleading clues and red herrings are therefore something readers would expect in Christie's fiction, and trying to separate true clues from false leads becomes as much part of the reader's detective activity as piecing together the correct solution to the mystery.[2] Christie's lists reflect this ambiguity; they can supply the reader with useful summaries of evidence gleaned by the detective or provided by the narrator, but they may also misdirect the reader's attention and distract from hints hidden elsewhere in the text.

Both Christie and Wheatley cast their readers as investigators who are at least potentially able to solve the problem the texts pose with nothing but the clues featured in the texts. The widely spread belief that Golden Age fiction allows its readers to take on the role of detective goes hand in hand with an "illusion of effective self-help and self-sufficiency" (Knight 1980, 110)—values which have great appeal to "an audience deeply imbued with [the] anxious individualism" that Knight sees as distinctive for Christie's largely bourgeois readership at the time her early novels were published (ibid., 127). The individual's power to restore order to a world that has been tipped out of balance is a strong ideological undercurrent that runs through detective fiction of the Golden Age, and the intratextual knowledge Christie's novels are steeped in suggests that restoring order in this way lies not only within the power of the detective but also within that of the reader.

Lists feature prominently as an organizing and tracking device in all kinds of self-help literature even today, and it is no coincidence that the list's affordances of tracking and organizing are the ones that feature most prominently in Golden Age detective fiction. Agatha Christie repeatedly employs lists as a device to allow the reader to track her detectives' thoughts step by step, for example, in the list of Poirot's ten questions in *Murder on the Orient Express* or in the list Miss Marple leaves behind before she disappears in *A Murder Is Announced*. Christie's detectives, furthermore, make lists to efficiently organize information and to thus have available at one glance a great number of details pertaining to their investigations. This practice can, for example, be observed in the list Poirot makes of the passengers' belongings in *Death in the Clouds* or in the list of stolen items he uses in *Hickory Dickory Dock*. Reordering those details correctly, that is, finding the organizing principle that is able to do so—or so the stories promise—will result in restoring order to the world that has been disturbed by the murder.[3]

Wheatley's *Herewith the Clues* also leaves no doubt about how its readers are expected to track and organize information with the help of the list-based dossier format. The score sheet the volume contains is a preorganized grid that allows readers to track the progress of their investigation—the investigation visibly progresses with each slot filled in—and to organize the evidence they examine according to which suspect can be associated with it. The entire dossier is organized into distinct sections that list different types of evidence and that are meant to serve as a finding aid for readers. The dossier format foregrounds the list's capability to track and organize information, and thus already co-defines the role readers are assigned in the crime dossiers. "[T]he material form of an expression," as Lisa Gitelman argues, hence tends to become conflated "with its linguistic meanings" (2014, 3). *Murder off Miami* is based on the same list-mechanisms and employs its list-affine structure to create verisimilitude by organizing its material in a way that emulates a real-world police file. This structure allows readers to chronologically track the information gathered by detective officer Kettering. Kettering's lists and summaries of times accounted for, alibis, personal profiles, belongings, and pieces of evidence enable readers to track the progress of his investigation in a similar way that Christie's lists provide readers with access to her detective's thoughts. To successfully identify the murderer, readers have to re-frame Kettering's collected information in the same manner that Christie's detectives reorganize the lists of facts they collect in order to solve the puzzle.

The lists in Adams's dossier novel *The Notting Hill Mystery* also have a strong disposition toward highlighting their tracking and ordering capacities, but a closer look at the different kinds of listing devices the novel employs reveals that it adopts a two-pronged strategy with regard to the knowledge it draws on. Adam's dossier relies on intratextual clues that the reader has access to for making its case against Baron R., but it also embeds sources of expert literature that exist outside the story world in order to support Henderson's claims to exactitude and meticulous documentation. This in-between position can be connected to the double role assigned to the reader in this text. In the position of investigating officer that the reader shares with Henderson, they are required to examine the textual clues they are presented with in Henderson's collected document to carefully construct their case against Baron R. In this role, readers have to draw their conclusions based on pieces of information scattered through the collected documents that need to be meticulously compared and cross-referenced to reveal the pattern they conceal. Henderson's footnotes and table of contents endow readers with listing tools to help accomplish this task, and exactitude or the ability to pay attention to details, rather than command over any kind of expert knowledge, is the key to succeed in this.

In the position of addressee and jury that the reader also shares, however, their task is to act as a judge on the reliability of the information Henderson collects in his dossier. In this role, the reader is to verify that Henderson's detective work is sound. Readers need to weigh the reliability of Henderson's meticulous work, which points to the Baron's guilt and the existence of mesmerism, against the conviction that such preternatural mesmeric powers cannot exist. Positing the reader as the addressee of Henderson's dossier blurs the boundaries between story world and real world. The references to documentation practices and expert knowledge that exists in the real world—the second body of knowledge that *The Notting Hill Mystery* draws on—further strengthen this fuzziness. The dossier, for example, includes a (correct) reference to a specific page of Alfred Swaine Taylor's *On Poisons, in Relation to Medical Jurisprudence* that serves as proof for the varying effects that antimony poisoning can have on a person's constitution and thus provides a plausible explanation for the symptoms one of the characters is experiencing. A meticulous reader is given the opportunity to verify this source and can thus fact-check some of Henderson's collected statements. References of this kind serve as a guarantor for the narrator's reliability and create the bias that other pieces of information that readers cannot verify outside the story world will nonetheless be accepted as reliable.

As a typical listing technique, referencing puts on display material that serves as a guarantor for knowledge of (or at least familiarity with) the sources being referenced. Lisa Gitelman calls this the "know-show function" and makes a case for visibility as a central aspect upon which (at least implied) reliability hinges (2014, 1). Referencing as a means to display knowledge employs a mechanics of "implied self-evidence that is intrinsically rhetorical" and based on a document's visible properties (ibid., 2); visibility, hence, becomes associated with truth. To unfold their potential as "epistemic objects" (ibid., 1) documents need to be displayed. *The Notting Hill Mystery* draws on this rhetoric of visibility and credibility to present extratextual expert knowledge as support for information that is situated within the story world. The dossier depicts two differently conditioned bodies of knowledge as provided by the same source—Henderson—and thus imbues the one that is constructed inside the story world with the verifiable reliability of the other.

When detective fiction features extratextual knowledge, this knowledge can generally be situated within the realm of science and professions associated with forensic investigations. Other areas of knowledge such as history or politics that may play a bigger role in the life of the average reader are rarely drawn upon in these stories. What I call extratextual knowledge thus usually comprises the professional knowledge of experts in a designated scientific field. Richard Austin Freeman's *Thorndyke* novels make the prominent display of such expert knowledge their unique selling point, and their prefaces and paratexts advertise the accurate depiction of scientific disciplines and forensic methods in the texts. The solutions Thorndyke proposes for his cases tend to be corroborated with an abundance of professional knowledge from a variety of scientific disciplines, and the texts present Thorndyke as a knowledgeable expert in all of them. The inclusion of such a broad range of scientific disciplines paired with the exceptional and specific details Thorndyke draws on for his solutions has a significant impact on the role of the reader in these texts. Unlike the novels of Agatha Christie, Dennis Wheatley, and Adams's *The Notting Hill Mystery*, the reader of a *Thorndyke* novel is not supposed to have any chance at figuring out the solution. With regard to the narrative situation, the reader usually shares the position of Thorndyke's assistant, who is considerably less knowledgeable than Thorndyke himself and frequently admires the detective's genius. Thorndyke's assistant implicitly invites the reader to share his admiration for both Thorndyke as a personality and the power of science as a tool for understanding, for example, when he describes the chemical procedure by which Thorndyke is able to determine a victim's identity from nothing but cremated remains in chapter 21 of *A Silent Witness*. To enhance the effect of such impressive feats of detection, Thorndyke's explanations occasionally contain pieces of information that have not been previously mentioned in the text. Instead of causing discontent and raising concerns about clues that have been concealed unfairly—as would certainly be the case if a Christie novel produced a clue in this way—this narrative technique further supports the use of extratextual knowledge (which most readers have no access to anyways) as a way to corroborate Thorndyke's status as an exceptional genius. Instead of inviting readers to become active as a detective and participate in finding a solution for the proposed case, Freeman's novels base their appeal on the awe and wonder that the explanatory power of science and reason can exert. Thorndyke as a character stands as the personification of those powers and thus incorporates the idea that (scientific) knowledge, or a person's expertise therein, is a way of restoring order to a chaotic world and of controlling circumstances that initially seem to elude our influence.

Thorndyke's deliberations at times take on a didactic quality the aim of which seems to be to both educate the reader about proper scientific procedures or dismantle common misconceptions and to lend credibility to Thorndyke's method.[4] Similar to the extratextual references in *The Notting Hill Mystery*, the extratextual knowledge Thorndyke draws on functions to bolster the validity of his investigative method in general, even in a case in which this knowledge is based on speculation and creative imagination rather than scientific procedures, as I have argued in my excursus about the *Thorndyke* novels.

Thorndyke's displays of scientific proficiency tend to occur toward the end of the novels, but the detective establishes his status as an expert much earlier in the texts through his use of language and particularly through the way in which he uses lists. The form of the list is closely entwined with a great number of scientific practices and is commonly regarded as an efficient ordering tool for providing concise and relevant information. Lists afford objectivity and mastery, and those two affordances take center stage when the *Thorndyke* novels incorporate extratextual expert knowledge in their representation of Thorndyke and his detective work. When Thorndyke interprets evidence, his deliberations often take the form of the list. Freeman's novels avail themselves of the aura of objectivity that is associated with the list form to endow Thorndyke's statements with similar claims to objectivity. Thorndyke's status as an expert that is frequently brought up in the texts and his abundant use of the list form to conjure up a sense of objectivity and control that is associated with scientific discourse mutually support one another.

Thorndyke's use of lists demonstrates his mastery over the subjects he talks about. The structured form of enumerations comes with the implicit suggestion that the creator of such a list wields control over the content being enumerated (see Mainberger 2003, 167; see also Stäheli 2016, 23). Behind this expectation stands the idea that breaking something down into its constituent parts and representing it in a brief and concise way is only possible if the list-maker is able to intellectually pervade the material to be presented. Freeman's novels thus implicitly validate the content of Thorndyke's statements through the list form, in which they are conveyed. Since readers have no insight into how Thorndyke compiles his lists, they are unlikely to question the list's authority.

Arthur Conan Doyle's *Sherlock Holmes* stories also present their detective as an expert and as a genius personality, but in conceptualizing the knowledge that backs up this status, they take a very different approach from what a reader might encounter in a *Thorndyke* novel. While Freeman's novels take great pains to communicate to their readers that the science Thorndyke uses to back up his claims is sound and represented exactly as it works in real life, Holmes lays claims to expertise in various subjects (such as Chinese tattoo art or types of tobacco ash) that are entirely without a referent outside the texts. Holmes's expertise furthermore differs from the intratextual clues that the novels of Christie and Wheatley make available to their readers and detectives. What Holmes calls his deductions is based on a body of knowledge that is referenced in the stories but neither exists in the real world nor is described in detail in the text. Consequently, as Ben Parker argues in his essay "The Method Effect: Empiricism and Form in *Sherlock Holmes*," "[t]here simply is no 'real' to the method that the Sherlock Holmes stories could be taken to be applying or failing to apply" (2016, 453). The body of knowledge Holmes's expertise is based on may thus appear to be extratextual and founded in real-world science, but it is in fact entirely undefined; it is part of the fictional world only by implication, but readers have no access to it, and its specific dimensions remain vague.

It is the *idea* of a method and of excessive knowledge behind Holmes's deductions rather than an actual method and concrete body of knowledge that Doyle's stories hinge on. This puts the reader in an interesting position: Holmes's repeated explanations about the seemingly sound and replicable method behind his genius suggest that readers should be able to arrive at the same conclusions as Holmes does. The ethereal quality of the knowledge that Holmes draws on and the way in which the detective presents his conclusions as the only possible interpretation of a given situation (even though there may be equally plausible alternatives), however, make it impossible for readers to emulate Holmes's inferences. The intended role of the reader thus appears to be similar to that of John Watson, whose perspective the reader shares in most stories: they are supposed to admire the brilliance of Holmes's feats of deduction and to consider his conclusions as reproducible without ever quite being able to reproduce them.

This reader model is more appealing than it might initially appear, at least in the context of the late nineteenth century, when the *Holmes* stories were first published. Sherlock Holmes is a projection surface for the hopes his contemporaries placed in science as the key to explaining and hence understanding the rapidly changing world around them. More than a 100 years later, the Sherlock Holmes character featured in the BBC show *Sherlock* takes on quite a similar role. While *Sherlock* cuts back on the notion prominent in Doyle's stories that there is only one possible explanation for any set of circumstances,[5] the show's protagonist basically adopts the same heroic role of the exceptional genius who is able to see (through) the structures behind seemingly inexplicable circumstances and to point out patterns in a world that seems impossibly complex to others. The show even replaces the original Sherlock Holmes's ethereal body of vague knowledge with an equally mysterious and unknowably vast contemporary source of information: the Internet.[6] *Sherlock* casts its protagonist's genius in terms of his ability to navigate great masses of information efficiently and his command over rapidly evolving technology, and thus mirrors the way in which Doyle's texts make the powers of deduction Holmes commands appear imitable and accessible.

The way in which Doyle's stories and the BBC show employ lists and listing techniques greatly contributes to achieving the aforementioned effect. Listing functions associated with paper technologies, such as selecting, sorting, and summarizing (see Blair 2010, 3), enable Doyle's Sherlock Holmes to evoke the idea of knowledge being called on through mere allusions to sources that remain ever vague and unverifiable. Moreover, the frequent referencing of printed reference volumes in Doyle and of the Internet as an unceasing source of information in *Sherlock* makes these non-verifiable sources appear as plausible explanations for the information the detective produces out of thin air. The paper technologies and listing techniques that both versions of Sherlock Holmes draw on are so central to the transmission of knowledge in real-world contexts that their appearance alone is enough to legitimize whatever stands behind them. Listing techniques thus make it possible to replace actual references, the function of which is to make sources verifiable, with the mere mechanics of referencing.

The omission of actual referents works so well because referencing devices and listing techniques make visible (and by implication accessible) in compressed form the material they refer to. The act of documentation, of writing something down and turning it into a file that can be referenced, has an authenticating effect (see Vismann 2000, 11) that is based on its materiality and, more specifically, on its visibility. Concrete descriptions of the reference volumes Holmes uses, such as the mention of the red cover of a volume (see "Bachelor", 217) or of his index as a material object that Holmes handles, establish them—and by implication their content—as palpable, unchanging entities that form part of the story world. Such descriptions distract from the fact that the reference works thus mentioned serve to back up ever-changing needs of the individual stories. The impression of infinity that lists can evoke (see Eco 2009, 363–369) and the idea of comprehensive knowledge that the mentioning of encyclopedias conjures up smooth over such omissions, and the technique of listing pieces of knowledge comes to metonymically stand in for the knowledge itself. In *Sherlock*, both the protagonist's ever-present smartphone that functions as a visible representation of the Internet Sherlock so frequently uses as a source of information and the screen overlays that make the detective's thoughts visible to the audience combine to achieve the same effect.

Visibility and comprehensiveness are the two affordances of the list most central to the presentation of knowledge in both *Sherlock Holmes* story worlds examined in chapter six. The reference works in Doyle's stories serve as proof for the comprehensive scope of Holmes's knowledge, and the conciseness and usefulness of his self-compiled index testify to his depth of understanding of the material the index comprises. Visualization is also the key to presenting Sherlock's knowledge in the BBC show. This becomes especially evident in the show's frequent incorporation of maps as visualization strategies for cognitive processes. Maps and indices share many affordances (see Mainberger 2003, 137), such as those of visualization and comprehensiveness, and they take on almost exchangeable functions in Doyle's *Sherlock Holmes* and BBC's *Sherlock*. The way in which *Sherlock* represents the memories in its protagonist's mind palace as a navigable field of searchable data, for example, aspires to the same kind of palpability that Doyle's stories try to award Holmes's case index. Lists and maps can both be employed as visualization techniques that draw their persuasive power from rendering the data they convey as immutable and mobile at the same time (see Latour 1990, 26). Both Doyle's stories and the BBC show rely on the affordances of visibility and comprehensiveness to present the bodies of knowledge their detectives resort to as substantial and clearly contoured, when in fact, they do not exist in any delimitable shape.

Since I started this book with a list, it seems fitting to conclude it with a table. The table on the following page displays my findings about the affordances and functions that lists take within the genre of detective fiction and highlights the respective roles of readers and detectives in connection to the various conceptions of knowledge the texts in my corpus operate with. As has been argued in this book, displaying information in the form of lists and tables necessitates a degree of compression that makes only the most salient points visible and is meant to summarize trends rather than represent the more subtle nuances of meaning. The following table is thus meant to be an overview over the key points argued in this book.

	Dossier novels	Christie novels	Dr. Thorndyke	Sherlock Holmes
List affordances	Tracking; organizing	Tracking; organizing; concealing	Objectivity; mastery	Visibility; comprehensiveness
Function of the list(s)	Summary; navigational tool; provide easy access to information	Directing the reader's attention; structuring tool for the detective	Generate the impression of scientificity	Referencing tool; placeholder for knowledge that is not displayed; "know-show function"
Role of the reader	Responsible for solving the case; reframe information	Compete with fictional detective to find the solution	Be educated about scientific methods; marvel at powers of science	Attempt but fail to emulate Holmes; admire Holmes's genius
Role of the detective	Arbiter; judge of suspect's guilt	Reader of clues	Representative of a professional field	Brilliant thinker; role model
Conception of knowledge	Intratextual; requires active manipulation of the material	Intratextual; clues often from the domestic realm	Extratextual; expert knowledge, often inaccessible to readers	Undefined or imaginary; only referenced, idea of knowledge is more important than actual knowledge details

My corpus of texts shows not so much a diachronic development of the use of lists in detective fiction as it illustrates various constellations of engagement and knowledge transmission that lists can facilitate between texts and readers. These constellations and the functions that lists take in these texts are not unique to the contexts in which they have been discussed here but constitute patterns that resurface in new contexts such as videogames. An approach such as the one taken in this book that focuses on narrative and literary forms within a particular genre can identify such patterns of meaning-making even when other factors (such as a change of medium) tend to obscure them.

As the abundance of listing techniques employed by the BBC series *Sherlock* already shows, lists in detective fiction are a restricted neither to the temporal domains of the nineteenth and twentieth centuries nor to printed media. The list-based interactive elements of storytelling that I have discussed in the context of dossier novels, for example, resurface in many videogames with a focus on investigative elements. Such games frequently use inventory structures to allow players to manage clues. The game *Sherlock Holmes: Crimes and Punishments* (2014) even employs screen overlays to display deductions that resemble those used in *Sherlock*. The game also features a "deduction space" where players can reorder clues and evidence displayed as unordered list in order to make deductions and unlock new tasks. An examination of list-based structures in (investigative) videogames could carry my findings further and tie them to current research on narrativity and interactivity in games.

As a cognitive tool, lists have the capacity to structure thought both within and outside the context of literary representation, and the form has been used to do so since antiquity. The detective fiction genre's concern with order makes it an ideal backdrop against which the affordances of this form can be examined. Even if different subgenres stress different affordances of the list form, the form itself appears timeless as a means for creating and representing patterns of thought both within and beyond the confines of the detective fiction genre.

Notes

1. Knight also argues that such domestic details tend to be associated with "the world of a woman's experience and understanding, at a time when women were largely restricted to household activity" (1980, 109) and thus invite Christie's largely female readership to make sense of them.
2. Especially in Golden Age fiction, readers are encouraged to compete with the fictional detective and try to find the solution to the mystery before it is revealed in the text. Stephen Knight ties this to the self-help ideology prevalent at the time and remarks that in the novels of Agatha Christie "[s]uccess in competition is valued because it implies the unaided personal solving of life problems, dramatises self-sufficiency and calibrates personal achievement" (1980, 117). John Gruesser (2020) discusses the element of competition in the detective stories written by Edgar Allan Poe.
3. The strategy of organizing details in a way that results in the greatest possible alignment is employed so frequently and so conspicuously in Christie's novels that later novels occasionally satirize it, as, for example, happens in *Death in the Clouds*, where Jane and Norman's attraction for one another is presented as based on a list of unrelated but matching details.
4. See, for example, the preface to *The Red Thumb Mark*, which informs the reader that the novel will address "certain popular misapprehensions on the subject of finger-prints" (7).

5. In "A Study in Pink," for instance, Sherlock makes a partly wrong guess about Watson's smartphone that acknowledges the possible existence of multiple explanations.
6. The Internet in itself is full of lists, and the way in which search algorithms display search results bears resemblance to the list-based presentation of entries in reference works.

WORKS CITED

Aarseth, Espen J. 1997. *Cybertext: Perspectives on Ergodic Literature*. Baltimore: Johns Hopkins University Press.

Adams, Charles Warren. 2012 [1865]. *The Notting Hill Mystery*. London: British Library.

Alber, Jan. 2016. Absurd Catalogues: The Functions of Lists in Postmodernist Fiction. *Style* 50:3: 342–358.

Alber, Jan, and Monika Fludernik. 2010. Introduction. In *Postclassical Narratology: Approaches and Analyses*, ed. Jan Alber and Monika Fludernik, 1–31. Columbus: The Ohio State University Press.

Alexander, Marc. 2009. Rhetorical Structure and Reader Manipulation in Agatha Christie's *Murder on the Orient Express*. *Miscelanea: A Journal of English and American Philology* 39: 13–27.

Auden, Wystan H. 1948. The Guilty Vicarage: Notes on the Detective Story, by an Addict. *Harper's Magazine*, May 1948. n.p. https://harpers.org/archive/1948/05/the-guilty-vicarage/. Accessed 31 January 2023.

Austin, J. L. 2004. How to Do Things with Words. In *Literary Theory: An Anthology*, ed. Julie Rivkin and Michael Ryan, 2nd ed., 162–176. Malden, MA: Blackwell Publishing.

Baker, Phil. 2009. *The Devil Is a Gentleman: The Life and Times of Dennis Wheatley*. Sawtry: Dedalus.

Barchas, Janine. 1996. Sarah Fielding's Dashing Style and Eighteenth-Century Print Culture. *ELH* 63:3: 633–656.

Barney, Stephen. 1982. Chaucer's Lists. In: *The Wisdom of Poetry: Essays in Early English Literature in Honor of Morton W. Bloomfield*, ed. Larry Dean Benson and Siegfried Wenzel, 189–223. Kalamazoo: Western Michigan University Press.

© The Author(s) 2023   191
S. J. Link, *A Narratological Approach to Lists in Detective Fiction*,
Crime Files, https://doi.org/10.1007/978-3-031-33227-2

Barthes, Roland. 1968. L'Effet de Réel. *Communications* 11: 84–89.

Barton, Roman et al. 2022a. Introduction: Epistemic and Artistic List-Making. In: *Forms of List-Making: Epistemic, Literary and Visual Enumeration*, ed. Roman Barton et al., 1–24. Cham: Palgrave Macmillan.

———, ed. 2022b. *Forms of List-Making: Epistemic, Literary and Visual Enumeration*. Cham: Palgrave Macmillan.

———. 2023. *Literary Lists: A Short History of Form and Function*. Cham: Palgrave Macmillan.

Belknap, Robert E. 2004. *The List: The Uses and Pleasures of Cataloguing*. New Haven: Yale University Press.

Binyon, Timothy J. 1989. *Murder Will Out: The Detective in Fiction*. Oxford: Oxford University Press.

Bily, Cynthia A. R. 2008. Austin Freeman. In *Critical Survey of Mystery & Detective Fiction*, vol. 2: *Lindsey Davis—Rupert Holmes*, ed. Carl Rollyson. Pasadena: Salem Press, 676–680.

Blair, Ann. 2010. *Too Much to Know: Managing Scholarly Information before the Modern Age*. New Haven: Yale University Press.

Bleiler, E. F. 1980. Gaboriau, Émile. In *Twentieth-Century Crime and Mystery Writers*, ed. John M. Reilly, 1540–1541. London: Macmillan.

Bochman, Svetlana. 2012. Detecting the Technocratic Detective. In *Sherlock Holmes for the 21st Century: Essays on New Adaptations*, ed. Lynnette R. Porter, 144–54. Jefferson: McFarland.

Bogost, Ian. 2009. Latour Litanizer: Generate Your Own Latour Litanies. 16 December 2009. http://bogost.com/writing/blog/latour_litanizer/. Accessed 31 January 2023.

Booth, Wayne C. 1983 [1961]. *The Rhetoric of Fiction*. Chicago: University of Chicago Press.

Borges, Jorge Luis. 1998 [1941]. The Library of Babel. In *Collected Fictions*, trans. Andrew Hurley, 112–118. New York: Viking.

Caracciolo, Marco. 2014. *The Experientiality of Narrative: An Enactivist Approach*. Berlin/Boston: de Gruyter.

Christie, Agatha. 1977 [1939]. *And Then There Were None*. London: Collins.

———. 2013a [1926]. *The Murder of Roger Ackroyd*. London: Harper Collins.

———. 2013b [1936]. *The ABC Murders*. London: Harper Collins.

———. 2015a [1934]. *Murder on the Orient Express*. London: Harper Collins.

———. 2015b [1935]. *Death in the Clouds*. London: Harper Collins.

———. 2015c [1955]. *Hickory Dickory Dock*. London: Harper Collins.

———. 2016 [1950]. *A Murder is Announced*. London: Harper Collins.

———. 2017 [1949]. *Crooked House*. London: Harper Collins.

Clark, Andy and David Chalmers. 1998. The Extended Mind. *Analysis* 58:1: 7–19.

Clarke, Clare. 2019. Doyle, Holmes and Victorian Publishing. In *The Cambridge Companion to Sherlock Holmes*, ed. Janice M. Allan and Christopher Pittard, 29–41. Cambridge: Cambridge University Press.

Codebò, Marco. 2007. The Dossier Novel: (Post)Modern Fiction and the Discourse of the Archive. *InterActions: UCLA Journal of Education and Information Studies* 3:1: n.p.

Coleridge, Samuel T. 2006 [1817]. Biographia Literaria. In *The Norton Anthology of English Literature, vol. 2*, ed. Stephen Greenblatt, 8th ed., 474–488. New York/London: W W Norton & Company.

Cox, Randolph J. 1989. Dennis (Yeats) Wheatley. In *Dictionary of Literary Biography, vol. 77: British Mystery Writers, 1920–1939*, ed. Bernard Benstock and Thomas F. Staley, 315–322. Detroit, MI:: Thomson Gale.

Curran, John. 2010. *Agatha Christie's Secret Notebooks: Fifty Years of Mysteries in the Making*. London: Harper.

Daston, Lorraine and Peter Galison. 2007. *Objectivity*. New York: Zone Books.

de Goede, Marieke, Anna Leander and Gavin Sullivan. 2016. Introduction: The Politics of the List. *Environment and Planning D: Society and Space* 34:1: 3–13.

Detection Club Oath, the. 1928. In *The Art of the Mystery Story: A Collection of Critical Essays*, ed. Howard Haycraft, 197–199. New York: Biblo & Tannen.

Diderot, Denis. 1964 [1755]. Encyclopédie. In *Encyclopédie, vol. 5*. Rpt. In *Rameau's Nephew and Other Works*, trans. Jacques Barzun and Ralph H. Bowen, 277. Indianapolis: Bobbs-Merrill.

Doležalová, Lucie, ed. 2009. *The Charm of a List: From the Sumerians to Computerised Data Processing*. Newcastle upon Tyne: Cambridge Scholars Publishing.

Donaldson, Norman. 1971. *In Search of Dr Thorndyke: The Story of R. Austin Freeman's Great Scientific Investigator and His Creator*. Bowling Green: Bowling Green State University Press.

Dove, George. 1990. The Detection Formula and the Act of Reading. In *The Cunning Craft: Original Essays on Detective Fiction and Contemporary Literary Theory*, ed. June M. Frazer and Ronald G. Walker, 68–85. Macomb: Western Illinois University Press.

———. 1997. *The Reader and the Detective Story*. Bowling Green: Bowling Green State University Press.

Doyle, Arthur Conan. 2010 [1890]. *The Sign of Four*. London: Penguin.

———. 2011 [1927]. *The Case-Book of Sherlock Holmes*. London: Penguin.

———. 2013 [1892]. *The Adventures of Sherlock Holmes*. London: Harper Collins.

———. 2014 [1887]. *A Study in Scarlet*. London: Penguin.

Eco, Umberto. 2009. *The Infinity of Lists*. New York: Rizzoli.

Eliot, T. S. 1934. Wilkie Collins and Dickens. In *Selected Essays*, 2nd ed., 422–432. London: Faber & Faber.

Erchinger, Philipp. 2018. *Artful Experiments: Ways of Knowing in Victorian Literature and Science*. Edinburgh: Edinburgh University Press.

Fludernik, Monika. 1996. *Towards a 'Natural' Narratology*. London: Routledge.

Fondanèché, Daniel. 2000. *Le Roman Policier: Thèmes et Études*. Paris: Ellipses.

Frazer, June M. and Ronald G. Walker, ed. 1990. *The Cunning Craft: Original Essays on Detective Fiction and Contemporary Literary Theory*. Macomb: Western Illinois University Press.

Frédéric, Madeleine. 1986. Enumération, Énumération Homologique, Énumération Chaotique: Essai de Caractérisation. In *Stylistique, Rhétorique et Poétique dans les Langues Romanes*, ed. Jean-Claude Bouvier, 103–117. Provence: Université de Provence.

Freeman, Richard Austin. 1976 [1924]. The Art of the Detective Story. In *The Art of the Mystery Story: A Collection of Critical Essays*, ed. Howard Haycraft, 7–17. New York: Biblo & Tannen.

———. 1989 [1911] *The Eye of Osiris*. Oxford: Oxford University Press.

———. 2001 [1914]. *A Silent Witness*. Cornwall: House of Stratus.

———. 2004a [1907]. *The Red Thumb Mark*. Rockville: Serenity Publishers.

———. 2004b [1912]. *The Mystery at Number 31, New Inn*. Greenville: JourneyForth.

———. 2017a [1909]. John Thorndyke's Cases: Original Preface. In *Dr. Thorndyke Collection, vol. 2*, 1. n.p.: Neo Books.

———. 2017b [1912]. A Wastrel's Romance. In *Dr. Thorndyke Collection, vol. 2*, 197–232. n.p.: Neo Books.

———. 2017c [1912]. The Case of Oscar Brodski. In *Dr. Thorndyke Collection, vol. 2*, 197–232. n.p.: Neo Books.

———. 2017d [1912]. *The Singing Bone*. In *Dr. Thorndyke Collection, vol. 2*, 196–340. n.p.: Neo Books.

Frogwares. 2014. *Sherlock Holmes: Crimes and Punishments*. Frogwares. Microsoft Windows/Playstation 3/Playstation 4/Xbox 360/Xbox One.

Gatiss, Mark and Steven Moffat, dir. 2010. *Sherlock*. Season 1. BBC.

———. 2012. *Sherlock*. Season 2. BBC.

———. 2014. *Sherlock*. Season 3. BBC.

Genette, Gérard. 1997. *Paratexts: Thresholds of Interpretation*, trans. Jane E. Lewin. Cambridge: Cambridge University Press.

Ghosal, Torsa. 2021. *Out of Mind: Mode, Mediation and Cognition in Twenty-First-Century Narrative*. Columbus: The Ohio State University Press.

Gibelli, Dario. 1992. Le Paradox du Narrateur dans Roger Ackroyd. *Poétique: Revue de Théorie et d'Analyse Littéraires* 23: 387–397.

Gibson, Eleanor J. and Harry Levin. 1975. *The Psychology of Reading*. Cambridge: MIT Press.

Gibson, James. 1979. The Theory of Affordances. In *The Ecological Approach to Visual Perception*, ed. James Gibson, 127–146. Boston: Houghton Mifflin.

Gitelman, Lisa. 2014. *Paper Knowledge: Toward a Media History of Documents.* Durham: Duke University Press.

Goody, Jack. 1978. What's in a List?. In *The Domestication of the Savage Mind,* ed. Jack Goody, 74–111. Cambridge: Cambridge University Press.

Griffiths, Eric. 2018. *If Not Critical.* ed. Freya Johnston. Oxford: Oxford University Press.

Gruesser, John. 2020. Not Knowing That They Don't Know: Narrators and Readers in Poe's Detective Fiction. Conference talk, ISSN International Conference, New Orleans, 7 March 2020.

Gutkowski, Emanuela. 2011. An "Investigation in Pragmatics": Agatha Christie's *The Murder of Roger Ackroyd. Clues: A Journal of Detection* 29:1: 51–60.

Hark, Ina Rae. 1987. Twelve Angry People: Conflicting Revelatory Strategies in *Murder on the Orient Express. Literature/Film* 15:19: 36–42.

Haycraft, Howard, ed. 1976. *The Art of the Mystery Story: A Collection of Critical Essays.* New York: Biblo and Tannen.

Herman, David. 2008. Description, Narrative and Explanation: Text-Type Categories and the Cognitive Foundation of Discourse Competence. *Poetics Today* 29:3: 437–472.

———. 2013a. Cognitive Narratology. In *The Living Handbook of Narratology,* ed. Peter Hühn et al., n.p. Hamburg: Hamburg University. https://www-archiv.fdm.uni-hamburg.de/lhn/node/38.html. Accessed 31 January 2023.

———. 2013b. *Storytelling and the Sciences of Mind.* Cambridge: MIT Press.

Hess, Volker and J. Andrew Mendelsohn. 2010. Case and Series: Medical Knowledge and Paper Technology, 1600–1900. *History of Science* 48:3/4: 287–314.

Humphreys, Richard. 2002. The Crime Dossiers of Dennis Wheatley and J G Links. http://www.denniswheatley.info/crimedossiers.htm. Accessed 31 January 2023.

Ingarden, Roman. 1931. *Das Literarische Kunstwerk: eine Untersuchung aus dem Grenzgebiet der Ontologie, Logik und Literaturwissenschaft.* Halle (Saale): Niemeyer.

Iser, Wolfgang. 1978. *The Act of Reading: A Theory of Aesthetic Response.* London: Routledge and Kegan Paul.

Jann, Rosemary. 1990. Sherlock Holmes Codes the Social Body. *English Literary History* 57:3: 685–708.

Jauss, Hans Robert. 2004. Literary History as a Challenge to Literary Theory. In *Critical Theory since Plato,* ed. Hazard Adams and Leroy Searle, 1237–1254. Belmont CA: Wadsworth Publishing.

Karpenko, Lara. 2017. "So Extraordinary a Bond": Mesmerism and Sympathetic Identification in Charles Adams's *Notting Hill Mystery.* In *Strange Science: Investigating the Limits of Knowledge in the Victorian Age,* ed. Lara Karpenko and Shalyn Clagget, 145–163. Ann Arbor: University of Michigan Press.

Kayman, Martin A. 1992. *From Bow Street to Baker Street: Mystery, Detection and Narrative*. Basingstoke: Macmillan.
———. 2006. The Short Story from Poe to Chesterton. In *The Cambridge Companion to Crime Fiction*, ed. Martin Priestman, 41–58. Cambridge: Cambridge University Press.
Knight, Stephen T. 1980. *Form and Ideology in Crime Fiction*. London: Macmillan.
———. 2004. *Crime Fiction, 1800–2000: Detection, Death, Diversity*. London: Macmillan.
———. 2006. The Golden Age. In *The Cambridge Introduction to Crime Fiction*, ed. Martin Priestman, 77–96. Cambridge: Cambridge University Press.
Knox, Ronald A. 1976 [1929]. A Detective Story Decalogue. In *The Art of the Mystery Story: A Collection of Critical Essays*, ed. Howard Haycraft, 194–196. New York: Biblo & Tannen.
Kovach, Elizabeth, Imke Polland and Ansgar Nünning, ed. 2021. *Forms at Work. New Formalist Approaches in the Study of Literature, Culture, and Media*. Trier: Wissenschaftlicher Verlag Trier.
Krajewski, Markus. 2016. Genauigkeit: Zur Ausbildung einer epistemischen Tugend im 'langen 19. Jahrhundert'. *Berichte zur Wissenschaftsgeschichte* 39:3: 211–229.
Kukkonen, Karin. 2013. Form as a Pattern of Thinking: Cognitive Poetics and New Formalism. In *New Formalisms and Literary Theory*, ed. Verena Theile and Linda Tredennick. 159–176. New York: Palgrave Macmillan.
———. 2020. *Probability Designs: Literature and Predictive Processing*. Oxford: Oxford University Press.
Kustritz, Anne and Melanie Kohnen. 2012. Decoding the Industrial and Digital City: Visions of Security in Holmes' and Sherlock's London. In *Sherlock and Transmedia Fandom: Essays on the BBC Series*, ed. Louisa Ellen Stein and Kristina Busse, 85–101. Jefferson, N.C: McFarland.
Laemmle, Rebecca, Cédric Scheidegger-Lämmle and Katharina Wesselmann, ed. 2021. *Lists and Catalogues in Ancient Literature and Beyond*. Berlin: de Gruyter.
Lanchester, John. 2018. The Case of Agatha Christie. *London Review of Books* 40:24: n.p. www.lrb.co.uk/the-paper/v40/n24/john-lanchester/the-case-of-agatha-christie. Accessed 29 January 2023.
Lanser, Susan. 2019. The (Ir)relevance of Narratology. In *Relevance and Narrative Research*, ed. Matei Chihaia and Katharina Rennhak, 3–17. Lanham: Lexington Books.
Latour, Bruno. 1990 [1986]. Drawing Things Together. In *Representation in Scientific Practice*, ed. Michael Lynch and Steve Woolgar, 19–68. Cambridge, MA: MIT Press.
Leighton, Mary Elizabeth. 2006. Under the Influence: Crime and Hypnotic Fictions of the Fin de Siècle. In *Victorian Literary Mesmerism*, ed. Martin Willis and Catherine Wynne, 203–226. Amsterdam: Rodopi.

Levine, Caroline. 2015. *Forms: Whole, Rhythm, Hierarchy, Network*. Princeton/Oxford: Princeton University Press.

Link, Sarah J. 2020. Detective Facts|Detective Fiction: Listing the Tools of the Trade. *a/b: Auto/Biography Studies* 35:3. https://doi.org/10.1080/0898957 5.2020.1815374.

———. 2022. Detecting Liminality: The List and Symbolic Form. In *Narrative Liminality*, ed. Katja Kanzler et al., 99–111. Bielefeld: Transcript.

Lovitt, Carl. 1990. Controlling Discourse in Detective Fiction, or Caring Very Much Who Killed Roger Ackroyd. In *The Cunning Craft: Original Essays on Detective Fiction and Contemporary Literary Theory*, ed. June M. Frazer and Ronald G. Walker, 68–85. Macomb: Western Illinois University Press.

Mainberger, Sabine. 2003. *Die Kunst des Aufzählens: Elemente zu einer Poetik des Enumerativen*. Berlin/New York: de Gruyter.

Maloney, Edward J. 2005. *Footnotes in Fiction: A Rhetorical Approach*. Diss. The Ohio State University.

Mandel, Ernest. 1987. *Ein Schöner Mord: Sozialgeschichte des Kriminalromans*. trans. Nils T. Lindquist. Frankfurt: Athenäum.

Manovich, Lev. 1999. Database as Symbolic Form. *Convergence*, 5:2: 80–99.

———. 2001. *The Language of New Media*. Cambridge, Mass.: MIT Press.

McHale, Brian. 2001. *Postmodernist Fiction*. London: Routledge.

McLuhan, Marshall. 1994. The Gadget Lover: Narcissus as Narcosis. In *Understanding Media: The Extensions of Man*, 41–47. Cambridge, Mass: MIT Press.

Miller, David A. 1988. *The Novel and the Police*. Berkeley/Los Angeles/London: University of California Press.

Milton, Heather. 2011. Sensation and Detection. In *A Companion to Sensation Fiction*, ed. Pamela K. Gilbert, 516–527. Chichester: Wiley Blackwell.

Moody, Susan, ed. 1990. *The Hatchards Crime Companion: 100 Top Crime Novels Selected by the Crime Writers' Association*. London: Hatchards.

Moretti, Franco. 1988. Clues. In *Signs Taken for Wonders: Essays in the Sociology of Literary Forms*, trans. Susan Fischer, David Forgacs, and David Miller, 130–156. London: Verso.

Müller-Wille, Staffan, and Isabelle Charmantier. 2012. Lists as Research Technologies. *Isis* 103:4: 743–752.

Oxford English Dictionary Online. 2020a. Fairness, n.6. Oxford University Press. https://www.oed.com/view/Entry/67729?redirectedFrom=fairness. Accessed 31 January 2023.

———. 2020b. List, n.3. Oxford University Press. https://www.oed.com/view/Entry/108988?rskey=Qbcmdz&result=3#eid. Accessed 31 January 2023.

———. 2020c. Table, n.14. Oxford University Press. https://www.oed.com/view/Entry/196785?rskey=lKhNn4&result=1#eid. Accessed 31 January 2023.

Oertzen, Christine. 2017. Die Historizität der Verdatung: Konzepte, Werkzeuge und Praktiken im 19. Jahrhundert. *International Journal of History & Ethics of Natural Sciences, Technology & Medicine* 25:4: 407–434.

Ousby, Ian. 1976. *Bloodhounds of Heaven: the Detective in English Fiction from Godwin to Doyle*. Cambridge, MA: Harvard University Press.

Parker, Ben. 2016. The Method Effect: Empiricism and Form in Sherlock Holmes. *Novel: A Forum on Fiction* 49:3: 449–466.

Priestman, Martin, ed. 2006a. *The Cambridge Introduction to Crime Fiction*. Cambridge: Cambridge University Press.

———. 2006b. Introduction: Crime Fiction and Detective Fiction. In *The Cambridge Introduction to Crime Fiction*, ed. Martin Priestman, 1–6. Cambridge: Cambridge University Press.

Propp, Vladimir. 2004. Morphology of the Folk-Tale. In *Literary Theory: An Anthology*, ed. Julie Rivkin and Michael Ryan, 2nd ed., 72–75. Malden, MA: Blackwell Publishing.

Purdon, James. 2016. Dossier Fiction. In *Modernist Informatics: Literature, Information, and the State*, ed. James Purdon, 55–88. Oxford: Oxford University Press.

Pykett, Lynn. 2006. The Newgate Novel and Sensation Fiction, 1830–1868. In *The Cambridge Introduction to Crime Fiction*, ed. Martin Priestman, 19–40. Cambridge: Cambridge University Press.

Rationalwiki. 2020. Holmesian Fallacy. Last modified 25 June 2022. https://rationalwiki.org/wiki/Holmesian_fallacy. Accessed 31 January 2023.

Reitz, Caroline. 2006. Detective Fiction. In: *The Oxford Encyclopedia of British Literature*, ed. David S. Kastan, n.p. https://www.oxfordreference.com/view/10.1093/acref/9780195169218.001.0001/acref-9780195169218-e-0134. Accessed 31 January 2023.

Rosch, Eleanor et al. 1976. Basic Objects in Natural Categories. *Cognitive Psychology* 8:3: 382–439.

Rüggemeier, Anne. 2020. Life Writing and the Poetics of List-Making: On the Manifestations, Effects, and Possible Uses of Lists in Life Writing. *a/b: Auto/Biography Studies* 35:3. https://doi.org/10.1080/08989575.2020.1815371.

Rushing, Robert. 2005. Traveling Detectives: The "Logic of Arrest" and the Pleasures of (Avoiding) the Real. *Yale French Studies* 108: 89–101.

Saint-Amour, Paul K. 2015. *Tense Future: Modernism, Total War, Encyclopedic Form*. Oxford/New York: Oxford University Press.

Sargent, Neil C. 2010. Mys-Reading the Past in Detective Fiction and Law. *Law & Literature* 22:2: 288–306.

Sayers, Dorothy. 1928. Introduction. In *Great Short Stories of Detection, Mystery and Horror*, ed. Dorothy Sayers, 9–47. London: Gollancz.

Scaggs, John. 2005. *Crime Fiction*. London: Routledge.

Schmid, Wolf. 2014. Implied Reader. In *The Living Handbook of Narratology*, ed. Peter Hühn et al., n.p. Hamburg: Hamburg University. https://www-archiv. fdm.uni-hamburg.de/lhn/node/59.html. Accessed 31 January 2023.

Schmidt, Sarah, ed. 2016. *Sprachen Des Sammelns: Literatur Als Medium Und Reflexionsform Des Sammelns*. Paderborn: Wilhelm Fink.

Schubert, Stefan. 2019. Narrative and Play in American Studies: Ludic Textuality in the Video Game *Alan Wake* and the TV Series *Westworld*. In *Playing the Field: Video Games and American Studies*, ed. Sascha Pöhlmann, 113–129. Berlin: de Gruyter.

Schütt, Sita A. 2006. French Crime Fiction. In *The Cambridge Companion to Crime Fiction*, ed. Martin Priestman, 59–76. Cambridge: Cambridge University Press.

Shpayer-Makov, Haia. 2010. From Menace to Celebrity: the English Police Detective and the Press, c.1842–1914. *Historical Research* 83(22): 672–692.

Sinfield, Alan. 1992. *Faultlines: Cultural Materialism and the Politics of Dissident Reading*. Oxford: Clarendon Press.

Sklovskij, Viktor Borisovic. 1991 [1925]. *Theory of Prose*, trans. Benjamin Sher. Elmwood Park, Ill: Dalkey Archive Press.

Smajić, Srdjan. 2010. *Ghost-Seers, Detectives, and Spiritualists: Theories of Vision in Victorian Literature and Science*. Cambridge: Cambridge University Press.

Spufford, Francis. 1989. *The Chatto Book of Cabbages and Kings: Lists in Literature*. London: Chatto and Windus.

Stäheli, Urs. 2011. Das Soziale als Liste: Zur Epistemologie der ANT. In *Die Wiederkehr der Dinge*, ed. Friedrich Balke, Maria Mühle and Antonia von Schöning. 83–101. Berlin: Kulturverlag Kadmos Berlin.

———. 2016. Indexing—The Politics of Invisibility. *Environment and Planning D: Society and Space* 34:1: 14–29.

———. 2017. Traveling by Lists: Navigational Knowledge and Tourism. *Zeitschrift für Literaturwissenschaft und Linguistik* 47:3: 361–374.

Starre, Alexander. 2017. Professionelle Kondensierung: Die Annotation als Wissensformat im Catalog Der American Library Association, 1893–1926. In *Kurz&Knapp: Zur Mediengeschichte Kleiner Formen Vom 17. Jahrhundert bis zur Gegenwart*, ed. Michael Gamper and Ruth Mayer, 229–250. Bielefeld: Transcript.

Stein, Louisa Ellen, and Kristina Busse, ed. 2012a. Sherlock *and Transmedia Fandom: Essays on the BBC Series*. Jefferson, N.C: McFarland.

———. 2012b. Introduction: The Literary, Televisual and Digital Adventures of the Beloved Detective. In Sherlock *and Transmedia Fandom: Essays on the BBC Series*, ed. Louisa Ellen Stein and Kristina Busse, 9–26. Jefferson, N.C: McFarland.

Stewart, Victoria. 2019. Objects, Things and Clues in Early Twentieth-Century Fiction. *Modernist Cultures* 14:2: 172–192.

Summerscale, Kate. 2008. *The Suspicions of Mr. Whicher: Or, The Murder at Road Hill House*. London: Bloomsbury.

Sweeney, S. E. 1990. Locked Rooms: Detective Fiction, Narrative Theory, and Self-Reflexivity. In *The Cunning Craft: Original Essays on Detective Fiction and Contemporary Literary Theory*, ed. June Frazer and Ronald Walker, 1–14. Macomb: Western Illinois University Press.

Symons, Julian. 1985 [1972]. *Bloody Murder: From the Detective Story to the Crime Novel*. Harmondsworth: Penguin.

Taylor, Alfred Swaine. 1859. *On Poisons, in Relation to Medical Jurisprudence and Medicine*. 2nd ed. Philadelphia: Lea and Blanchard.

Taylor, Rhonda Harris. 2012. The 'Great Game' of Information: The BBC's Digital Native. In *Sherlock Holmes for the 21st Century: Essays on New Adaptations*, ed. Lynnette R. Porter, 128–143. Jefferson, N.C.: McFarland.

Theile, Verena, and Linda Tredennick, ed. 2013. *New Formalisms and Literary Theory*. New York: Palgrave Macmillan.

Todorov, Tzvetan. 1966. The Typology of Detective Fiction. In *Crime and Media: A Reader*, ed. Chris Greer, 291–301. London: Routledge.

Underwood, Ted. 2016. The Life Cycles of Genres. *Journal of Cultural Analytics* 1:1: 1–25. https://doi.org/10.22148/16.005.

van der Linde, Gerhard, and Els Wouters. 2003. Variations on Three Bodies of Knowledge. *International Fiction Review* 30:1/2: 76–91.

Van Dine, S. S. [Willard Huntigton Wright] 1928. Twenty Rules for Writing Detective Stories. In *The Art of the Mystery Story: A Collection of Critical Essays*, ed. Howard Haycraft, 189–193. New York: Biblo & Tannen.

Vismann, Cornelia. 2000. *Akten: Medientechnik und Recht*. Frankfurt: Fischer.

von Contzen, Eva, ed. 2016. Lists in Literature from the Middle Ages to Postmodernism. *Style* 50:3.

———. 2017. Grenzfälle des Erzählens: Die Liste als Einfache Form. In *Komplexität und Einfachheit*, ed. Albrecht Koschorke, 221–239. Stuttgart: J.B. Metzler.

———. 2018. Experience, Affect, and Literary Lists. *Partial Answers* 16:2: 315–327.

———. 2021. Theorising Lists in Literature: Towards a Listology. In *Lists and Catalogues in Ancient Literature and Beyond*, ed. Rebecca Lämmle, Cédric Scheidegger-Lämmle and Katharina Wesselmann, 35–54. Berlin: de Gruyter.

———. 2022. Don't Trust the List: The Politics of Enumeration and Capitalist Discourse in the Novel. In *Forms of List-Making: Epistemic, Literary and Visual Enumeration*, ed. Roman Barton et al., 129–149. Cham: Palgrave Macmillan.

———. n.d. *The Epic Catalogue: List Form, Cognition, and Reception from* Paradise Lost *to* Beowulf. Unpublished manuscript.

Weber, Max. 1978 [1921]. *Economy and Society, vol 2*. ed. Günther Roth and Claus Wittich. Berkeley: University of California Press.

Wheatley, Dennis. 1979 [1936]. *Murder off Miami*. Planned by J.G. Links. London: Hutchinson/Webb & Bower.

———. 1980 [1937]. *Who Killed Robert Prentice?*. Planned by J.G. Links. Exeter: Webb & Bower.

———. 1982 [1939]. *Herewith the Clues*. Planned by J.G. Links. Exeter: Webb & Bower.

Willis, Martin and Catherine Wynne. 2006. Introduction. In *Victorian Literary Mesmerism*, ed. Martin Willis and Catherine Wynne, 1–16. Amsterdam: Rodopi.

Worthington, Heather. 2011. Reading the Body of Narrative: Seeking Scientific Evidence in Early 19th Century Criminography. In *The Case and the Canon: Anomalies, Discontinuities, Metaphors between Science and Literature*, ed. Alessandra Calanchi et al., 125–135. Göttingen: Vandenhoeck & Ruprecht.

Young, Liam Cole. 2017. *List Cultures: Knowledge and Poetics from Mesopotamia to BuzzFeed*. Amsterdam: Amsterdam University Press.

——— 2013. Un-Black Boxing the List: Knowledge, Materiality and Form. *Canadian Journal of Communication* 38: 497–516.

Zielinski, Sarah. 2014. The Secrets of Sherlock's Mind Palace. *Smithsonian Magazine*, 3 February 2014. https://www.smithsonianmag.com/arts-culture/secrets-sherlocks-mind-palace-180949567/. Accessed 31 January 2023.

Index[1]

---

[1] Note: Page numbers followed by 'n' refer to notes.

Milton Keynes UK
Ingram Content Group UK Ltd.
UKHW050043201023
430832UK00006B/30

9 783031 332265